Mike Gayle has contributed to a variety of magazines including *FHM*, *Sunday Times Style* and *Cosmopolitan*. His bestsellers, *My Legendary Girlfriend*, *Mr Commitment*, *Turning Thirty*, *Dinner for Two*, *His 'N' Hers*, *Brand New Friend* and *Wish You Were Here* are available in Hodder paperback. To find out more about his novels, visit Mike's website at www.mikegayle.co.uk

Praise for *The To-Do List*

'Brilliantly funny' *Daily Mail*

'Put ''buy it'' at the top of your to do list'
Radio 4, Loose Ends

Also by Mike Gayle

THE TO-DO LIST

MIKE GAYLE

HODDER

First published in Great Britain in 2009 by
Hodder & Stoughton
An Hachette UK company

First published in paperback in 2009

1

A CIP catalogue record for this title is
available from the British Library

ISBN 978 0 340 93675 7 (B format)
978 0 340 98084 2 (A format)

Typeset in Benguiat by Hewer Text UK Ltd, Edinburgh
Printed and bound by Clays Ltd, St Ives plc

Hodder & Stoughton policy is to use papers that are natural,
renewable and recyclable products and made from wood
grown in sustainable forests. The logging and manufacturing
processes are expected to conform to the environmental
regulations of the country of origin.

Hodder & Stoughton Ltd
338 Euston Road
London NW1 3BH

www.hodder.co.uk

In memory of Barbara Richards

who knew more about getting things done

than I'll ever know.

Acknowledgements

Thanks to the following: Sue, Swati and everyone at Hodder; Simon and all at United Agents; Jane B.E; the Sunday Night Pub Club; Mark Forster aka The Time Management Guru, Alexa the Canadian, John and Charlotte; the O'Reillys, the Board, Team Gayle, Susie Dent, Jackie, Danny, Sam, Hassan, Nadine, Chris McCabe, Sharon, John, Richard and everyone everywhere that I might have missed out who helped out during my year of To Do Listing. The drinks are on me!

I don't like the sound of all those lists he's making —
it's like taking too many notes at school; you feel
you've achieved something when you haven't.

Dodie Smith, *I Capture the Castle*

Prologue

It feels odd packing my bags for a trip that's going to take me so far away from my family. Before Claire and I had kids going away on my own used to be easy. Exciting even. Who wouldn't have been thrilled at the prospect of a work jolly abroad? Getting ready for these trips I used to throw a few things into a suitcase, happy in the knowledge that Claire would use her time living in a Mike-free world to indulge in a spot of part-time bachelorette activity featuring long baths, hour upon hour of *America's Top Model*, marathon phone conversations with her friend Charlotte and the opportunity to get a good night's sleep without having to wrestle the duvet from anybody.

Now of course things are different. Not only does my going away even for just a couple of nights to somewhere as close as London make life difficult for my wife in terms of looking after the kids (although thankfully for this trip Claire's mum is at hand to help out), it also feels like the hardest thing in the world to do. What if something happens in the middle of the night and one of the kids needs me? What if I'm not there to witness first-hand some new and amazing development in Maisie's abilities now that she's already started walking? What if I just miss the everyday to and fro of family life? In recent years I've turned down trips abroad for these very reasons so why is it that I am about to fly all the way to

America for the sake of a $12 coffee mug? The answer, to me at least, is simple: love. I'm doing it all for love. Because no matter how you say it and how often it gets said, actions will always speak louder than words and right now, though some might call it pointless, frivolous, or just plain stupid, flying to the other side of the Atlantic for the sake of a $12 coffee mug is the one thing I want to say in the loudest possible way.

PART ONE

October

(During which a birthday, some
new neighbours and a toothpaste-
encrusted T-shirt led me to write
a 1277-item-long To-Do List)

Chapter 1: 'Realise that you've got a problem.'

The events that led me to jump on a plane to New York in pursuit of a $12 coffee mug had their origins in the Saturday before my thirty-sixth birthday. It was just after six in the morning and I was lying on the sofa in the darkness of the living room watching TV. By which I actually mean that I was slavishly working my way through the DVD box set of the second season of 24 which I had been given for Christmas some two years earlier. In the course of those two years I had not only failed to watch a single episode; I'd also failed to so much as remove the polythene wrapping. Every time I walked past the shelves in the living room where the DVDs lived I'd immediately feel guilty. I'd wanted that DVD box set more than anything. I'd imagined some unspecified point in the future when I'd have nothing better to do than sit down and catch up with the latest antics of Jack Bauer and his Kevlar body armour, yet that time was still to come around. The box had sat unloved and unopened for two whole years. Still, it was in good company. There was a box set of the first season of *The Wire*, the US import version (that's how badly I'd wanted it) of the *Die Hard Trilogy* and the first series of *Spooks*. All unwatched. All still in their wrappers. And all making me feel guilty. So guilty, that having woken from a restless sleep at three o'clock in the morning, my first thought was whether I could get up early every day for the next twenty-four days, watch an episode of the second series of *24*, and still find the energy to work, play with my three-and-a-half-year-old daughter Lydia, spend time with my pregnant wife and undertake the hundred and one different tasks that found their way onto my daily To-Do List. Reasoning that in my current state of mind I was never going to get back to sleep and finding myself in agreement with the adage that there's no time like the present, I slipped out of bed, headed downstairs, turned off the burglar alarm, made my way to the DVD shelf in the living room, unwrapped the second series of *24*, slid the first disc into the DVD player, settled myself down on the sofa and pressed 'play'.

When the hinges on the door behind my head screeched open I paused the on-screen action and made yet another mental note to buy a can of oil the next time I was some-where that sold cans of oil and sort out the hinges. It was only a small thing, not exactly the hardest task in the world, yet it had remained unchecked on my mental To-Do List for the best part of five years.

'Morning, babe.' My wife entered the room. 'You're up early. Couldn't you sleep?'

I shook my head.

'What time did you get up?'

'About three. It's getting ridiculous. This is the third day in a row. No matter what time I get to bed, come three o'clock I'm wide awake and there's not a single thing I can do to get back to sleep. I mean, what time did we go to bed last night?'

Claire stretched and stifled a yawn. 'We had dinner at five, played with Lydia for a bit before taking her up for a wash, then we read her stories and put her to bed, then I came down and tidied up while you did some work in the loft and then Lydia called down to say that she'd done a poo so I went back up to deal with that, and then she said that she was thirsty so I got her a cup of water and then carried on tidying up and you came downstairs and said, "Let's watch telly", and so I asked you what you wanted to watch and you said, "Let's watch stuff that makes us want to shout at the TV," so then you found an old episode of *Property Ladder*, and the couple they were featuring was really annoying but during the ad break you said that you were going to close your eyes for five minutes so I did too and the next thing I knew it was ten to ten and I said we should go to bed and you said, "Just five more minutes," so I closed my eyes again and then the next thing I knew it was ten to eleven and you were waking me up saying that we should go to bed.' She paused to laugh her beautiful laugh. 'Did I leave anything out?'

'No, babe, I think that's pretty much everything.'

This way of life had been pretty much *de rigueur* for Claire and me ever since we first became parents three and a half years earlier. Not that we were living a rock 'n' roll lifestyle before that, far from it – we were probably the least rock 'n' roll people you could hope to meet – but at the very least life pre-Lydia used to consist of a bit more than falling asleep on the sofa in front of the TV.

'Do you think we've done the right thing having another baby?' Claire mused.

'Yeah, of course,' I replied confidently even though I wasn't sure at all. 'Everything will be fine.'

'I know it will,' said Claire rubbing her tummy fondly. 'But . . . I don't know . . . before I got pregnant again I felt like we were on the home straight. We knew what we were doing. We had it all sorted out and were having so much fun. But now, well, I'll be a "mother of two". You'll be a "father of two". This baby's going to turn us into proper grown-ups.'

Later that morning, when we'd both calmed down a bit,

eaten breakfast and showered, I found myself thinking about what Claire had said. There really was no turning back. In a few weeks we would be responsible not just for one small life but two and that prospect suddenly seemed scary.

But at the age of thirty-five and thirty-three respectively weren't we already 'proper adults'? Technically I suppose we were. My thirty-sixth birthday was less than twenty-four hours away, I was already a father of one, a 'propelling-you-into-adulthood' responsibility in itself; yes, like most of my fellow thirtysomethings I was being slowly crushed by the weight of a hefty mortgage. But other than that (and enjoying playing Scrabble and finding property programmes 'relaxing') I was pure kid. I mean, would a so-called 'proper adult' spill milk under the fridge and let it sit there for weeks? Would a 'proper adult' take the best part of *three years* to post a solitary Christmas card to a close friend? Would a 'proper adult' have underwear in active service that was well over a decade old?

So there I was: neither flesh nor fowl; neither Big John nor Little John; neither man nor boy. Instead I was stuck between two camps – able to laugh at jokes about breaking wind and yet eligible for Big Boys' prison should I ever find that I've committed murder.

That evening, as we tidied our bedroom having just put Lydia to bed, I turned to Claire. 'Do you know what I think the problem is?'

'The problem with what?'

'With us. I think the problem with us is that we're scared to commit.'

'To what?'

'To the idea of full adulthood.'

'Rubbish,' replied Claire. 'Of course we're not. Whatever gave you that idea?'

I led Claire to the full-sized mirror in the corner of the room and pointed. 'That's what gave me the idea,' I said pointing at our reflections. 'Look at us! What do you see?'

Claire peered hard in the mirror. 'I see you and me.'

'Exactly! You see "me and you". Now answer this: do you think that Derek and Jessica look like this?' I jabbed a finger in the direction of the T-shirt that I and my reflection were wearing. 'Do you think that right now Derek is wearing a T-shirt depicting Sid James riding on a BMX?'

Claire began picking at a white blob of something just above my right nipple. 'Even if he was I don't think he'd have toothpaste encrusted onto it. How do you do that by the way? How do you get toothpaste over every single item of clothing that you wear?'

'The toothpaste isn't the point,' I replied impatiently. 'The point, babe, is us. We're a mess. I mean do you really think that Jessica is wearing a pair of comedy tiger-claw slippers?'

'But I like my slippers,' said Claire indignantly, looking down at her feet, 'they're comfortable!'

'I know that. You're preaching to the choir here. But you have to admit that they're just not very Derek and Jessica are they?'

Derek and Jessica were our new next-door neighbours as of approximately six weeks ago. Our previous next-door neighbours, Tony and Jane, a pair of grumpy but nonetheless amusing middle-aged comprehensive school teachers, had moved to Bath to open a B&B and despite our jovial request to sell their home to someone 'fun' had opted for the highest bidders. Financial consultant Derek and his wife, marketing consultant Jessica, in their mid-thirties, were it.

It wasn't just that they turned up in top-of-the-range executive cars, or that pretty much every Saturday night since they'd moved in they would throw dinner parties for which a stream of glamorous-looking friends would arrive clutching expensive bottles of wine while Claire and I lay slumped in a post-chicken-dhansak-induced coma in front of *X-Factor*. It wasn't even that they too had a three-year-old child with another baby on the way, and yet possessed a home that was permanently immaculate. No, what really depressed me was that both Derek and Jessica were unmistakably 'proper grown-ups'. I couldn't imagine either of them taking three years to post a Christmas card, owning underwear over a decade old and as for leaving spilt milk under the fridge, I was pretty sure Jessica would have a heart attack at the very thought.

'We need to be more like them,' I said as I gazed gloomily at our reflections. 'We need to start acting like proper grown-ups and doing grown-up things instead of carrying on like teenagers waiting to be found out.'

'Great,' said Claire succinctly. 'Maybe you can begin your journey into adulthood with a bout of kitchen cleaning because that milk you spilt under the fridge is really starting to honk.'

At the end of the night, as I put our takeaway cartons into the kitchen bin and tried not to gag at the smell wafting up from underneath the fridge, I resolved that this was it: make or break time. The eve of my thirty-sixth birthday was when I was finally going to have to decide whether I was a man or just a boy in long trousers.

'Are you coming up to bed?' Claire put her arms around me.

'Not yet,' I replied, patting her tummy. 'I've got a few things to do.'

'Like what?'

'Nothing much, just a few things.'

As Claire headed up to the bathroom to get ready for bed I

made my way into the living room, picked up an old diary that Lydia had been doodling on and one of her felt-tip pens and made my way to the loft. After sweeping a pile of discarded newspapers and sweet wrappers onto the floor, I settled myself at my desk and in large capital letters wrote the words that would change my life: 'TO-DO LIST.'

It was sometime later and I was still feverishly working away when Claire popped her head around the door.

'What are you doing?'

'I'm writing a list.'

'At three o'clock in the morning?'

I looked at my watch. It was indeed three o'clock in the morning.

'I didn't realise,' I replied. 'That said, it *is* a pretty important list.'

'What kind of list can be that important?'

'It's a To-Do list.'

Sighing, she entered the room and sat on the edge of the spare bed, rubbed her eyes and ran a hand through her hair which was flying off in all directions as though trying to make a break from her head. Clearly confused by the sight of me sitting at my desk in my pants and an old band T-shirt frantically scribbling on a notepad she assumed a pained expression and focused her full attention on me.

'A To-Do List?' she prompted.

'Yeah, you know, because I've got a lot of stuff *to do*.'

My wife's eyebrows began to knit together in a mask of disbelief and confusion. My explanation obviously hadn't explained why her husband of nearly ten years was up at three in the morning on his thirty-sixth birthday making . . . of all things . . . a To-Do list.

11

'I don't understand.' She rubbed the underside of her belly in the manner an old gypsy lady might use to polish her crystal ball. 'Exactly what stuff is it that you've got to do? And when have you got to do it?'

I looked down at my notepad. When Claire had entered the room I'd just finished Item number 253: 'Get old baby clothes out of the cupboard in loft' and was in the middle of Item number 254: 'Have a go at growing a beard'.

I knew she would be pleased that I was giving considered thought to the arrival of the new baby, but when it came to the idea of my cultivating facial hair, I was on less certain ground.

'It's just stuff.' I sounded sulky. 'Not interesting stuff. Just stuff.'

'Right. Well much as I'd love to sit here talking to you all night about "stuff", I'm badly in need of sleep. I only got up because I needed a wee – this baby is pressing down on my bladder something rotten – and now I need another one so I'll leave you to your list making.'

'Cheers, babe.' I got up from my desk, walked over and put my arms around her.

'Look, I won't be long. Ten, maybe fifteen minutes tops and then I'll be back in bed.'

'Fine, but no more than that, okay?'

'Scout's honour.'

It was two and a half hours and an extra two hundred or so items on the List later, not to mention having taken Lord Baden-Powell's name in vain, that I finally slunk back into bed without rousing my wife. I was exhausted. Shattered. Good for absolutely nothing other than sleep. But also elated. And alive. And excited. Because for the first time in a long while I felt as though I'd got a bit of direction in my life. As though I'd got a plan.

Chapter 2: 'Do something about the aforementioned problem.'

Waking up just after nine on the day of my birthday I was struck by how much energy I felt I had despite getting far less than my preferred seven hours sleep. As I pondered why this was, I heard my daughter scrambling up the stairs and within a few moments she'd appeared in the room, carrying a pen and pad of paper.

'Because it's your birthday Mummy said I can be a waitress and take your breakfast order,' she explained in her best 'proper' voice. 'What would you like to eat, sir?'

'What's on the menu?'

She looked down at the pad. 'Eggs.'

'What kind of eggs?'

She shrugged. 'Just eggs.'

Opting for 'just eggs' and 'just orange juice' I got a big kiss on the lips from my waitress, who wished me a happy birthday and left the room.

Half an hour later, I'd polished off my breakfast, opened my presents and listened to Lydia singing her best rendition *of Happy Birthday*, and was bouncing up and down on the bed with Lydia in time to music coming out of the i-Pod. It was weird. I'd gone to bed very late indeed and by rights should be completely shattered yet the tiredness didn't seem to want to come. I felt good about life. In fact I felt *great* about life. It wasn't just about it being my birthday. It wasn't that I'd had a rare lie-in combined with breakfast in bed. In mid-bounce, out of the corner of my eye, I spotted Lydia's old doodling book and remembered the reason for my new-found energy.

I picked up the notebook and scanned the last few entries: '409: Take all unwanted books to Oxfam because you've got too many'; '410: Get magazine subscription for *Vanity Fair* because it has long articles and it's not just about music'; '411: Start reading *Private Eye* again so you can work at being both humorous and topical'; '412: Give blood because you know it makes sense'; '413: Try wearing hats more often because you look good in them'.

It was odd reading these messages from my late-night self. What had possessed me to spend from eleven at night through to five thirty in the morning writing a To-Do List? I was reminded of the scene from *Memento* where Guy Pearce's amnesiac character notices that his body is covered in tattoos reminding him of things he needs to know. This notebook was my version of Guy Pearce's tattooed body. And oddly enough it was the reason that I was feeling happy.

The truth of the matter was that I'd always loved To-Do Lists. Always. I'm pretty sure that the second thing I did after learning to scrawl my name was to write a list of things I wanted to achieve. It probably went along the lines of:

1. Learn to read.
2. Take a nap.
3. Watch *Rainbow*.
4. Play with toys.

And though I might not have learned to read before I'd taken a nap or indeed watched *Rainbow* before playing with my toys, the very act of taking a pencil and paper and writing these things down one after the other gave me an immense amount of pleasure.

To me a list is a statement of intent, a plan, a map to point you in the right direction. Without my To-Do Lists I'd be lost. Without my To-Do Lists I would just be making stuff up as I went along and that, as far as I'm concerned, is no way to live a life.

My early To-Do Lists tended to be lists of books that I wanted to read, and each time I read one I got a tick. Now, while the writing of a list can be a reward in itself, as any veteran To-Do Lister will attest, the real pay-off is the satisfaction that comes from ticking, crossing, or scribbling an item off your list. With one neat action a task that has been bugging you for the longest time is utterly obliterated. *Pow!* It's gone. Nothing beats a hard-won tick off the list.

Soon after reaching secondary school in the early eighties, I came to realise that the making of To-Do Lists wasn't just an idle pastime but rather a means of survival, the significance of which I learned the hard way.

Set the arduous homework task by the Biology teacher, Mr Mason, of drawing margins on every single page of my exercise book, I decided that I would save time and effort by simply adding it to the To-Do List inside my head. At the time my mental To-Do List was populated by things like:

1. Learn how to dance like Michael Jackson.
2. Watch *Grange Hill*.
3. Read the *Lord of The Rings* trilogy.

4. Decide whether you're too old to still be playing with *Star Wars* figures.
5. Persuade parents to buy a video recorder.

I should have known that I was on a hiding to nothing. But it was only when the next Biology lesson came along and Mr Mason asked us to present our homework for inspection that I realised my mistake. My punishment was to write a five-hundred-word essay during lunch break entitled 'My favourite animal'. As punishments aimed at twelve-year-old boys go, it wasn't that bad but it was enough to demonstrate conclusively that when it came to keeping track of things you need to do, there is no better invention than an actual, written-down-on paper, To-Do List.

Years later, having ticked off items like 'get a girlfriend', 'get a degree', 'get a girlfriend who's in a band', 'get a job as a journalist', 'get married and buy a house' and 'write novel', all by the time I was thirty, I smugly thought I was doing pretty well with the whole To-Do-List thing. Of course there were a few items along the way that never got ticked off such as 'write music reviews for the *NME*', 'write a sitcom', and 'Go out with Kylie Minogue' but on the whole tickwise I thought I was doing okay. In fact, I thought I was doing so okay that there really was only one more thing left on my life list, and that was 'Have a baby'. And while ticking that one off was a lot less straightforward than I hoped it would be, once it happened in the spring of 2003, and Lydia was born, I felt ready to retire from the world of To-Do Lists. After all, I reasoned, what else is there? What I failed to realise of course was the first undeniable truth of To-Do Lists: 'Unless you're dead there's always going to be stuff that needs doing.'

As Claire and I got on with the business of raising our daughter, I took my eye off the To-Do-List ball, so to speak. After six years without a To-Do List to my name, a three-and-a-half-year-old daughter in the mix, another child on the way and a whole lot of stuff that I'd been putting on 'the back burner', there was no doubt that I'd probably stored up enough 'trouble' to last me an entire life time.

Returning to my breakfast leftovers I managed a few mouthfuls of toast before I found myself reaching for the list and writing in purple wax crayon (the only writing implement to hand): '414: Put pens in every room because I'm sick and tired of not being able to find anything to write with'; followed by '415: Tidy Lydia's crayons away before they all end up getting walked into the carpet', before scribbling a completely random '416: Overcome prison phobia so that you don't have to keep coming up with excuses for why you're not watching *Prison Break* like everyone else'.

I was fine for a while after that. In fact I'd had a shower and was almost dressed before succumbing to the urge to add items such as: 'Have a facial': 'Sample all the milks'; 'Be someone's mentor'; 'Text Richard'; 'See Darren and Emma', and 'Replace broken remote control'. I re-examined what I'd written and was confused. I understood why I wanted a facial (because I'd never had one and well, why not?) but where would I get one done and how would I avoid feeling like an idiot while receiving it? What exactly did I mean by sample all the milks? I'd done pasteurised, semi-skimmed, skimmed and gold top but I'd never tried Guernsey, goat or soya. But when I said 'all the milks' did that include camel, donkey, yak, water buffalo, reindeer, thistle, and . . . breast? And whose mentor was I going to be? What would it involve me doing? Would I have to put an advert in the paper? Would they know I was mentoring them or would I mentor by stealth? Texting my friend Richard sounded easy, but would it really be that straight-forward given that I hadn't worked out how to send or receive text messages since getting my new phone? I had found it hard enough to see Emma and Darren when they lived in Manchester so what was I going to do now they were in New Zealand? Finally, where on earth was I going to find a replacement remote control for my TV?

Problems. Problems. Problems. It was tempting to give up before I'd begun and yet despite the many obstacles to completing my ever-growing list I couldn't seem to stop adding to it. I added to it in the tapas restaurant that Claire took me to for my birthday lunch; I pulled over and added to it in the car on the way home from the park; I added to it as I prepared Lydia a tea-time snack and I carried on adding to it for what was left of the rest of the day. The following morning I added to it as soon as I woke up (admittedly less able to dance on the bed); I added to it when I was supposed to be getting on with work, and I added to it when I was supposed to be spending 'quality time' with Claire. In fact I added to it for more than six and a half days. Then I wrote Item 1398: 'Ride on world's fastest rollercoaster,' stopped, and felt very strange indeed.

PART TWO
Early November

(During which I try and work out what to do next with my to-do list and come up with a plan)

Chapter 3: 'Speak to a Canadian (they are nice).'

What exactly was I going to do next, now that I had this ludicrously long list? Perhaps the best thing was to put it in a drawer and forget about it. After all, it wasn't as though I was going to do all this stuff, was it? It was hard enough doing the essentials let alone actively seeking out stuff that – while it might improve my quality of life – wasn't exactly urgent. I mean, was it urgent to buy a few shirts that actually fitted? Couldn't I just carry on with the ones that were two sizes too small? And while I did appreciate that my parents wouldn't always be around, was there a desperate need to tell Mum and Dad that I loved them right this very second? Couldn't I just carry on giving them the thumbs-up sign whenever I nipped round to theirs? Yes, it would be great to play my bass guitar like Flea from the Red Hot Chilli Peppers, but given that it had been at least fifteen years since I'd bought it and no longer harboured the desire to appear on *Top of The Pops*, shouldn't I just let the whole thing lie?

The drawer was definitely the best place for the List so I stuck it in the one by the back door which was always overflowing with takeaway menus (Item 498: 'Empty drawer by back door of takeaway menus and bits of old junk') and told myself to forget about it until I could see a way forward that made some kind of sense.

I didn't have to wait too long. A few days later, when I least expected it, the way forward presented itself from a most unlikely source: Claire's friend, Alexa.

Alexa is Canadian. I mention this because as far as I can work out, being Canadian is a pretty good thing and the more I learn about my wife's friend (and about Canadians in general) the more I wonder why they aren't running the world. Canadians appear to be not only incredibly sensible but also really nice. Trust me, every home should have one.

Anyway, along with being Canadian, being a wife and mum to two kids and something of a master baker, Alexa also occasionally helps me out with some general administration. By which I mean pretty much everything work related that isn't to do with the actual writing of books: filing the important papers I'd neglected to put away; replying to letters that I hadn't answered; paying the bills I'd long been ignoring; and doing magical things with the huge plastic carrier bags of receipts that sat unlogged on the floor of my office, all so I could get on with the incredibly taxing business of being creative.

Anyway, what with the summer holidays, her having the kids at home to look after and my lax attitude to deadlines, it had been quite a while since Alexa had been over to help out. After receiving a particularly alarming demand from my accountant, telling me that I needed to email him some figures or risk handing over my family and home to the Inland Revenue, the first thing I did was set Alexa on the case.

'So what is it that you're working on?' she asked as I typed away on the computer.

'Looking up trips to Antarctica on the internet.'

'Any particular reason?'

'It's on my To-Do List, which I'm supposed to be ignoring at the moment but finding hard to let go,' I confided.

'Ah,' said Alexa knowingly, 'the To-Do List! Claire told me you're going through something of a mid-life crisis.'

'It's not a mid-life crisis,' I objected. 'It's me making a decision to become a fully fledged adult by finally sorting my stuff out.'

'And going to Antarctica is on there because . . .?'

'It's Antarctica.'

'Do you think that's a good enough reason?'

'Who wouldn't want to go to Antarctica?'

'Well, me for one.' She perched on the edge of my desk. 'I mean come on, Mike, you're a guy who likes his creature comforts. You can't tell me that you'd be happy in Antarctica?'

She made a good point. I do like my creature comforts and in order to go to Antarctica I'd have to fly to Buenos Aires in February, make my way to some remote town at the bottom of the country, then meet the boat and share a cabin with a total stranger for upwards of the three weeks (weather dependent) that it would take to get there. All of which, I strongly suspected, would feature a distinct lack of creature comforts.

'Now you put it like that I suppose the answer is no. And while I'm thinking about it, I'm pretty sure that I don't want to have a ride on the world's fastest rollercoaster . . . fly to Las Vegas and gamble everything I own on one single roll of a dice . . . go bungee jumping . . . or pet a dolphin . . . or drive a Ferrari at top speed . . . or even buy a pet monkey.'

'You really thought of buying a monkey?'

'Not a big one. Probably a chimp of some kind. Though I'm guessing even the small ones are quite messy.'

'So if you don't really want to do these things,' Alexa fixed me with a bemused grin, 'why are they on your To-Do List?'

'Aren't these the kinds of things that we're all supposed to want to do?'

Alexa shook her head. 'They're not on my list and I'm pretty sure they shouldn't be on yours either. Can I be honest with you? When Claire first told me what you were doing I thought, "Here we go, yet another guy trying to regain his youth by going on lots of *Boys Own* adventures"; then she told me how normal and everyday some of the things on your list were and I found myself thinking, "Good on you, Mike." I could get behind this. It's the kind of thing I would love to do. I can understand wanting to get things done, things that *need* to be done rather than stuff you just quite like the look of.' She paused and smiled. 'I do think you ought to do this list, but I don't think you should spoil it by getting too self-indulgent.'

'So you think the Antarctic stuff should go?'

She nodded.

'And the stuff about wanting to touch a fake breast?'

She rolled her eyes exactly like Claire does.

'And the monkey?'

'I think you know the answer to that one, Mike. Just keep it real.'

After Alexa had gone home, I headed downstairs, took the List out of the takeaway drawer and started checking through the entries. While most of the early items were okay, somewhere around the late eight hundreds an increasing number of 'less real' items had sprung up and continued to do so with alarming regularity, reaching a climax with the last hundred or so entries which wouldn't get me a single step closer to my goal of being a 'proper grown up'. So I set about scratching off every item that failed to reach my new standard of 'keeping it real'. In a bid to separate hardcore items from the kind of everyday stuff which I would probably get round to doing eventually anyway, I struck off anything that hadn't spent a good six months or so hanging around in To-Do-List purgatory. By the end of the day, although I was some 121 items poorer, I was in fact all the richer for having a list that now positively gleamed with an integrity of which Alexa and her fellow countrymen would be proud. I could feel it, I was nearly there. Now all I needed to do was to test out the plan slowly forming in my mind to make sure that it didn't have too many holes in it. Who better to test my theory on than the Sunday Night Pub Club?

Despite its title the Sunday Night Pub Club isn't so much a club as a loose collective of friends who get together once a week in the Queen's Head pub (commonly known as the Queen's), for a drink and a chat. At first this was a strictly boys-only affair that convened on a Thursday night but then Thursdays got too busy so Sunday became the new Thursday (which in itself had been the new Friday) and somewhere along the way we were joined by various girls who in spite of their fundamental fragrance could drink pints and hold their own in conversations that required them to rank pretty much everything into a Top Ten. Having gone through several line-up changes over the six years that we'd been in existence we were now down to a relatively solid (but classic) line-up of nine members: Arthur, Amy, Danby, Gary, Jo, Henshaw, Steve, Kaytee and Amanda.

'So what exactly are you saying?' said Arthur. 'That you've written a To-Do list?'

'It is a To-Do List of sorts, but actually it's much more than that.'

'In what way?'

'In every way.'

'Yeah, but in what way exactly?'

'Well, in the way that it's probably more like a manifesto.'

'A manifesto for what?'

'A manifesto for life . . . a manifesto for anyone who has ever sat down and thought to themselves "If only I had more time I'd do this or that" . . . in fact it's a manifesto for people like us.'

'He means a manifesto for grumpy thirtysomethings in ill-fitting clothes who hate their jobs,' said Danby dryly.

'And this manifesto,' asked Henshaw, 'has got how many things on it?'

I coughed nervously, aware of the mockery I was about to receive.

'At the last count, it was 1,277.'

The whole table exploded with laughter so violent it threatened to upturn several pints.

'You've honestly got a one-thousand-two-hundred-and-seventy-seven-item-long To-Do List?' said Kaytee. 'Mine usually max out around thirty.'

'This is brilliant!' laughed Arthur. 'That will take you forever!'

'I was thinking I'd give myself until my next birthday.'

'Actually.' Henshaw pulled a contemplative face. 'To give Mike his due that works out roughly to about three and a bit things a day, which I reckon is pretty doable.'

'If they're easy-to-do things,' countered Arthur. 'Is everything on the list easy to do?'

I shook my head. 'There's loads of stuff that will take weeks if not months. Stuff like losing weight, getting hold of lost friends and learning basic Italian.'

'Is parachuting on your list?' asked Amanda, reaching into her bag for a pen. 'If it's not I'll put it on for you.'

'No,' I replied sternly.

'Why not?' Amanda looked hurt.

'Because it's not about jumping out of planes or any of that business, it's about more everyday things. The kind of stuff that you ought to do but can always find a good excuse for not doing.'

'Like cleaning out the guttering?'

'Exactly.' I scanned my list. 'Item number 970: "Clear leaves from gutter".'

'Or sorting out damp patches in your hallway,' suggested Danby.

'Right on the nose. Item 125: "Sort damp patch in bathroom".'

'Right,' said Amanda, 'I get you now. I've got a To-Do List of my own like that as long as my arm.'

'But I bet it's not 1,277 items long,' said Danby adopting his usual stance as the Sunday Night Pub Club's resident cynic. 'Who really has that many things on their To-Do List? This just sounds made up.' He held out his hand. 'Come on, show me the list! Let's see what kind of stuff is on there that you think you need to do.'

'Hands off! Lanky one! Until it's over no one gets to see the full list but me.'

'So no one's seen the list? Not even Claire?'

'She's seen bits of it – before I really knew what I was doing – but not the full thing . . .' I paused for a moment. 'Oh, and Claire's friend Alexa has seen bits of it too.'

'Okay,' said Gary (who is often quite quiet on a Sunday night given that his Saturday nights tend to go on until ten or eleven on a Sunday morning). 'You've got your list and now it's got integrity, so what's next?'

I surprised myself by the determination in my voice. 'Well it's this: I'm actually going to do it.'

Chapter 4: 'Regardless of how ill prepared you are, head off like a bull in a china shop.'

Every now and again, when friends drop by for a cup of tea, Claire likes to share with them a pair of amusing stories that don't exactly show me in the best possible light. The first, referred to as 'the bull incident' involves a charging bull and an allegation (which I strongly deny) that several years ago when the aforementioned bull charged us as we crossed a field, I abandoned my wife-to-be at the first sign of danger and leapt over a fence to save myself. The second story (which I admit is true) concerns a spectacularly awful attempt at DIY.

Waking up on a Good Friday morning in a pre-kid world filled with the cheer of the forthcoming long weekend, I decided that I would take action on the myriad DIY tasks that needed doing around the house. And while there were window latches to fix, pictures to put up, leaking taps to attend to and a loo flush that sounded like a foghorn to sort out, I decided that the most pressing job lay somewhere else entirely. Today, I was going to paint the ugly brown floor tiles in the conservatory.

Most normal people would have done some minor investigation into the world of tile painting but I wasn't exactly normal people. Before Claire was even out of bed I'd got up, showered, breakfasted, made my way to B&Q and returned

28

home with eight litres of brilliant white paint. Now, you'd be forgiven for thinking that even with a cursory knowledge of the nature of tiles, I'd have bought a special tile paint or at a push a floor paint specifically designed to adhere to non-porous floor tiles. Sadly, I did neither of those things. Reasoning that all paint was pretty much the same, I purchased a brilliant white paint with an eggshell finish designed to be applied to internal walls and ceilings. Nowhere on the tins did it say that it was okay to use it on floors and when Claire pointed this out, having entered the kitchen in her dressing gown to find me on my hands and knees daubing huge dollops of paint all over the conservatory floor, my reply was a casual comment along the lines of, 'You worry too much, it's paint. How wrong can paint be?'

Two days later, having persuaded Claire to finish off the job that I was no longer interested in, we found out.

As we placed the conservatory furniture on the pristine white floor for the first time, we were horrified to notice huge swathes of white paint lifting up the second they came into contact with anything abrasive. Within a matter of hours the conservatory floor went from looking like an expanse of newly fallen snow to the slushy mess left behind on a busy urban street a day or two later.

I share this story in order to illustrate an important fact about myself: when it comes to an undertaking, I am the very definition of: 'Act first. Think later'. And the To-Do List was no exception.

The morning following my announcement to the Sunday Night Pub Club I'd felt on top of the world. Fired up by the commitment that I had made in front of my friends and with my mind racing with anticipation at getting stuck in, I shared my good news with Claire over breakfast.

'So you're actually going to do this list thing?'

'Absolutely. I really think tackling the List is going to be the making of me.'

'I'm sure it will be,' said Claire dryly. 'So what's the plan? If you are going to start as of today may I suggest, ''Help Claire out with the ironing because the To-Do ironing basket upstairs is bursting at the seams''.'

'I'd love to, babe,' I replied, 'but I'm afraid ironing is not on the List.'

'It wouldn't be, would it? So what exactly is your plan of attack? Have you got any strategy?'

'Other than looking at the List and doing stuff on it?'

'Trust me, Mike, I know you better than you know yourself and I'm telling you that you'll need a plan of attack if you're not going to get bored with the whole thing after ten minutes. Just remember the tile-painting episode.'

'That was different,' I protested, but had to stifle a smile.

'Different how? Different because you tackled a job in a half-cocked manner without having a plan? Or different because it wasn't you that got bored halfway through and talked me into finishing it off while you watched TV?'

This woman was definitely raining on my parade.

'Just different. The To-Do List is a different kettle of fish altogether, okay? It's not a brown-tiled floor, it's a To-Do List.'

'It doesn't matter, you still need a plan,' said Claire giving me her best ''this will all end in tears'' shake of the head. 'You can't just race headlong into the List hoping that a bit of luck and sheer momentum will take you all the way through to your next birthday.'

'Oh, really?' I replied in a high-handed manner. 'Well, we'll have to see about that.'

*   *   *

I made my way upstairs to my office in the loft, sat down at my desk and began looking around for inspiration. Before it struck, I accidentally knocked my computer mouse and within a few moments I was notified by electronic 'ding' that I had seven emails waiting.

There wasn't anything exciting: some spam; a number of invitations to buy stuff from John Lewis and Amazon; and a mocking message from Arthur offering a hard cash bet that I would fall on my face with this To-Do-List thing before the month was out.

Fighting talk! I dashed off a dismissive reply to Arthur and then the following email to friends, family and work colleagues, in fact everybody in my online address book:

> Dear all,
> Just wanted to let you know that having come to the conclusion that it's about time I joined the world of fully functioning adults on a permanent basis, as of today I will be undertaking a 1,277-item To-Do List (while continuing with my regular 'day job') which I plan to have completed by my 37th birthday in approximately twelve months' time. The reason I'm telling you lot this is to give me the inspiration and motivation to succeed, knowing full well that should I fail my task I will look like a complete and utter buffoon in front of you all and will afford you the right to mock me (as some have done already) to within an inch of my life.
> See you all soon
> Mike x

I read and re-read the message several times before pressing send and then watched keenly as my computer's email programme flung the hundred or so messages it had loaded up out into cyberspace. There was no going back. Right there on the spot I was officially motivated. Feeling as though I was still riding the crest of a wave I replied to all the emails in my in-box and then permanently deleted all 122 items of spam from the rubbish bin. It was almost as if things that needed to be done seemed to be lining themselves up just to have me knock them straight back down and, although none of them was on my official To-Do List, getting them done was a good feeling nonetheless.

Keen for this euphoria to continue, I took a look through the List for any items particularly suited to being ticked off from where I was sitting and eventually found Item 109: 'Be a better correspondent with people that you don't get to see every day because even a single email once a month is better than nothing.' I decided to email my friend Lisa.

Since Lisa had emigrated to Australia six years earlier we'd been terrible at keeping in touch. Every time I'd come across her name in my address book I'd feel a pang of guilt and think to myself, 'I really must drop her a line and see how she's doing' only to get distracted moments later by something seemingly more pressing. Well, not any more. I put some music on quietly and wrote Lisa a long letter asking about her news, telling her all mine and even adding in a selection of pictures of Lydia.

I now felt positively glowing. No one writes long emails any more and yet I had just written *and* sent what was almost a novella to Lisa. And even though this solitary email might not constitute a tick (there were friends in New Zealand, South Africa, south Wales *and* Manchester who needed emails plus the tenor of the entry was that I had to correspond on a *regular* basis) I was entitled to feel that I wasn't just a good person. I was well on my way to becoming a great person.

   I briefly contemplated a celebratory lap of the house but just as I was about to stand up the following email popped up on screen:

> All right, Mate?
> Just read your email! 1,277-item To-Do List! You have got to be joking! I'll keep my fingers crossed for you, fella! Good luck.
> John-boy

Which was quickly followed by this one from Nadine:

> Mikey babe!
> Are you mad? A 1,277-item To-Do List! I hope Item 344 is: 'Nip down to London and have lunch with Nadine as I haven't seen her in ages?' It better had be!
> Best of luck!
> Nx

Which was followed by this one from Chris:

> 1,277 things! You've got no chance! Let's meet up for a beer sometime to discuss!
> See you soon.
> Chris

Message after message pinged into my in-box. It was great. Everyone knew what I was doing. There really was no backing out, even if I'd wanted to, which of course I didn't. So in the spirit of doing things now rather than later I decided to tackle Item 173: 'Sort out garden because it's a jungle out there'.

*   *   *

Having donned my green parka, army surplus hat and old trainers, I opened the back door and peered outside at the patio. It was covered in a thick carpet of leaves from the huge oak tree at the side of the house. Despite my strenuously wishing that they would magically disappear they had remained in situ, mocking my lack of gardening skills for some time now.

I ventured down to the bottom of the garden and opened my shed (like me, it had seen better days) and rummaged around for the rake (a wedding present from my parents).

Looking at the sheer volume of leaves (you couldn't see any of the blue brick patio at all) and factoring in the leaf fall on the garden itself (three times the size of the patio) I concluded I had the wrong tool for the job. Okay, it was a rake of sorts but it clearly wasn't designed for heavy-duty leaf clearance. On a recent drive to town I had passed a couple of council workmen and briefly admired their huge leaf-retrieval system that looked like a pair of broom handles with scoops at the end. That was exactly what I needed and as the wind began to blow, swirling the leaves at my feet and making my eyes water, I decided that a trip to B&Q was in order.

Even though my local B&Q was relatively quiet it still took me the best part of three quarters of an hour to make it out of the store. This had less to do with leaf-picking-up devices (I managed to pick up one called 'Big Green Hands', that looked like a huge pair of plastic claws) and had more to do with the fact that I got distracted.

There's something incredibly comforting about DIY stores. I like the way they're set out in aisles that you can wander up and down, I like the way that you can rarely tell what the weather's doing once you're inside but most of all I like the fact that they are filled with a hundred and one solutions to everyday problems and though I had 1,277 pressing problems, I couldn't resist a few solutions to problems that I didn't have yet which explains why, along with my 'Big Green hands', I left the store with two tubes of No More Nails, a scart plug, two bedside lamps, a device for detecting electrical cables behind walls, two packs of discounted Christmas baubles and a new set of Christmas lights, a cork notice board and a mini potted palm. I didn't actually do any gardening that day because by the time I reached home it had started to rain.

This haphazard, start-a-million-different-projects-but-finish-none-of-them attitude continued not just through the first day of the To-Do List, but through the first week and well into the second. But it wasn't until the beginning of the third week as Claire and I sat down after putting Lydia to bed, that I finally admitted that perhaps Claire had made a good point about the necessity of a plan.

'So how are you getting on with that List of yours?' This was the first reference that she had made to the List since she'd reminded me of the Tile-Painting Incident.

'Not great,' I confessed. 'Today I thought about learning Italian, I got a few tools out of the shed, I bought a load more stuff from B&Q that I neither needed nor wanted, I half wrote a letter to my Uncle Churchill in Jamaica whom I haven't seen in thirty-odd years and I'm getting a bit sick of the fact that the loft still looks like a tip since my attempt to clear out the under-eaves space. It's been a great couple of weeks for procrastination but not a brilliant one for getting things done. Okay, I admit it. You were right, I was wrong. There is no way that I'll be able to keep this up if I don't come up with a plan to fool myself into staying on course, so I've made a couple of decisions.'

'Like what?'

'Well, the first is that I'm not going to do anything more today, tomorrow, or for the rest of the week.'

'So, some kind of less-is-more philosophy?' joked Claire. 'Let me know if it works!'

'No.' I narrowed my eyes in mock menace. 'I do need a plan and I think I've finally got one.'

'Which is?'

'To take it one step at a time.'

'And your first step is . . .?'

'Get some expert advice.'

'From whom?'

'Well, that's the genius part,' I said, tapping the side of my nose in a knowing fashion. 'I'm planning to get my expert advice from the best in the business.'

'What business would that be?'

'The time business,' I replied. 'I'm going to get me some face time with a genuine Time Management guru.'

Chapter 5: 'Get some advice from people who know what they're talking about.'

A couple of years ago, around the time I was turning thirty, I had a few moments similar to my current To-Do-List obsession when I thought I should sort my life out. I can see now it was the whole turning thirty 'Where am I going? Where have I been? Where am I right now?' thing but at the time it seemed like the moment to get myself organised.

My first step was to head for the shops in the hope that purchasing useful things would miraculously change my life. This was a daft theory and one all too well understood by those who churn out work-out DVDs in January. Just as my wife purchasing Davina McCall's *Power of Three* work-out DVD and leaving it gathering dust on the shelf didn't help anyone but Davina McCall, buying Mark Forster's book *Get Everything Done and Still Have Time To Play*, reading the first two chapters and then not going back to it because (irony of ironies) I couldn't find the time, doesn't help anyone but Mark Forster.

Luckily I didn't take Forster's book to Oxfam along with Claire's Davina DVDs and her *Mr Motivator* box set, but retained it for use in possible future emergencies just like this one. But of course I had to find it first.

I began the search in the living room because that's where we keep most of our books. Like many young couples who prefer people not to think they spend their evenings watching property programmes or yelling at the characters on *EastEnders*, we owned a lot of books that we liked to keep on display. There were upwards of a couple of hundred of them in the living room alone and others scattered at various locations around the house. The clever-clever stuff (Zola, Dickens, Carver, etc.) and feminist stuff belonged solely to Claire; the occasional smart modern stuff (Smith, Amis, Eggers, etc.) along with the stuff that seemed more than a little bit random (an original copy of *Everything You Wanted To Know About Sex But Were Afraid To Ask*, *The Collected Andy Capp* and *Gary Wilmot's Guide to Doing Impressions*) were mine; and finally the *Lonely Planet* and *Rough Guides* that gave the impression we were a well-travelled cosmopolitan couple (South Africa, Russia, Crete, Thailand and the USA) were jointly ours.

The problem with this many books was that if you wanted a specific tome and hadn't organised them into some kind of order (Item 818. 'Organise book shelves so that you can find a specific book without looking through everything') you were pretty much stuffed.

I started with the main shelf above the stereo but it wasn't there nor on the ones by the French doors; I checked the three IKEA shelves in our bedroom but it wasn't there nor in Lydia's room (she had been known to pluck a random book off the shelf in order to spend an entire afternoon pretending that she was reading *The Collected Works of Aphra Behn*); finally I headed up to the office/spare room and checked out the books stacked against the wall by the sofa bed and the ones piled on the wonky IKEA Lack shelving. No luck. About to give up, I racked my brains to remember where I'd had it last and began to see disconnected images of me in a tidying frenzy some months earlier when I'd grabbed a bunch of stuff that had been sitting on the floor at my feet and tossed it into a box before ceremonially dumping it in . . . *the under-eaves storage space.*

Twenty minutes later with half of the contents of the storage cupboard once again strewn around the room, I finally found what I was looking for.

'Time is what our lives are made of', said the blurb on the back of the book, 'and yet our failure to use time properly can have disastrous effects on our happiness and sense of well-being. This book is written for everyone who has to juggle different demands in a busy schedule, including advice on finding an effective system while making allowances for human psychology and the unexpected.'

It was hard to believe how right this book was for me given my situation. I called Claire upstairs and read her the blurb.

'*Get Everything Done* is a book written for everyone who has to juggle different demands in a busy schedule,' I said pointing to the relevant part of the blurb. 'See that? A book for me.'

'That's great,' said Claire. 'Now all you have to do is read it.'

Good point. This book was only going to work for me if I actually read it but I hadn't got the time to read it so I was a bit stuck.

I woke up my computer and typed Mark Forster's name into Google hoping to find an audio version of *Get Everything Done* so I could multi task. Instead I found something far more useful: the author's email address. Within minutes I was composing a message to him:

Dear Mr Forster

My name's Mike Gayle and I've got a list of 1,277 things I need to do before my next birthday. I was wondering whether you might be free at some point quite soon to have a chat in person about what I'm attempting to do.

Cheers

Mike Gayle

'Do you think he'll reply?' Claire was reading the message over my shoulder.

'I'm hoping so.' I turned over the book and examined his author photo. He looked cheery, the sort of man that you'd definitely trust with your car keys. 'He certainly looks like the sort of man who would write back.'

'So, are you going to carry on with the List in the meantime?'

'No way. I'm on a roll so my plan is to use my time wisely and head off right now for a chat with another, more local, expert but one whose field is more organisational. And I'll give you a clue: she's Canadian, married with two kids under three, and easily, hands down, the most organised person we know.'

It was just after eight by the time I arrived at Alexa's. After ushering me into her front room, she headed off to get us some coffee while I looked around, wearing different eyes from the ones I had worn here on previous occasions. Suddenly everything spoke of Alexa's organisational skills. The books were all in alphabetical order with the bottom shelf reserved for oversized books. I wondered idly if Alexa (whose postgraduate degree had been in Librarianship) had also made miniature library tickets for them all; on the table next to the sofa, fanned out in a decorative fashion that you might find in an upmarket hairdressers, were half a dozen magazines: *Martha Stewart's Living*, Oprah Winfrey's *O*, *Canadian Living*, *Canadian Interiors*, *Patchwork Monthly* and *Red*; in the corner of the room were three pairs of shoes all lined up in ascending size from left to right. This was a woman who knew about being organised. This was a woman who would definitely be able to assist me on my mission to conquer the List.

'So come on then,' she said, cradling her coffee as she leaned back in her armchair. 'You were very cryptic on the phone. What exactly can I do to help you?'

'Well, you know that list? The one with the 1,277 things on it? Well, I've sort of run into trouble and I need advice about how to be organised and given that you're the most organised person I know . . .'

'I wouldn't say that exactly . . .'

'I would. I bet if I went into your loft right now I wouldn't find half a cast-iron fireplace, would I?'

'No, you wouldn't,' replied Alexa, baffled. 'Would I find one in yours?'

I raised my eyebrows in a show of guilt. 'All I'm trying to demonstrate is that you're organised. I bet you even know exactly where your birth certificate is.'

'Top left-hand drawer of the sideboard in the dining room.'

'And how about last year's tax return?'

'In a box file underneath my side of the bed.'

'And what about . . .?' I struggled to find something obscure, '. . . I know, what about . . . a pen? We can never find a pen for love nor money in our house. So come on, Alexa, show me a pen.'

She plucked one from the shelf behind my head and handed it to me.

'I got sick of not being able to find a pen when I wanted one so once a week, usually on a Tuesday, I go around every room and leave pens at pre-designated pen-dropping spots. I know it's not normal behaviour but it makes me happy.'

'You see?' I wanted to offer her a round of applause. 'This is why I've come here tonight. Because you can do stuff like this. So come on, Alexa, what's your secret? What's the secret of being a proper grown-up?'

Like any guru worth their money Alexa took a moment to consider her answer. 'For me,' she began, 'the real secret is routine. For instance I always stick the kid's lunch bags in the same places. And I always put them out before we go to bed and have everything organised the night before so that when I'm on auto-pilot in the morning I don't have to think.'

'Right,' I said wondering how to apply this theory to the List. 'Use routine.'

Alexa grinned as though she'd read my mind. 'I'm guessing that for your list the key thing will be making sure that you get into the routine of doing things every day.' She took a sip of her coffee and looked guilty. 'Since we're talking lists, I will tell you something that I don't tell many people because they'd laugh at me: I make To-Do Lists all the time and sometimes when I'm feeling particularly low I put things like ''Take a shower'' just to have the satisfaction of ticking it off. It's my kick-start for the day.'

'So you're saying I should make sure not to do all the easy stuff straight away? Otherwise I'll have used all of my kick starts?'

'Exactly. When you've got as many things as you have, you've got to pace yourself. In fact I would break them up into the things that you're excited about and the things that you're not so excited about and then alternate them so there's always something to look forward to. It's like eating your pudding before your tea. If you do, there's no incentive to eat your tea.'

'Food metaphors – now you're talking my language. Though I have to admit between the ages of nineteen and twenty-five before I met Claire I regularly ate my pudding before my tea.'

'Not one for delayed gratification then?'

'This is probably where I've fallen down these past few years.'

'Well, you're going to have to get that sorted pronto, my friend, because getting things done is all about delayed gratification. Put the work in now for a pay-off in the future.'

Feeling like a soldier on the front line after a stirring motivational speech from my general I rose to my feet and just about stopped myself from giving her a salute.

'Thanks, I feel really inspired.'

Alexa nodded sagely. 'That's good but remember to pace yourself.'

'What are you doing now? Sorting out your sock drawers or some such?'

'No, it's knitting club tonight.'

I couldn't help myself. I laughed. Alexa was no longer a general, she was back to being my wife's super-organized, constantly baking, Oprah-loving best friend and figure of fun.

'You're going to knitting club?' I scoffed. 'Isn't the first rule of knitting club not to talk about knitting club?'

'Like I haven't heard that a million times! It's just me and some mom friends. I'm knitting a cardigan. We talk about all kinds of interesting things. You should try it some time.'

'Yeah, right,' I replied. 'Me in a knitting club?'

*　　*　　*

When I got home I checked my emails and found the following message:

> Dear Mike
> Thanks for your email, and I'd be very pleased to help you with this. It sounds a fascinating idea. Presumably you're thinking in terms of a phone conversation? If so, when's a good time for you to talk?
> Best wishes,
> Mark Forster
> The Time Freedom Coach

I couldn't believe it. Mark Forster, a man so skilled in Time Management that he referred to himself not as *a* Time Freedom Coach but *The* Time Freedom Coach had agreed to talk to me! I suddenly pictured myself doing all my normal work, spending half an hour a day demolishing the List in small but efficient nuggets of time and then taking the afternoon off to do the things I really like doing like falling asleep in front of the TV. This wasn't just good news. This was the best news ever. I typed a reply straight away:

> Dear Mark,
> Thank you for your speedy reply. I was actually thinking of coming to see you but then it occurred to me that given that you're The Time Freedom Coach in Chichester and I'm a writer in Birmingham, that probably wouldn't be a particularly useful way of making the maximum possible use of the time available to either of us! How about we speak at your earliest convenience?
> Best wishes
> Mike Gayle

Moments later:

Dear Mike

I've put you down for tomorrow at 10am. If another time would be better for you, please let me know, though I can't do earlier than that.

Best wishes,

Mark

Things were really starting to come together.

'A lot of it is to do with imposing order on chaos,' said Mark on the phone the following morning. 'Life is pretty chaotic but if you make a list it's imposing order on life. I tell people who feel overwhelmed that the first step is just to sit and write everything down: it helps you calm down and see what action you need to take. That said, amongst my students and the people I work with I have to admit that I don't actually encourage the use of To-Do Lists.'

I was horrified.

'Why not?'

'What I do instead is encourage people to have a closed list, by which I mean a list of things that you are actually going to do. If it's done properly that can be used to control the amount of work they take on in a day because most people take on more than they could ever hope of dealing with properly.'

'Like me and my 1,277 things?'

'Yes, indeed,' laughed Mark. 'What you need to do is balance the work coming in with the work you're actually doing.'

It was a good point but it wasn't much help to me, given that I'd already taken on more than I could ever hope to deal with properly.

He sensed my disquiet. 'The thing is, Mike, a To-Do List should not be the be all and end all. You need a life beyond

45

the list. You need to be wary of becoming so list-bound that you lose all creativity. I encourage people to put on their list to "think" about things and "explore" so that the list is creative in itself.'

I checked to see if I'd actually written down anything at all about 'thinking' or 'exploring'.

I hadn't.

Resigning myself to doing my 'thinking' and 'exploring', in my own time without the benefit of a tick earned, I persuaded Mark to open up more about his theories on time management before finally quizzing him about the one demon I most needed to conquer if I was ever going to succeed: Procrastination.

'The thing is,' I began, 'I feel like procrastination is my number-one enemy – my Achilles heel and the one thing most likely to scupper my mission. As one of life's chief procrastinators, how can I hope to overcome it for good?'

'That's a good question,' chuckled Mark. 'I've found you don't need to procrastinate when you're on top of things. The example I always use is washing dishes. If you leave the dishes unwashed for a month you'll be resistant to doing them but if you wash up immediately after every meal then you will be less resistant.'

'That's great,' I said, 'but my list, to use your analogy, is actually a very, very big pile of washing-up. It's probably the equivalent of having not washed a single dish for a good three or four years.'

'Looks like you're out of luck then!'

I really had thrown myself in at the deep end by attempting to tackle the List. In a bid to try to end our conversation on a high I asked one final question that I hoped would send me off feeling refreshed and focused.

'If there was one single thing I could do that would help to achieve my goal what would it be?'

'That's easy. The best thing is to tell every single person you know what you're doing so that you commit yourself fully to the project.'

'Like for instance sending out a mass email to your entire address book explaining how you're going to complete a 1,277-item To-Do List?'

'Yes, that might work.'

I didn't have the heart to tell Mark that I'd already tried this.

'Anything else you can think of? Any final words of wisdom?'

Mark mulled the question over for a few moments. 'Well, there is one thing . . .'

'Yes?'

'Try picking some buddies to help you along the way, so you are accountable to them for getting this list done.'

'How about a bunch of layabouts and n'eer-do-wells in a pub in Moseley?'

'Will they keep you on the straight and narrow?'

'I reckon they'll have a go.'

'Then they sound like exactly the sort of people you'll need.'

'So the list is back on?' asked Kaytee as I revealed my big news to the Sunday Night Pub Club the following weekend. 'I didn't know it had stopped.'

'It didn't. I just paused it while I gathered my thoughts properly.'

'That's brilliant, I'm really chuffed for you.'

'You see, I spoke to a Time Management bloke recently and he said I should get you in as cheerleaders.'

'Do we get uniforms and pom-poms?' asked Steve.

'You can have whatever you want, but right now we need to work out the rules.'

The exact rules for tackling the list had been on my mind for some time. For instance, there were things that are easy to define as being crossed off, for example Item 399: 'Tell Mum that I love her.' But at what point exactly would Item 70: 'Lose weight', be crossed off? After I'd lost one pound? Or eight? And given that I now had 1,260 things left to do and roughly nine months in which to do them, that equated to roughly 4.5 things every single day, even if I didn't take a single day off between now and my birthday (a big if), wouldn't I be tempted to give up if I got behind? After all, 4.5 things is fine if they are all to do with tidying drawers or painting woodwork but if one of those things happens to be Item 655: 'Digitise the best of your old mix tapes' or Item 1006: 'Build something out of wood for Lydia', then I was going to be pretty much stuffed.

One hour, two rounds, and a diversionary conversation based on the question: 'If you could wear one celebrity's head on your shoulders for a whole day whose would you choose and why?' we finally came up with the following set of rules for tackling the To-Do List.

1. Everything on the List must be attempted at least once.
2. To allow a greater degree of flexibility a ninety-nine-per-cent tick rate or above will be considered a success.
3. But to make sure that Gayle doesn't just sit on his backside for nine months, a ninety-eight-per-cent

tick rate or below will be considered a complete and utter failure.

4. As of today Arthur, Gary, Henshaw, Steve, Danby, Amy, Kaytee, Jo and Amanda are all officially appointed judges of the To-Do List.
5. The judges' words are final.
6. Judges do not have to wear silly wigs unless they really want to (thanks, Steve).
7. To make sure Gayle doesn't give up halfway, there will be an audit at the end of April just to make sure that he's on track.
8. On completion of the challenge, Gayle must hand over the List in its entirety to the judges.
9. No fibbing.
10. And no getting behind on the real everyday stuff that you have to do either.

There in front of me spread across six half-torn beer mats on the table were the rules that would be my constant companions for the next nine months. And now that I had my rules, and expert opinions from both a busy mum of two and a Time Management Guru, I felt as though there was nothing that could stand between me and a completed 1,277-item To-Do List. But that night as I crawled into bed and settled down to sleep, Claire whispered something in my ear that made me reconsider: 'I think my contractions have started.'

PART THREE

Late December

(During which an offer is made, a lot of sleep is missed and the list sort of goes by the wayside)

Chapter 6: 'Remember failure is just another word for . . . failure.'

As I stared out of the loft window at the rotten December weather (rain, hail *and* snow) while contemplating the fact that there were only seven shopping days left until Christmas and I hadn't bought a single present, my mobile rang and brought me back to earth. The screen said: 'Agent Mobi calling'. Sadly, this was no James Bond style assignment coming my way but my literary agent Simon calling me. I knew this was likely to be bad news, possibly even the kind of bad news that might see me having to get a day job, because in my experience literary agents are not prone to shooting the breeze for the sake of it, so when one calls you on an actual *telephone* rather than contacting you by email it is usually for a reason: they either have news or are looking for news *from* you.

If Simon was indeed looking for news *from* me then that would undoubtedly be because he had been prompted into action by an enquiry from my editor, Sue, relating to the book that I still hadn't finished and was due to be delivered three months ago. Even if he was looking to deliver news *to* me there was still no reason to relax: it would probably mean trouble anyway.

'Mike,' boomed Simon (who incidentally once trained as an actor), 'how are you, good sir?'

'Great, thanks.' I stared blankly at the half-typed sentence on my computer screen. 'How about yourself?'

'Me? Never better. All ready for Christmas?'

'Absolutely.'

'And how's that new baby of yours?'

'Fantastic.'

'And how's the new book going?'

'Great,' I replied. 'Shouldn't be too long before it's all wrapped up.'

This wasn't exactly true, given that it was probably going to take another couple of weeks to finish.

'Good to hear it,' boomed Simon. Small talk time was over.

'So, Mike, that book proposal you emailed me a while back . . . I just wanted to let you know that I loved it.'

I was confused. 'Which book proposal?'

'The email that you copied me in on telling all your mates that you were doing those 1,277 things. It's a great idea.'

'That wasn't a book proposal, that was just me spouting off like a lunatic.'

'Really?' Simon seemed unfazed by this news. 'Well, if it wasn't, it certainly is now because I've just this minute finished pitching it to your publishers. They love it. They think it will really be a lot of fun. What do you think?'

'It sounds . . . it sounds . . . great.'

'Good!' boomed Simon. 'That's what I like to hear. Anyway, no point me wasting your time yakking. Get cracking on that list of yours because you've got another book to write!'

To describe the last couple of weeks that culminated in my agent pitching a non-existent book idea to my publishers as 'something of a whirlwind' would have been a major understatement. It had been more like a tornado ripping through my relatively tranquil life and turning various objects (small cows included) upside down and ripping the roof off everything that had a roof to rip off.

The whirlwind began with Claire's contractions and continued throughout the rest of the night and the following day and saw not only the arrival of my second daughter, Maisie Gayle (9lbs) at 8.58p.m. on the Monday night but also various altercations with Tory party canvassers, maternity hospital parking meters and overly complacent nurses who thought we were exaggerating when we told them that our baby daughter's arrival was imminent.

Following my day of excitement I'd left the maternity hospital just after midnight and stopped off at the local chip shop for a celebratory kebab (in lieu of a cigar), eaten it on the way home and then had promptly fallen asleep. The following morning I was still somewhat shell-shocked but pretty well rested. Little did I know that this would end up being the last full night's sleep that I would get.

Heading to bed at around ten on the evening of baby Maisie's first day at home, Claire and I hoped with all our strength that she would be our ticket to joining that small but perfectly formed group of parents known as the Smug Parents Club, group motto: 'Our babies slept through the night from day one.' Our friends Leona and Paul had been members of the Smug Parents Club from the birth of their first baby in January 2002 and had remained fully fledged members despite two more children. Our NCT friends Tracey and Stefan were equally fortunate when Tracey gave birth to baby Jake a fortnight after Lydia was born in the May of 2003. 'What? You've not slept a wink since Lydia was born?' they both asked in disbelief as we explained to them her erratic sleeping patterns (or should that be non-sleeping patterns). 'Jake slept through the night from day one.'

Alas, Maisie wasn't the slightest bit interested in facilitating our membership of the Smug Parents Club. Utilising her own unique hybrid scream (part-tortured fox gnawing off its own foot and part-cat being strangled) she proceeded to wake us up every twenty minutes until somewhere around four o'clock in the morning, having tried everything in the book (and by book I mean the entire library of baby literature that Claire had accumulated from the moment that she first became pregnant with Lydia), I picked Maisie up, headed downstairs, turned off the burglar alarm and decided that now was as good a time as any to tackle something from the List.

Item 897 was 'Get round to watching those DVDs that Danby gave you because you've had them from the best part of eighteen months', which on the surface you'd be forgiven for thinking would be an easy tick, given how much I liked watching TV. Sadly, these were no ordinary DVDs of the quality US TV box set variety. These were 'art' DVDs that were loaned to me by Danby in his role as Professor Higgins to my Eliza Doolittle as part of an earlier self-inspired attempt to get myself 'into' culture. The first DVD was called *The Cost of Living* and was a piece of performance art by the DV8 dance company. It was hailed by *Time Out* as being: 'EXCEPTIONAL . . . nothing less than visual poetry.' The second DVD, *Rivers and Tides*, was a film about the artist Andy Goldsworthy who, according to the back of the DVD box, was 'one of Britain's best-known sculptors'. At the time when Danby handed these DVDs to me he said, 'Listen, these are the most astonishing performances that you will ever see. Watch them now.' And I really did mean to watch them because I wanted to be the kind of person who could make small talk about how there are dance companies 'breaking down the barrier between dance and theatre' as well as wanting to be able to name at least one well-known British sculptor.

Despite my ambition to be interested in stuff that wasn't about buying or selling houses or that featured explosions of some description, I'd never managed to watch either of these two DVDs but all this time later, as I looked at the digital display on the DVD player that said '04.12' and then at the baby in my arms who showed no interest in sleeping, I reasoned that if ever there was a good time to watch these DVDs this was it. So dropping the first DVD into the player, I settled myself on the sofa, propped the baby up so that she could see the TV and settled down in preparation for a late night dose of high culture. Needless to say we were both asleep within a matter of moments.

From that night onwards Maisie proved to be the worst sleeper ever. In fact if there had been a club for not-so-smug parents who wanted to crow: 'Oh, my baby has kept me awake from day one!' then Claire and I would have been made presidents of it in a shot. Though Maisie did sleep, it just wasn't at night, and with Lydia awake and alert from six in the morning there were times when Claire and I were convinced that our kids were deliberately trying to keep us up for twenty-four hours seven days a week in some kind of Olympic endurance test. It was no way to live at the best of times and certainly no way to live if you had a book to write and a 1,277 item-long To-Do List to whittle down to some-thing more sensible.

*　　*　　*

After my conversation with Simon I leaned back in my chair and began searching through the pile of debris on my desk (a broken fax machine, a week's worth of newspapers, half a banana and a half-drunk bottle of Evian with bits floating in it) until I finally found the List. As I scanned its pages I could feel myself beginning to panic; it was starting to sink in that I had just informed Simon that not only would I be continuing with the To-Do List but also writing a book about it. Why? Why hadn't I just said, 'No, Simon, it wasn't a pitch for a book but a daft email about a daft idea that I no longer want to do?' I can only imagine that my subconscious wanted to motivate me to greater things. Or possibly it was down to the simple fact that I was so shattered from being up with the baby that I truly could no longer tell my arse from my elbow.

In a bid to (as the Time Management Guru had put it) 'impose some kind of order' on the chaos that was threatening to take me over, I grabbed a loose sheet of paper from my printer tray and wrote down a list of all the things that I needed to do *right now* that weren't on my original To-Do List:

1. Buy a new mobile phone to replace the one that Claire put in the washing machine.
2. Phone old phone company about porting number.
3. Sort out problem with laptop.
4. Cancel old phone insurance Direct Debit.
5. Email editor.
6. Send Connie a birthday card.
7. And a present.
8. Send publisher receipts for library event.
9. Invoice BA.

10. Make appointment to see accountant.
11. Invoice *The Express*.
12. Print out photos.
13. Write short story for charity book.
14. Write other short story for charity book.
15. Edit page proofs for short story for the other charity book.
16. Send biog stuff to Simon.
17. Buy the kids' Christmas presents.
18. Decide what we're doing about Christmas.
19. Decide what we're doing about New Year.
20. Book hotel for London trip.
21. Call Dyson about vacuum cleaner.
22. Reply to website email.
23. See Nadine.
24. Get together signed copies of books for Danny's charity thing.
25. Sort present for Lauren and Greg's wedding.
26. Book Claire's theatre tickets.
27. Chase council about parking ticket.
28. Send camera back to Amazon.
29. Wait in for gas man.
30. Do Phil's DVD.
31. Pay web people.
32. Sort out TV aerial.
33. Take Lydia swimming.
34. Sort out problem with disappearing cursor on Word.
35. Finish novel.
36. Spend time with kids.
37. Spend time with wife.
38. Find time to sleep.

Even just looking at the List made me hyperventilate. I'd been putting off some of the stuff ever since I'd first started the To-Do List and those things had become more and more pressing until now there really was nowhere left to hide. And to top it all I had just informed Simon that I was going to turn the To-Do List into a book too.

I was in trouble. Big trouble. And whatever happened over the course of the next twenty-four hours, the one thing of which I was sure was that I was going to have to make some pretty huge decisions very, very soon.

'I've made a decision,' I said, sitting bolt upright in bed at just after five in the morning.

'Urrrrggghhh?' said Claire.

'I said I've made a decision.'

'You've . . . waarrrggghhhh?'

'Don't worry, just go back to sleep.'

At this Claire opened one eye and fixed me with it. 'Don't worry about what?'

'About nothing. Just go back to sleep.'

'How can I go back to sleep when you've just told me there's nothing to worry about?' She too sat bolt upright. 'What is it exactly that I shouldn't be worrying about?'

'The To-Do List,' I replied.

'Oh that,' sighed Claire flopping back on the pillow. 'I thought you were worrying about something important.'

'It is important. I didn't tell you this earlier because I was trying to make up my mind, but Simon called yesterday morning and told me that he's pitched the To-Do List to the publishers as a book idea.'

'Well, that's good isn't it?'

I shook my head.

'Why not?'

'Because if I do it as a book then I'll have to actually do it, won't I?'

'So what are you saying?' Claire gave me a full-on 360-degree eye roll. 'That you don't want to do it? What about all that stuff about how this birthday of yours and Maisie being born and us being married ten years were real milestones that meant that you had to pull your finger out and start being more like Derek and Jessica?'

'That was before I realised how much work it must take to be Derek and Jessica. Basically I think that you and I need to set our sights a little lower.'

'Isn't that what we're doing already?'

I shrugged. 'I suppose what I'm trying to say is that I just can't see how it's going to work. I'm three months late with the book I'm writing, I've got another novel to write after that and then I have to find the time to do all the stuff on my To-Do List and write a book about it. It's just not going to happen.'

'So knock it on the head then,' said Claire.

'That's exactly what I said.'

'Good, we're on the same page then. Now, listen, Mike, I love you, you know I do, but right now I really, really, really have to go to sleep. So if you wake me up again with any more revelations I can't be held responsible for my actions, okay?'

'Yeah,' I replied. 'Okay.'

When Lydia woke up twenty minutes later saying that she couldn't sleep because her hair 'felt funny' I realised that I'd made the right decision in giving up on the To-Do List. There was no time left in my life for anything other than the bare minimum. So when I returned home from dropping Lydia off at pre-school I headed straight upstairs and began working on the book that I was supposed to be writing. I'd barely written a dozen words when I admitted I was simply trying to postpone the inevitable, so I reluctantly picked up the phone and dialled Simon's number.

'Hi, Simon, it's me,' I said trying to sound jovial. 'How are things?'

'Mike, how are you, sir?' boomed Simon. 'Cracking on with that list of yours I hope. You must nearly have the whole thing done.'

'Not quite.' I laughed nervously. 'The thing is . . . I've been thinking about it all night and well . . . as much as I appreciate everything you've done I've sort of come to the conclusion that I don't really want to do it.'

'You don't want to do it?'

'No. It's practically Christmas. Everyone I know is looking forward to a bit of time off and then there's me trying to finish a book that's already late while trying to help out at home with a brand-new baby. I can't afford to be spending time doing stuff on the List when I've already got a list of stuff to do as long as my arm.'

'I understand,' said Simon. 'Maybe it's something you could do another time?'

'Yes, yes, of course. Another time, definitely.'

But even as the words left my lips I knew that 'another time' was never going to happen.

With a heavy heart I composed the following email message:

The To-Do List

Dear all,

As you may well remember a while back I sent out an email letting you know that I'd made the decision that it was about time that I joined the world of fully functioning adults and that along with my regular day job I would be undertaking a 1,277-item To-Do List which I planned to have completed by my thirty-seventh birthday. Sadly, for reasons too mundane to go into I have decided to give up the challenge. I feel like a complete and utter buffoon and you should feel free to exercise your right to mock me to within an inch of my life.

Have a great Christmas
Mike x

Within a few minutes I received my first reply, from my friend Cath in London.

Mate! Don't give up. I was really rooting for you! I've got a To-Do List as long as my arm and was hoping that you'd inspire me to pull my finger out a bit and get things sorted!
Have a great Christmas
Cath xxx

An email from Jackie quickly followed.

Mikey baby! Say it ain't so! I was so in love with your To-Do-List idea. I even drew up a list of my own but then I lost it for ages and by the time I picked it up again the moment was gone! You should definitely carry on. If not for your sake then for mine. Otherwise how will I ever get around to finding the time to do any of the things on my list without you as an inspiration?

Finally, from my friend Chris:

Waster! I knew you'd give up! Let's meet up sometime over Christmas for a drink so that I can mock you in person.

Chris was right. He'd said that I would give up on my list and sure enough I had. Part of me would like to prove him wrong, show that I could complete my To-Do List in the allotted time but I genuinely didn't think I could. At least not without something else giving way in the meantime. After all, there are only so many hours in the day and all of mine were double-booked already.

Chapter 7: 'Go to a ridiculously glamorous woman's house and find inspiration.'

A week into my new list-less life I received an email from my friend Nadine asking me when I was next going to be in London because she hadn't seen me in ages. I started a reply suggesting a date in January once the Christmas rush was out of the way but halfway through I changed my mind and deleted the lot: Nadine was a really good friend and rather than fobbing her off with some distant date in the future I knew I should make an effort, so I asked her what she was up to the following Tuesday. A reply came back within a few minutes: she had a few bits of work to do but was free for lunch and instead of braving the crowds of Christmas shoppers currently clogging up the West End she suggested that I should come over to her house in Chiswick and she would make lunch for the two of us.

Nadine should have been exactly the kind of person I avoided like the plague: compared to her Derek and Jessica were practically messy teenagers. But Nadine is one of those rare things: a really nice person who had a very fabulous life.

Nadine's house (which I'd never been to before) was like something out of a posh interiors magazine. All the walls in the large hallway, living room and kitchen were painted in an off-white colour that I could tell was not just expensive but hideously expensive. The German-made kitchen units were a gleaming gloss white and there wasn't a single item of cutlery or crockery out on show on the pristine gleaming black granite work surfaces. The living room, with its un-treated ash flooring, the huge leather sofa and expensive looking occasional table; the tastefully decorated bedrooms upstairs and the bathroom that could have come straight out of a designer hotel all had the same opulence about them as the kitchen. I sat down on her posh sofa and Nadine looked at me expectantly awaiting my verdict on her home.

'You love it don't you?'

'Love it?' I replied. 'I want to marry it. It's like . . .'

'Something out of a posh hotel?'

'Exactly.'

'So why the frown?'

I hadn't been aware that I was frowning but now that she pointed it out . . .

'Well the thing is, mate . . .'

'What?'

'I don't understand: where's all your stuff?'

'What stuff?'

'You know, stuff? Where are all your books and CDs? Where's all your ornaments from tacky holidays and piles of unread newspapers and magazines?'

'You're describing your house aren't you?'

'I thought I was describing everyone's house until I saw yours,' I replied. 'Everyone in the world has a house full of stuff apart from you. How come?'

Nadine shrugged. 'We've got no CDs because all our music is on our i-Pods, we've got no DVDs because we rent them from Blockbuster, we've got no books because once I read them I take them down to Oxfam and we've got no magazines because if I see an article I'm interested in I rip it out and then recycle the rest. I've never been a hoarder. I just can't see the point.'

Once I got over the shock that my friend of the past decade is a closet non-hoarder we settled into our normal groove of conversation and laughter pausing only to consume the posh lunch she'd prepared. Around five, I decided it was time to leave and, kissing her goodbye, made my way to the tube station. As I walked along Chiswick High Street picking my way through the Christmas shoppers I found myself thinking about Nadine's pristine home and her comment about having never been a hoarder. How can she never have been a hoarder? Isn't hoarding what normal people do? And I thought about my house and the hundreds of books and CDs and DVDs in the living room and then I thought about the various bedrooms and all of the stuff in there too but then my mind came to rest at the top of the house and I found myself deciding that tomorrow was going to be the day that I would begin de-stuffing my entire house, starting with the area with the highest concentration of stuff and the number-one plague of my life: the loft.

De-stuffing the loft a week before Christmas wasn't the smartest move ever, especially as there were plenty of things that were a higher priority like reassembling the cast-iron bed frame in the front bedroom. This was so that when Claire's mum came to stay over Christmas she wouldn't be reduced to sharing a bed with her granddaughter the human octopus. Still, mother-in-law or no mother-in-law, my current enthusiasm wasn't aimed at bed maintenance and was instead focused on the myth that having a loft marginally less filled with crap might somehow make me feel more Zen and less jealous of the lady-with-no-stuff.

I started by taking everything out and doing a kind of inventory, which made for quite a depressing read:

1. Non-working Apple Computer tower and monitor × 1
2. Cast-iron fireplace × 1
3. Large suitcases filled with crap × 4
4. Cardboard boxes filled with crap × 12
5. Non-working video recorders × 2
6. Box of broken Christmas decorations × 1
7. Fake Christmas Tree × 1
8. Thirty-year-old fake Christmas Tree rescued from bin at parents' house several years earlier × 1
9. Comic books × 345
10. Cardboard boxes filled with books × 3
11. Cardboard boxes filled with CDs that I no longer listen to but don't want to give away × 2
12. Vinyl albums × 450
13. Vinyl singles × 280
14. Black bin liners filled with Lydia's old clothes × 8
15. Cardboard box filled with pre-recorded videos × 1

This was a depressing read because I'd once cherished quite a lot of the so-called crap. The comics, records and videos had been amongst my most beloved possessions during my twenties and just seeing them brought back floods of memories from my university days and beyond. Whole evenings spent in darkened rooms listening to The Smiths, lost afternoons re-watching *Betty Blue*, wondering why I couldn't find a girl mad enough to poke her own eyes out, and whole days lost in the imaginary world of the X-men wondering whether one day I'd discover my own superhuman power. Broken computers and bits of electrical cabling aside, the contents of the loft *was* me.

I called Claire upstairs to ask her advice.

Claire was aghast. 'What are you doing? You told me you were putting the bed together so that Mum's got somewhere to sleep next week.'

'I was but . . . I got distracted.'

'By a loft filled with rubbish?'

I was about to explain about Nadine's stuffless life but then I saw her point. 'I'll put it all back and sort out the bed, eh?'

Claire leant across to offer me a kiss of consolation that communicated her appreciation of my actions no matter how misguided but before her lips could reach my cheek a familiar tortured-cat scream filled the air.

'I'd better go.'

'Yeah,' I replied. 'You better had.'

Later that evening Claire and I were on the sofa watching TV and half discussing our plans for Christmas.

'Do you want to know something weird?'

'Like what?'

'Like the fact that even though I've officially given up my To-Do List in an odd sort of way I've actually been doing it.'

'How?'

'Item 303 was "Try to see Nadine before the end of the year"; Item 34 was "Sort out loft"; Item 210 was "Take down bed in front room and put in loft" but I only did half of that. It's the List. I've been unconsciously doing the List all this time and never even noticed.'

'Maybe it's possessed like that Stephen King book, *Christine*,' laughed Claire.

'How can a notebook filled with stuff to do be possessed?'

'I'm guessing the same way that a 1958 Plymouth Fury gets possessed,' replied Claire. 'Who knows?' She widened her eyes and pulled what I assumed was her spooky face. 'All I know is this: you might have given up the List but the List doesn't seem to have given up on you.'

Chapter 8: 'Buy champagne flutes . . . or failing that a couple of plastic beakers from IKEA.'

'Which one should we get the boys to sing next?' sniggered Claire. '"Islands in the Stream" or "Total Eclipse of the Heart"?'

It was a little after eleven on New Year's Eve and with an hour to go before midnight I was trying my best to stay awake on the long haul to the big bongs. To entertain ourselves Claire and I, along with our 'also-with-child' friends John and Charlotte, were playing the PlayStation karaoke game that I'd received for Christmas.

'We're not singing either of those,' complained John plucking the box from his wife's hands. 'Us boys need something to rock out to. A bit of Whitesnake, AC-DC or maybe even some of Motorhead. What do you say, Mike? Are you ready to rock out to Motorhead?'

'Yeah, why not?' I yawned and stretched as Claire lined up 'The Ace of Spades' through the controller and Charlotte handed me the blue microphone. 'I could definitely do with a bit of Motorhead to liven myself up.' I braced myself to rock out to the classic heavy metal anthem but before I could even put the microphone to my lips a strangled cat scream filled the air.

'I'll sort it out,' said Claire.

'No, it's my turn. You sorted the last five times.'

'Are you sure?'

I handed her the microphone. 'Motorhead are all yours, babe.' Up in our bedroom, I propped my daughter against my shoulder and patted her back. Was it Derek and Jessica's fireworks that had woken her? Or was she hungry? Or was it colic? Or was she simply over-tired? Or was she under-tired after that long nap she'd had this afternoon? Too many questions and not enough answers but I was definitely glad that I had given up on the To-Do List.

A huge weight had been taken off my shoulders; I could get back to the business of being me: a crumpled, slightly overweight thirty-six-year-old man with a tonne of things to be ignored for as long as possible. Every time the wardrobe door jammed (Item 984: 'Fix wardrobe sliding door',) I just smiled, relieved that it wasn't a high enough priority for me to bother with; every time I glanced up at the damp patch in the bathroom (Item 125) I just shrugged and carried on showering; and every time I was heading up to work and Lydia asked me to 'play babies' with her (Item 3: 'Spend more time with number-one child so that she doesn't grow up to be attracted to emotionally distant men') I just sighed and carried on up the stairs to my office.

After all it wasn't as if there hadn't been plenty of things that I had given up on in the past. In my early twenties I got it into my head that I wanted to be a model when some quirk of fate resulted in me featuring in a catalogue and cinema advertisement for Benetton. Not for a second did it occur to me that the fact that I was only five feet eleven inches tall, had a slightly chipped front tooth and possessed the kind of physique that came hand in hand with a diet that regularly featured Jammy Dodgers would stand in my way. No, in possession of the kind of self-belief that you can only possess in your early twenties, I marched into a modelling agency, handed them a 4" × 4" picture of my face taken from the campaign and told them to ring me. The call never came. In fact much to my shame I had to call them in order to get my picture back. And since then, I had managed to give up on a multitude of things (wanting to be a TV presenter, the music and artistry of the band Radiohead and the third book of *Lord of The Rings* to name but a few) and in doing so I felt I had become richer (at least in terms of time not wasted fannying about) rather than poorer, so as far as the To-Do List was concerned that really should have been the end of my efforts.

It took me roughly twenty minutes or so to calm Maisie down and as soon as she was drifting back to sleep I headed back downstairs for karaoke fun. But instead of being bombarded by appalling renditions of classic Eighties hits, the TV was off and Claire, John and Charlotte were sitting on the sofa huddled around a photograph album.

'Motorhead did us in,' explained Claire looking up, 'so now Charlotte and I are taking a walk down memory lane while John laughs at our hairstyles and the size of our glasses.'

'You should see some of these pictures of your wife when she was in the sixth form with Charlotte,' said John, 'she looks like she's just stepped out of a John Hughes movie.'

We spent a good half hour looking through photos and it was great fun. There were Claire and Charlotte crying after receiving their 'A' level results, which was featured in the *Leicester Mercury* under the headline 'City teenagers in "A" Level joy!'; me dancing at a barbecue wearing slightly camp red velour trousers paired with a brown jacket; young versions of Claire and me dressed in old clothes decorating the front bedroom of our first house; me in a daft hat hanging out of a tent at Reading Festival while my friend Jackie looked on. It was a history of me and of Claire; of who we were then and who we were now; and it made me feel nostalgic for the past. We hadn't always been the people we were now.

Tidying away in preparation for midnight I vowed that I really would sort out the photo albums. They were, to be frank, possibly the worst photo albums in existence. The covers were plastic and the photos were supposedly held in place by sheets of transparent sticky stuff that appeared to be better at sticking to itself than to the photos.

'Sorting this lot was on my To-Do List,' I told Claire as a flood of unstuck photographs poured out onto the floor. 'Item 509: "Organise photo albums so that when the kids are older they can see a time before they even existed presented in some kind of order." Still,' I scrabbled around on the floor trying to pick up the escaped photos, 'I suppose I've got a bit of time before it becomes urgent.'

Heading to the kitchen I pulled the bottle of champagne that John and Charlotte had brought out of the fridge and searched the kitchen for the champagne flutes that we'd received as a wedding present from Claire's great uncle Clarke. It was only after five minutes of hunting through every single cupboard that I remembered we'd managed to break every single one. We didn't own champagne flutes any more.

'I bet you Derek and Jessica have got champagne flutes,' I ranted as Claire came to find out why I was taking so long. 'I bet you they've got ordinary everyday champagne flutes and champagne flutes that they keep just for special occasions! And do you know what's worse? It was on the To-Do List.

Item 846: "Buy new glassware so that when people come round we can look like we give a crap".'

'Come on, Mike,' coaxed Claire, 'we don't really need champagne flutes do we? What about that set of tall glasses from Habitat that your parents bought us a while back?'

'Those things are long gone,' I replied. 'We smashed two of them at the barbecue in August, the dishwasher killed another one, two have just disappeared into thin air and the only one in the cupboard has a big chip in it. And before you ask about that set of six wine glasses your mum bought us last Christmas, there are only two left.'

'Two?'

'Yes, two.'

'We'll just have to make do with whatever we can find then.'

As the four of us stood in front of the TV watching the masses at Trafalgar Square, and I poured out the champagne into two huge red wine glasses and a pair of plastic children's beakers, it occurred to me that the drinking-receptacle fiasco was symbolic of the mess my life was in. While other proper grown-ups the world round celebrated utilising the correct glassware Claire and I, as a result of our self-inflicted infantilisation, were seeing in the new year with green and yellow plastic beakers from IKEA. How long would this 'plastic beaker phase' of our life continue? Months? Years? Decades? Or would New Year's Eve 2030 see us swigging champagne from saucepans or straight from the bottle? It really didn't bear thinking about.

And so as the final Big Ben bongs rang out and Claire, John, and Charlotte cheered and hugged and attempted to clink wine glasses with beakers, I was in no mood for celebration. The brand-new year that we had just heralded was going to be one big lump of more of the same. I was sick of it. I was tired of it. I was never going to be a proper grown-up like Derek and Jessica.

I was about to drown my sorrows in a world of bubbles when something lying on the floor caught my eye. A piece of notepaper. I bent down and picked it up.

'What's the matter?' asked Claire. 'You look like you've seen a ghost.'

'I think I have,' I replied handing her the paper.

John and Charlotte crowded around Claire to get a better look.

'What is it?' asked Charlotte.

'It's a To-Do List.'

'You're joking,' said Charlotte. 'What does it say?'

Under the title: 'Where am I going exactly?' and in frankly rubbish handwriting, I'd written down in blue marker pen a list of everything I wanted to do when I was twenty-three:

1. Become a journalist.
2. Write a novel.
3. Write for the *NME*.
4. Write a sitcom called *Sibling Ribaldry*.
5. Write for *Smash Hits* or *Just Seventeen*.
6. Develop a radio show called 'The Pop Show'.
7. Become a TV presenter.
9. Read *The Misanthrope*.
10. Read *Fear and Loathing in Las Vegas*.

'Are you okay?' asked Claire.

'Yeah, I'm fine,' I replied. 'I just feel a bit weird.'

'Because of this To-Do List?'

'Do you know what? I actually did some of the things on

there. I actually did become a journalist, I actually did write a novel, I actually did write for *Just Seventeen* and though I didn't actually read *The Misanthrope* or *Fear and Loathing in Las Vegas*, write a sitcom, make a radio show or write for the *NME* I did at least have a couple of goes at being a TV presenter.'

'That's great,' said Claire. 'So why do you look so down?'

'Because I'm not that guy any more, am I? That guy had a go and didn't care if he failed. Some things he ticked off the list and some things he didn't. What he didn't do was give up at the first sign of a problem.' I slipped the list into my back pocket, picked up my champagne and raised a toast.

'Here's to New Year's resolutions.'

'I know that face, Mike.' Claire looked worried. 'What is it that you've resolved to do? Not the Antarctic thing again is it?'

'No,' I replied. 'It's better than that. It's the To-Do List. I'm actually going to do it! And though I appreciate that I might not tick all 1,277 things off the list, I'm going to give every last one of them my best shot.'

When John and Charlotte had gone I sat at my desk and fired up my computer and wrote the following email which I sent to everyone in my online address book:

Dear all,

Just wanted to let you know (again) that having come to the conclusion that it was about time that I joined the world of fully functioning adults on a permanent basis only to change my mind a few months later, I've once again "about turned" and as of today will be focusing ALL of my efforts on the previously mentioned 1, 277-item To-Do List. This time round I really am hoping that my fear of being mocked twice over will provide me with sufficient inspiration

and motivation to succeed where I have previously failed.
Cheers, guys!
Mike x
P.S. Happy New Year!
P.P.S. The only way is up!

PART FOUR
January–April

(During which a new year begins, I get
stuck into the To-Do List and try my
very best to make it to the first audit)

Selected Highlights from Mike's To-Do-List Diary (Part 1)

Monday 1 January

5.15 a.m. Woke up and headed downstairs to tackle my first To-Do-List item of the New Year. 943: 'Find the instruction manuals for the video recorder and DVD player and work out how to put the correct time on the clocks because they've been telling the wrong time now for five and a half years.'

5.55 a.m. Have turned the whole house upside down looking for the aforementioned manuals and although I have located instruction manuals for a bread maker (that we no longer own), the condenser boiler and two kettles (how stupid can you be that you need instructions to turn on a kettle?), no sign of the ones I want.

9.00 a.m. Have finally located instruction manual for the DVD player inside a book called *Play bass guitar in three months!* Video player instruction manual still nowhere to be seen.

9.23 a.m. Have officially earned my first half tick! The 'half' is based on the fact that while the DVD player now displays the correct time the video player doesn't as without the manual I still can't work out how to programme the clock.

9.46 a.m. Problem solved. Have given away our video player to John and Charlotte and decided to move on and attempt Item 254: 'Try growing a beard because you will look good with one'.

Tuesday 2 January

3.21 p.m. I am in the car on the way over to Arthur's house (because Arthur owns every sci-fi/geeky TV series DVD in the world) in a bid to fulfil Item 1041: 'Find out what happened at the end of the *X-Files* because it might actually have been interesting'.

3.49 p.m. I am currently arguing with Arthur (who takes his TV sci-fi series about as seriously as the Pope takes Catholicism) because he claims I can't just watch the last episode on its own because it won't make any sense. In order to understand the 'full narrative flow' of the final episode, I need to watch all 23 episodes of the final series.

4.33 p.m. After much heated 'debate', Arthur and I have reached a compromise: he will let me watch the final episode (which is actually in two parts!) without watching all the others if I allow him to verbally explain the 'narrative thread' running through all NINE series of the *X-Files*.

4.55 p.m. Arthur has been talking now for a good twenty minutes and although I am trying my very best NOT TO LISTEN TO A SINGLE WORD HE IS SAYING occasionally a phrase like 'The smoking man', 'The Lone Gunman' or 'Black oil' manages to permeate my ear drums. This despite my attempt to block out the white noise of sci-fi fandom with internal choruses of 'La, la, la, I'm not listening! La, la, la! You think I'm listening but I'm not!'

5.19 p.m. Arthur puts the disc with the final episode into his DVD player. I settle down and prepare to be blown away.

6.00 p.m. I am officially bored out of my skull. Nothing makes any sense even with Arthur pausing to explain EVERY SINGLE significant plot point.

7.00 p.m. It is over and I am none the wiser. Are the aliens real? What did happen to Mulder's sister? And okay, so they've tied up a few loose ends but none of it (at least to an outsider) makes any real sense. Still, it's another tick in the box.

Wednesday 3 January

4.23 p.m. I am sitting at my desk with a pen and paper in a bid to tick off Item 948: 'Write a letter to the Chadwick family who have been sending Christmas cards to the Smiths who used to live at our address to tell them that the Smiths no longer live here.' This is a hard letter to write. How do I begin to explain that while I've appreciated the last seven years' worth of Christmas cards and round robins (I was especially pleased to hear that young Gilly had returned from Australia but was saddened to hear the news that Dixie the dog had passed away) the Smiths don't even like the Chadwicks enough to let them know that they've moved house SEVEN YEARS after the event? I decide to go with the following: 'Hi, I'm Mike Gayle the new owner of The Smiths' former house. Sadly, the Smiths have moved away without leaving a forwarding address. However, feel free to carry on sending the cards because we're really keeping our fingers crossed that Auntie Margaret pulls through. Cheers, Mike Gayle.'

Thursday 4 January

7.43 p.m. I am on the phone with my friend Richard in a bid to get his address and postcode in order to fulfil Item 817: 'Get yourself an address book and write down people's addresses'. I used to have an address book with people's addresses in it. It was great. If I wanted to write to someone I could open it up find their address and send them a letter. Fifteen years on not only do I not have an address book (I got sick of crossing stuff out whenever they moved rented accommodation) but I don't actually have anyone's addresses either. I have their mobile number or, if I'm really lucky, a land line number which means that come Christmas (or if they're lucky their birthday) I have to call them up to find out their address thereby spoiling any surprise that they might have enjoyed on discovering a card from me.

9.43 p.m. I am only halfway through this endeavour and I have learned several things:

1. No one can remember their postcode.
2. No one answers their phone any more.
3. This is a good way of catching up with people who, the second you hear their voice, you remember just how much you like them.

10.45 p.m. Tick.

Friday 5 January

11.55 a.m. I am down in the basement looking for my toolbox in a bid to tackle Item 550: 'Try to open the rear bedroom window that hasn't been opened in the three years since you painted it shut'. At the time it had occurred to me that it wasn't exactly the wisest thing to do, but I told myself I would try moving it later so that it wouldn't stick. Of course I never did move it later and of course it stuck.

12.08 p.m. The window won't budge for love or money. It's as though it's been superglued to the frame. I look in my toolbox for inspiration and spy a screwdriver.

12.31 p.m. I am in B&Q looking for wood glue. Who knew that if you jabbed a screwdriver into a wooden pine frame and wiggled it about, a massive chunk would splinter off so easily?

Saturday 7 January

7.21 a.m. I am by the tap in the kitchen looking at a pint of water because Item 483 is 'Drink more water because it's healthy'. I drink the water in one go and await feelings of intense inner healthiness.

9.45 a.m. I am in the newsagents buying a two-litre bottle of Evian. I determine that I will polish one of these off every day.

10.00 a.m. I am having a wee. Normally it looks a bit like Lucozade. Today it is straw coloured, just like so-called experts say it should be. I am pleased.

11.13 a.m. I am having another wee (it is still straw coloured).

13.23 p.m. I am having yet another wee (still straw coloured).

14.55 p.m. I am talking to my wife about what colour her wee is. 'Is it straw coloured?' I ask. 'I'm not telling you.' 'It should be straw coloured' I tell her. 'If it's not your kidneys must be knackered.'

7.30 p.m. Straw coloured or not, I am bored of weeing. I am also bored of drinking and thinking about drinking. In fact I'm actually fantasising about being thirsty. It is no fun at all being fully hydrated.

Sunday 8 January

8.21 a.m. I am checking out my burgeoning beard in the bathroom mirror. I think it looks great in a sophisticated and mature kind of way as though I might be a captain of industry having a weekend off from being a captain of industry.

9.21 a.m. I've just picked up Lydia to give her a kiss and she's pulled a face, rolled her eyes just like her mum and asked Claire why Dad has got his 'scratchy face' on? 'I don't know,' says my wife despondently. 'I really don't know.'

11.45 p.m. Just in from a night out with the Sunday Night Pub Club. Beard has gone down very well indeed. Kaytee said I looked distinguished and Jo and Amanda said that I looked 'handsome'. The boys loved the beard so much that they have all made a pact to grow beards too. 'We'll be the beard gang,' said Steve. 'And have a secret beard handshake and everything.'

Chapter 9: 'Get rid of your AOL account because it's just beyond ridiculous that you've been paying them £11.99 a month for a service that you don't even use any more.'

I had been with the multinational internet service provider AOL ever since one of their CDs dropped out of a magazine I'd been reading back in the mid nineties. Back then people had been going on about this thing called 'the internet' and how it was going to change the future and in a short space of time I'd moved from being unconvinced (dismissing it to one friend at the time as 'a bit like CB radio for computer geeks') to a full-on convert as everyone I knew began to get email addresses. Within a few hours of my dial-up being installed I was surfing, sending emails *and* downloading a solitary four-minute Coldplay b-side in just under six hours. I was in love.

In spite of having pledged my troth to AOL with a monthly direct debit of £11.99, when the opportunity came along a few years later to get a faster broadband service through my cable provider for £15.99 a month I grabbed the opportunity with both hands. But rather than cutting all ties with AOL and moving on to a new life with Telewest, I carried on paying AOL.

For the first month or two my reasoning was that I couldn't afford the time to mess about changing email addresses and exporting address books. As those months became two years I began to wonder whether I was suffering from some kind of mental illness which led me to confuse the act of cancelling my direct debit with dumping a particularly tear prone girlfriend. Fearful that my actions might result in tears and tantrums, like any good bloke I avoided any opportunity for conflict and decided that rather than come out with the truth ('I'm just not that into you any more') I'd go with the old 'extrication two-step': Step 1) present the person/multinational you wish to leave with an insurmountable problem that explains why you want to call it off. Step 2) cross your fingers and hope that they can't come up with a solution.

For ages now email access via my computer had been very unreliable, and having set up an alternative email address in preparation, now was the time to let AOL know the situation was unacceptable. It was a no-brainer. Victory would be mine.

'Hello, Mr Gayle,' said the man from AOL, 'you're through to AOL and my name is "Steve", how may I help you today?'

'Hi, Steve,' I replied even though it didn't take a genius to work out that he was based in Bombay and wasn't really called 'Steve' at all. 'My email's not working.'

'I see,' said Steve. 'That is a problem. Mr Gayle, can I ask are you using an Apple Mac or a PC?'

'A Mac.'

'Ah,' replied 'Steve'. 'I can only deal with problems related to PCs. I will have to put you on to my colleague.'

And before I could reply I was put on hold.

After what seemed like an age I was put through to 'Jason', their Apple Mac specialist who took me through a number of procedures which didn't work before suggesting that I re-installed the software.

Even though all I wanted to do was leave I felt the very least I could do was go through with this suggestion and so I searched high and low for the AOL software disk, undertook a clean re-install and then attempted to check my email. It still didn't work.

Punching the air with glee I called AOL straight back.

'Hello, Mr Gayle, you're through to AOL and my name is "Robert", how can I help you?'

'I'm calling because my email's not working—'

'I see,' said 'Robert', cutting me off. 'That is a problem. Mr Gayle, can I ask, are you using an Apple Mac or a PC?'

'A Mac,' I replied.

'Ah,' replied 'Robert'. 'I can only deal with problems related to PCs. I will have to put you on to my colleague.'

And before I could tell him that it didn't matter whether he only worked with PCs or not because I wanted to leave, he put me on hold and after a decade I was put through to 'Andy' who, claiming that he had no record of my previous call, attempted to take me through exactly the same procedure that 'Jason' had previously taken me through.

'But I've already done this!'

'Mr Gayle,' said 'Andy' calmly, 'we must follow the procedure exactly if we are going to be able to help you.'

'Even if I've already done it? And know for a fact it doesn't work?'

'If it doesn't work this can be something that we can find out together.'

'But I don't want us to find this out together because I already found it out together with the last bloke I spoke to.'

'I understand your frustration, Mr Gayle,' replied 'Andy' 'but I still have to take you through the process otherwise I wouldn't be doing my job.'

'Fine,' I replied. 'Let's do it your way.'

'Andy' took me through the exact same procedures that

'Jason' had previously taken me through (all of which still didn't work) before suggesting that once again I re-installed the software.

'You want me to re-install the software even though it's been . . . oh, I don't know, the best part of twenty minutes since I last re-installed it?'

'Yes, please, Mr Gayle. Please re-install the software.'

There was something about the confidence in Andy's voice that made me think, 'Well perhaps he knows what he's talking about.' So once again I searched out the AOL software disk, undertook a clean re-install and then attempted to check my email. It still didn't work.

Now I really was furious. I called AOL straight back.

'Hello, Mr Gayle, you're through to AOL and my name is ''Mark'', how can I help you?'

'I'm calling because my email's not working—'

'I see,' said 'Mark'. 'That is a problem. Mr Gayle, can I ask are you using an Apple Mac or a PC?'

'A Mac,' I replied.

'Ah,' replied 'Mark'. 'I can only deal with problems related to PCs. I will have to put you on to my colleague.'

'But—'

It was too late. 'Mark' had put me on hold and in one swift movement I found myself well and truly beyond furious and now officially in the land of the livid.

'Hello, Mr Gayle, you're through to AOL and my name is ''John''. I'm an Apple Mac specialist, how can I help you?'

'Listen ''John'',' I said pointedly. 'It's like this: my email is not working, I've called three times now and have been passed from pillar to post to find a Mac specialist who then proceeds to take me through a bunch of procedures that don't work before suggesting that I re-install the AOL software again.'

'Mr Gayle,' said 'John' calmly, 'we must follow the procedure exactly if we are going to be able to help you.'

'Even if I've already done it? And know for a fact it doesn't work? Because it doesn't, you know?'

'If it doesn't work this can be something that we can find out together.'

'But I don't want us to find this out together!' I yelled. 'I already know it doesn't work and so would you if your stupid computers were updated properly!'

'I understand your frustration, Mr Gayle,' replied 'John', 'but I still have to take you through the process otherwise I wouldn't be doing my job.'

I couldn't believe it.

'Are you telling me that you're going to make me go through this whole process again?'

'Mr Gayle,' said 'John', still calmly. 'It is the only way.'

'Well, let's see about that, because I'm taping this conversation we're having right now and I think it would make interesting reading in my local newspaper!'

I was lying of course. I wasn't recording anything. The idea had just sort of sprung into my head and refused to leave and now it was out there. Suddenly 'John' no longer sounded quite as cool and calm as before.

'Mr Gayle.' 'John' sounded distinctly ruffled. 'Did you say you were recording this conversation?'

'What if I am? You are too, aren't you? There's that long speech before you pick up saying that you record calls for "training purposes".'

'Mr Gayle,' he said forcefully, 'could you please answer my question: are you recording this conversation?'

I could tell from the severity in his voice that he wasn't going to let it go and I was so annoyed that I wasn't going to let it go either.

'For the sake of argument, let's just say that I am recording this telephone conversation. What exactly are you going to do about it?'

'Mr Gayle, if you are recording this conversation then I will have to terminate this call immediately.' He put the phone down on me.

The sound and fury of a thousand and one expletives being released in one almighty roar quickly brought my wife rushing up the stairs to see who or what had died.

'What's the matter, babe?'

'They've just put the phone down on me!' I raged.

'Who?'

'Some bloke in Mumbai!'

'Why were you calling some bloke in Mumbai?'

'I wasn't. I was calling AOL and I got put through to some bloke in Mumbai.'

'Why did he put the phone down on you?'

'Because I told him I was recording the call.'

Claire looked puzzled. 'Why were you recording the call?'

'I wasn't, I was just pretending so that the bloke at the other end of the line would stop trying to make me do things to my computer that I'd already done.'

'But I thought you were trying to leave them anyway?' reasoned Claire. 'Why would you even be trying to fix the problem?'

'That's not the point,' I spluttered. 'But they'll soon find out what the point is when I call them back!'

'Why don't you wait until you're a little calmer?'

'Because I don't want to be calm! I've just had the phone put down on me! Have you any idea how outrageous that is? What kind of world do we live in where people can put phones down on other people just because they're record- ing phone calls? This isn't Communist-era eastern Germany you know? I've got rights! This is England!'

'But they're in Mumbai,' sighed Claire, giving me a roll of the eyes quickly followed by a 'This-will-all-end-in-tears' headshake. 'Look, I don't care what you do. But try to keep the noise down and remember that if our daughter starts cursing like a sailor any time soon, having AOL put the phone down on you will *definitely* be the least of your problems.'

As I picked up the phone and mentally prepared myself to give 'John' or whomever else they put on the line a piece of my mind I began to feel guilty. After all, this wasn't Mumbai 'John's' fault at all. He was probably just some student trying to make a bit of money in his spare time so that he could go out for a drink with his mates. He couldn't help having to stick to AOL's rage-inducing script. His bosses were probably listening in to make sure he didn't deviate. He more than likely found the situation just as frustrating as I did and was probably dying to say: 'Look, mate, I feel your pain but my hands are tied.'

With all this in mind, I told myself that whatever happened I was going to stay calm.

'Good evening, Mr Gayle, you're through to AOL and you're talking to "Paul", how may I help you today?'

'Hello, "Paul",' I began calmly. 'First off I'd like to say that I genuinely hope you're having a good afternoon yourself and secondly I'd—'

'Mr Gayle,' said 'Paul' talking over me, 'before I can help

you with your query this evening can I ask are you recording this conversation?'

'What?'

'Mr Gayle,' repeated 'Paul' coolly. 'According to your notes you are recording telephone conversations. Is this true?'

I couldn't believe it! 'John' had flagged me up on the AOL database as being 'someone who records phone calls'!

'I'm what?' I feigned outrage.

'Mr Gayle, according to your notes on the system you are recording telephone conversations. Is this true?'

'Now, hang on a second, mate!' I felt myself lose all sense of proportion. 'You can put a note on your system saying "Mr Gayle is recording phone calls", but you can't manage to put a note on the system that says, "Please don't wind Mr Gayle up any more because he's called on three separate occasions and already we've made him jump three times through the same hoops like some kind of performing monkey!"'

'Paul' was unmoved. 'Mr Gayle, I must repeat: are you recording this telephone conversation?'

I opened my mouth hoping that some manner of cleverness would leap from my lips but to no avail. Not only did I know that 'Paul' would put the phone down if I said yes but I knew 'Paul' knew that I knew too and, unless I was prepared to just keep phoning AOL's Mumbai base only to have them put the phone down, I was going to have to give in at some point.

'No,' I replied weary and broken. 'No, I am not recording this call.'

There was a long silence. Probably just enough time for 'Paul' to cover the mouthpiece, punch the air in victory and then high-five 'Steve', 'Jason', 'Robert', 'Andy', 'Mark', and 'John'.

'That is good to hear, Mr Gayle,' said 'Paul'. 'Now, how exactly may I help you this evening?'

The upside of my encounter with AOL was that having wasted the best part of a whole afternoon battling its Mumbai-based Outpost of Evil in an effort to fix a software problem that I didn't want rectified in order to have an excuse to get rid of a service that I no longer needed, I failed to experience even a shred of guilt when I reached the point in my conversation with 'Paul' when I got to tell him that I wanted to leave. That said, the little screen that shows the duration of the last phone call revealed that my battle with AOL had wasted forty-seven minutes of life that I was never going to get back, time that could have been better spent writing my novel, playing with my kids or simply staring into space. I may have earned another tick, but it had been hard won.

That evening, as we were sitting down to watch TV, Claire turned to me and smiled. 'It's a good thing, this list of yours.'

I was surprised. Since my encounter with AOL I had started to think that it was a huge pain in the backside.

'Do you really think so?'

'Absolutely. I think it's brilliant. You're getting things done and making things happen. Just think about it: that's the best part of £120 a year that you've saved by leaving AOL. You might not have gone about it the right way but it's definitely a result.' Claire stifled a huge yawn. 'Anyway, so what's next, List Master? Learning to play tennis? Kissing the Blarney stone? Writing a letter of complaint to Tony Blair about the missing bin from outside the newsagent at the top of the road?'

'None of those things are even on the List, babe, let alone ear-marked for my next big tick-off.'

'So what is your next big "tick-off"?' said Claire, clearly amused by my growing List-inspired vocabulary.

'Something I've had on my mind for quite a while now.' I stifled a huge yawn of my own, 'Items 42 to 50: "Catch up with lost friends because you know what? They used to be great friends".'

Chapter 10: 'Catch up with lost friends because you know what? They used to be great friends.'

My list of lost friends was long. Very long. It included every kind of lost friend imaginable: Ian and Scott (rubbish summer job lost friends); Monica and Paige (over-worked and under-paid bar working lost friends); Jane, Mia and Simon (camping holiday in Anglesey lost friends); Sarah, Alex and Maria (working on teen magazine lost friends); Sam, Richard and Tall Mike (lost friends inherited from other lost friends); Emma, Jo, Anthony and Alison (university lost friends); Cath, Susie and Sarah (sixth-form lost friends); Mick, Mark and Simon (secondary-school lost friends) and Lisa, Steve and Jen (early days in London lost friends).

I decided to start with the easy ones: those with email addresses. This still left an awful lot of work to do, as the last time I saw some of these people, email had yet to be invented. I began to try to type a suitable message but found myself stuck. What exactly was I supposed to say to people that I hadn't spoken to in years? And what reason was I going to give for contacting them now? Would they be pleased that they were on my 1,277-item-long To-Do List, or would they be vaguely insulted? I decided to put the question to Claire, who was usually pretty good at working out whether or not I was insulting people.

'Just tell them that you were thinking about them and

want to say hello and hope that they're well.' I stood slack jawed in awe at how easy women find anything to do with relationships.

'You're right,' I replied. 'That's exactly the thing to do.'

Inspired, I wrote the following email and sent it to everyone that I had addresses for:

> Dear [insert name of missing person here], It's me, Mike Gayle, I was thinking about you recently and how ace you are and so I thought I'd just drop you a line to say, 'Hello!' Hope you're well and would love to hear your news.
> All the best,
> Mike x

I sent this to five out of the twenty-six lost friends and for a moment or two felt really good about myself. Then four of the five messages were immediately bounced straight back. It was disheartening to say the least. To put it bluntly I was stuffed and I was about to embrace failure when an idea hit me. This was the age of social networking and what better way to catch up with old friends than to join every single social networking website on the internet? So that was what I did. I joined Facebook, MySpace, Bebo, Friends Reunited, Blogger, WAYN and even ancestry.co.uk and hoped against hope that at least a few of them would be on there. Sure enough I got lucky. Within an hour of joining MySpace I found four different old friends, and a few hours after joining Facebook I found another six, which given that neither website had even existed when I first became friends with these people made me feel really old. Gathering my wits about me, I copied and pasted my original email into messages to all those whose profiles I'd managed to locate, pressed send, then crossed my fingers and waited. Ten minutes later I got my first reply.

I first met Sam in the autumn of 1992. Having just graduated that summer and moved back home to Birmingham I'd been feeling a bit lost without the security of university life with its easygoing daily structure of lectures and nightly array of readily available social activities. Though most of my Birmingham friends had moved on, the few that remained did so because this was the town that they had moved to for university and had now adopted as their own. Out in Moseley one Saturday night with my friend Monica, I was introduced to Sam. Sam had long straight shoulder-length auburn hair, grey-green eyes and a cheeky smile that seemed even cheekier once she started talking with her broad Yorkshire accent. Though she dressed like a student (in all the time I knew her I don't think I ever saw her wear anything other than jeans or cords) she actually worked for the local dole office and had moved down to Birmingham from Keighley a few years earlier to be with her boyfriend.

I can't really remember what we talked about although I suspect that at some point we must have discussed the fact that she came from Keighley because I'd visited Brontë country with a couple of university mates only a few months before and had walked all the way from Keighley to Top Withens which was supposed to be the location of the main house in *Wuthering Heights*. I used to like to think the fact that I had ticked *Wuthering Heights* off my To-Do List of places to visit marked me out as some kind of literary romantic but I suspect that it actually marked me out as someone who needed to get out more.

After the pub we all went to a nightclub called Snobs, but then Monica had some kind of melt-down to do with her boyfriend so Sam and I spent the evening hanging out together. Sometime in the early hours of Sunday morning most of the group left but Sam and I decided to go for a walk at about three in the morning. We were both tired and more than a bit cold but we headed to Cannon Hill Park and ended up sitting on the swings talking about everything and nothing as though we'd known each other forever. From that moment onwards we were firm friends.

Sam's message to me via Facebook perfectly captured the essence of the person I knew back then.

> It's you! How are you? I've been hoping that one day you'd pop out of the woodwork! I'm well, thanks, living in Leeds, working in IT and driving a Ford Fiesta! Still like good music though. Tell me your news! Seethee, Sam x

Though it was short it was both warm and funny (I particularly liked that word 'seethee' as though she were an eighty-year-old Yorkshireman). I replied outlining everything that had happened to me since we had last seen each other (the best part of fourteen years ago) and suggested that we meet up. Within a few minutes I received the following message:

> Would absolutely love it if you came up to see me! How long has it been? Feels like forever. Whatever day you fancy just let me know and I'll book the day off work and cancel my spin class (I go most days after work). Give my love to your Missus and your very, very, very cute kids! Sam x

A short flurry of emails later we'd arranged a date.

It was just after eleven a.m. on the last Wednesday in January when I found myself standing in front of the departure board at Leeds railway station scanning the hundreds of faces milling around on the concourse. There were girls of every sort but not one matched the face that I had pictured in my head. Suddenly there she was: the long auburn air was now bobbed, the silver nose stud gone and her skinny frame, though fuller, was more healthy looking (this version of Sam didn't look for a moment as though it survived on a diet of Silk Cut and microwave pizza rolls). The only thing that remained unchanged were the clothes (less obviously studenty but still recognisably Sam's style), her smiling eyes and the filthy big grin. For a moment I was speechless because it really was the weirdest sensation to see someone whom you'd once seen practically every day for a year after a fourteen-year gap. I was expecting to see the Sam that I'd known then and though the person in front of me was vaguely like her, the resemblance was more that of an older, wiser sibling. What I looked like to her I had no idea but there was considerably more of me now than there had been back then. As for the way I was dressed (army jacket, jeans, trainers) I guessed I looked grown up but not exactly like a *grown-up*.

As we walked along the street towards Leeds's Corn Exchange for a coffee I commented on how the city had changed. As a student in Manchester I used to come here all the time for gigs or to see friends at the university and knew it quite well but the huge swathes of glass and steel were unfamiliar. Always keen to adopt a clumsy metaphor, I wondered whether Sam might see me in the same way.

We wandered around various shops selling everything from Goth clubwear to comics before heading down to the café on the lower ground floor. As we waited for our drinks Sam filled in the gaps of how she had left Birmingham to go back to Yorkshire and how she ended up in IT support. She told me all about her house in a little village to the west of Leeds, how she'd given up smoking and got into Pilates. She told me she'd been seeing a guy for a while but wasn't sure where it was going and that she might like to have kids one day if both the guy and the timing were right. Midway through an anecdote about a recent gig she paused as though she'd remembered something important, picked up her bag from the floor, and pulled out a large grey folder.

'Have a look at this.'

I opened the folder and a smile spread across my face. Inside were the letters that I'd sent to her when I'd first moved to London the summer after we became friends. The letters were filled with nonsense that at the time I thought was funny: drawings of stick men, detailed descriptions of things I'd eaten for breakfast and information leaflets for local swimming baths. At the bottom was something that really took me back: a homemade birthday card (from photocopied pictures from the Jamie Hewlett comic, *Tank Girl*) that I'd sent to Sam on her twentieth birthday.

Sam grinned. 'That is still one of the nicest cards I've ever had.'

'Cheers,' I said examining my handcrafted effort. 'It took me forever to make but I remember really enjoying it. I miss doing stuff like that – making cards and mix-tapes and writing friends long letters – I miss doing things for no other reason than because they're fun.'

There was a bit of a silence and I wondered whether Sam

had picked up on what I was trying to say: that as well as missing making stupid birthday cards I missed having a mate as good as her, but then the waitress arrived and we got distracted.

'I'm definitely going to come and see you again, you know.'

'Why? Are you thinking of leaving already?'

'No,' I laughed, 'it's just . . . it's just . . . I dunno.'

'It's all right, I know what you mean. I was thinking the same thing: it seems pointless making so many good mates when you're younger just to let them all go without putting up a fight.'

'Exactly,' I replied. 'What I'm trying to say is let's not leave it another fourteen years before we do this again.'

On the 18.10 back to Birmingham New Street, squeezed in next to a plump business man with a bright red face and opposite a pair of students sharing iPod headphones, I reflected not only on the day but on the whole of this last month. From that momentous change of heart on New Year's Eve I'd ticked off dozens of items from the To-Do List and moreover stuck to the plan for a whole month. Maybe this To-Do List wasn't going to end up like every other here-today-gone-tomorrow whim of mine. Maybe this really was different.

Excerpt from Mike's To-Do-List Diary (Part 2)

Thursday 1 February

1.21 p.m. I am searching for my old debit card for my First Direct bank account in order to find their number so that I can call them and tick off Item 320: 'Close First Direct account that you haven't used in about six years'. I'd opened the account because at the time they were offering customers £20 to do so. Sensing a bargain I put £50 in there, waited until they put in the £20 then planned to withdraw the lot and close the account. Obviously me being me, I didn't get round to closing it but then the strain of having two different PIN numbers to remember took its toll and after about six months I stopped using it altogether.

1.35 p.m. I have found the card. It was in the kitchen drawer by the back door.

1.38 p.m. I'm on the computer Googling the bank's phone number which has changed from the one on the back of the card.

1.42 p.m. I am on the phone with First Direct:

FD: Hi, how can I help you?

Me: I'd like to close my account and get my money back please.

FD: Of course. Could you give me the details?

Me: Okay (I then proceed to give her the details).

FD (after a pause): Oh, you haven't used it in a while.

Me: Er . . . no.

FD: I see. Well it's been marked as a dormant account so I'll have to put you on to my line manager.

FD line manager: Hi, how can I help you?

Me: I'd like my money back please.

FD: Right. (Long pause). There's £3.72 in there. (Laughs) Will a cheque do?

Me: That would be lovely.

Friday 2 February

2.28 p.m. Item 398 on the To-Do List is: 'Buy new pants because walking around acting like you haven't got a care in the world when your underwear is over a decade old is just plain wrong!' Therefore I am on my way to Birmingham's Bullring shopping centre in search of pants. I can't quite understand how this old pants situation came about given that when it comes to outerwear I've always been pretty much on the money. Perhaps the thing is, given that in any one day a man might have 5,000 or so different thoughts, very few of them tend to be about pants. Claire on the other hand is always buying new pants. Rarely does a week pass without a telltale Marks and Spencer carrier bag appearing in the house. The last time I bravely asked why she bought so many pants when there are only seven days in the week and she's only got one bottom. She didn't reply. She just narrowed her eyes, pursed her lips and carried on unpacking her pants.

2.45 p.m. I am in Selfridges looking at Calvin Klein underwear. They want the best part of fifteen quid for a single pair! I do the maths in my head and work out that if I want a pair for each day and an extra pair for good luck it will cost me

£120. I don't want to spend £120 on pants and so I head to M&S.

3.03 p.m. M&S do okay pants. In fact the ones I've got on now are the ones that I wore on my wedding day just over ten years ago. Apart from various bits of fraying they are still going strong. I examine the various designs: boxers, briefs, trunks, hipsters and slips. I immediately discount slips on account of them being called 'slips' and briefs too on account of them being plain old nasty. Having always been a fan of 'a place for everything and everything in its place', I ruled out boxers and was left with trunks and hipsters (which pretty much looked like trunks). Faced with the further options of 'climate control' cotton or 'RealCool Cotton' (Did I really need the ability to manage the temperature in my pants or could I get away with them just being constantly cool?) I thought about calling Claire and asking her to try to get a look at Derek's smalls somehow but, unsure of how this could be safely accomplished, I decided against it and bought three sets of each.

4.05 p.m. I'm in the changing room at Next allegedly trying on a jumper but in fact changing into my new pants. Boy, do they feel great. I can't believe that I've been missing out on the world of proper support and climate-control cotton for a whole decade. I love my new pants!

Saturday 3 February

1.55 p.m. I am on my way to my folks in the car as today I am planning to mostly do Item 119: 'Remove crap from parents' house that you insist on keeping there as if there might come a day when you would ever consider moving back in with them.'

2.16 p.m. I am in my parents' garage looking at a huge box filled with old school exercise books wondering exactly what to do with them. Mum thinks I should throw them out. Dad thinks I should keep them for posterity. I open up one that says: ENGLISH, Mike Gayle, 1S and flick through to the back page where someone has scrawled the words: 'Gayle is a Slaphead!' This makes me laugh. I can't possibly take this lot home and yet I can't stand the idea of throwing them away either. I am conflicted.

2.45 p.m. I am up in my parents' loft holding the 5-in-1 microscope that I got for my thirteenth birthday. I had a lot of fun looking at onion cells and microscopic amoeba with this microscope but nowhere near enough fun to warrant me bringing it back home. Should I chuck it? Once again I feel conflicted.

3.15 p.m. I'm in my parents' shed looking at my old racing bike. Blah. Blah. Blah. Conflicted.

3.58 p.m. I now have an inordinate amount of stuff that I have to decide what to do with. 'But this is what parents' houses are for,' I try to explain to Mum. 'When Lydia and Maisie move home they'll leave loads of crap at our house too. It's the circle of life!' My mum is having none of it. 'If you leave it all here even one more day I'll put it out for the bin men.' 'Fine,' I sigh. 'I'll take it.'

Sunday 4 February
3.15 p.m. We're off to the park with the kids. 'What's all this stuff in the back of the car?' asks Claire. 'My childhood,' I say mournfully. 'It can't stay there.' 'I know,' I sigh. 'I'm working on it.'

Monday 5 February
9.55 a.m. The good news: the postman has just arrived with my cheque from First Direct. I am so taken aback by their

startling efficiency that I almost rejoin them. The bad news: my childhood is still in the car.

Tuesday 6 February

15.21 p.m. Inspired by my success with First Direct I am searching out the phone number for my bank in order to tick off Item 819: 'Call bank and get rid of any old direct debits.' I've always hated direct debits. The idea that some institution can just whip money out of my bank at will seems wrong.

15.25 p.m. I am now on the phone with my bank and the woman on the phone is going through my list of direct debits. Most appear legitimate but then she comes across one (taking out the sneaky sum of £1 a month) for insurance cover for a TV that we don't even own any more. In a fit of righteous indignation I cancel it straight away and tell the lady on the end of the phone that yes, indeed I will write to the company to let them know what I've done (even though I have NO intention of doing so). I can't believe it! With one short phone call I have saved myself £10 and prevented my account from being potentially raided by old direct debits.

Wednesday 7 February

19.05 p.m. Claire and I are in London for a posh book-award ceremony that I had been a judge for earlier in the year. I see a number of people in the trade that I know and they are all without exception impressed by my facial hair. The beard is a definite hit.

Chapter 11: 'Spend quality time with your mum because she's not always going to be around.'

It was the Monday morning of the second week in February and having woken up a little later than normal due to a post-Sunday Night Pub Club visit to Arthur's, I headed downstairs for breakfast to find Claire and Lydia in the kitchen eating cereal.

'So what are you up to today?' asked Claire as she re-placed Lydia's empty cereal bowl with a plate of toast and Marmite. 'Any big List plans?'

As I watched Lydia licking the Marmite off her toast I pretended that I was mulling the question over. Not only had I got my entire day planned, I'd got my entire week planned out too.

'Today and in fact for the rest of the week I will be mostly concentrating my efforts on ticking off Item 26.'

'So what's that then?' Claire was nonplussed. 'Jumping out of a plane? Rounding up your old school mates? Learning to ride a uni-cycle? You're forgetting that you still haven't let me see the List yet.'

'I didn't forget.' I raised my right eyebrow archly. 'I was being mysterious.'

'Listen, mate. I haven't got time for you to be mysterious. I've got to get Lydia to pre-school and then go to Sainsbury's before the Ring and Ride lot turn up. It's always packed

109

when they get there. So come on, Mr Mystery, just cough it out so I can get on with my business.'

'Fine,' I relented. 'Item number 26 is this: "Spend more time with my parents because they're not going to be around forever".'

She smiled. 'That's a good thing to have on your list.'

'I think it might be too good.'

'How do you mean?'

'Well, half of me just wants to get the tick and move on, but the other half feels guilty that in doing Mum and Dad at the same time I'm trying to kill two birds with one stone.'

'So do them separately. Do your mum now and maybe do your dad later in the year.'

'But isn't that just making work for myself?'

'Probably,' replied Claire. 'But it'll be worth it. It can't all be just about getting ticks can it? I'm pretty sure that some things on your List will be worth more than any number of ticks in the long run if you actually do them.'

'You're right,' I replied kissing her fondly. 'I'll do Mum now and Dad later.'

'So what are you going to do? Take her out somewhere nice for the day?'

I shook my head. 'I thought about that but then I thought it would probably freak her out more if I turned up and just hung out with her for a few days without telling her why.'

'What reason could you possibly have for wanting to freak your mum out? She's your mum. You're her son. And she's seventy years old. You shouldn't want to freak your mum out.'

'Suffice it to say,' I tapped the side of my nose in a knowing fashion, 'I have my reasons.'

My reason was simple: nothing – not a single thing in the world – ever surprised my mum. After her time as a nurse she wasn't fazed by blood, guts or gore. After raising three boys she wasn't fazed at being left in sole charge of four grandchildren under three. And after a lifetime of being uninterested in TV she wasn't the slightest bit fazed when the producers of Channel Four's Big Breakfast once asked her to pop out of an oversized Christmas present live on national TV. Honestly, you could take my mum out to the park and say, 'Look, Mum, a dinosaur eating a caramel,' and she would undoubtedly look the other way just to underline how unfazed she was.

My mum didn't do fazed. She did unfazed. So much so that for the majority of my thirty-six years it had been my greatest wish to do something that might get her to raise her eyebrows and think, 'Well, I didn't see that coming.' In the past the news that I was getting married and, later, making her a grandmother had failed to make her even pause for breath let alone appear surprised, so I was relishing the opportunity to catch her out by turning up on her doorstep and without explaining my actions, spending quality time with her whether she liked it or not.

Pulling up outside my parents' house just after ten I let myself in, turned on the TV and arranged myself casually on their posh new leather sofa.

'Morning,' greeted my mum as though it was an everyday occurrence to walk into her own living room and find her thirty-six-year-old son watching the opening credits to *Homes Under The Hammer*. 'How are you?'

'I'm good thanks. What are you up to today?'

'Minding my own business,' she grinned. 'How about you?'

'I had planned to do some work, but minding your business seems as good as any idea I've got. So what are we doing today?'

I had no idea if Mum's curiosity was even vaguely piqued by my declaration that I was spending the day hanging out with her because she didn't let on. What she did say was, 'Well if you're going to make yourself useful, as it turns out I have got a few things that I need to do,' and before I knew it I was being sucked into her world. But whereas on previous occasions when I had promised to take her places or run errands I would end up getting frustrated because she seemed to think nothing of wasting my time and patience taking forever to make up her mind about what to buy, or where to go next, this time the small boy with the bad temper that dwells within every son was nowhere to be seen. Even though I say so myself I was a perfect delight to be with and that was because I had nothing planned other than to lavish time and attention upon my mother. So if that meant spending three hours in T.K.Maxx watching Mum looking for clothing bargains that was what we did. If it meant being her general taxi service on visits to Sandwell to see my aunt Cynthia, Handsworth to do some shopping, or Southampton to see my cousin Marjorie, then we did that too. In fact, whatever was on her own personal To-Do List of things that she had never had the time, energy or transport (neither of my parents drove) to do, we did. And as the days drifted by ferrying her from one place to the other we talked about the kind of things that are only possible when you've spent all day with someone and have long since passed the point where everyday conversation will do. Instead I got to dip into the mysterious reservoir of topics that I just didn't get access to via my usual ten minute 'popping not stopping' flying visits, my regular 'Mum, do you mind having the kids for a couple of hours?' telephone conversations or even my occasional appearances for Sunday lunch that were always dominated by the kids.

There were no earth-shattering revelations of the 'Did you know I always wanted to be a dancer at the Moulin Rouge?' kind, instead there were a lot of snapshots of a version of my mum that I never knew. The little girl growing up in rural Jamaica in the 1940s making clothes from torn rags for dolls made from twisted strands of corn; the teenager having to look after a brood of six younger siblings while her mum worked the land; the young woman leaving the warmth and the vibrancy of her country of birth to arrive in dull, grey 1960s Wolverhampton.

All too soon, however, our day-to-day companionship drew to a close. Fortunately I had one last trick up my sleeve that would ensure that neither of us would forget the week in a hurry.

'So are you coming up again tomorrow or have you got other plans?' asked Mum as I dropped her off after an afternoon spent hunting for curtain material and cushions in Dunelm Mill.

'I was going to ask you the same question,' I replied. 'Have you got any plans for tomorrow?'

'No, not really. I was thinking about taking some of those things we bought from T.K.Maxx back because I've changed my mind about them but I could leave that until next week. Then I got to thinking that I might quite like you to take me to visit my friend Sandra in Coventry but I'm not fussed really. What have you got in mind?'

'How do you feel about a trip to London?'

'London?' she replied. 'What do I want to go to London for?'

'To meet the Chancellor of the Exchequer,' I replied. 'Because tomorrow you and I are going to Eleven Downing Street to meet Gordon Brown.'

The reason I was inviting my mum down to London to meet the next prime minister of England had nothing to do with having friends in high places and everything to do with the fact that when you write books for a living you get involved in all manner of charitable activities. Ninety-nine per cent of the time this means giving talks to bored secondary-school kids but every now and again you get a corker of an invitation that combines doing something good for charity whilst getting to poke your nose around the home of the Chancellor of the Exchequer as though you're auditioning for a job presenting *Through The Keyhole*.

A year earlier, out of the blue, I received an invitation to contribute a piece to a charity anthology about mums that was being edited by the Chancellor's wife Sarah Brown. A few months after handing in the piece (the same piece which sat on my everyday work To-Do List for the best part of six months before I actually got round to it) I received a letter on Downing Street-headed notepaper inviting contributors, authors and their guests to a tea-time reception at 11 Downing Street as a thank you. My initial thought was to take Claire as there are few things that she enjoys more than the opportunity for a good dress-up, but then I realised this was my chance for a genuine gasp of surprise from my mum. So with Claire's blessing I put the invitation away until I was ready to reveal all.

*　　*　　*

Mum barely raised an eyebrow at my invitation to Gordon Brown's gaff and so having resigned myself to the fact that I was never going to crack my mum's obstinate façade of unsurprise, I took her down to Euston by train and across London by taxi to Downing Street. We were scanned and frisked by security and then finally allowed to wander Downing Street at our leisure.

Walking past number 10 I noticed that the front door was open and so Mum and I automatically slowed down in the hope of catching a glimpse of either Tony or Cherie Blair. Neither of them was anywhere in sight but I did get a big smile and a nod from a policeman armed with a machine gun.

Entering the large crowded downstairs drawing room of number 11 in which the reception was being held I switched into star-spotting mode. I whispered the names of a few big-time authors into Mum's ear but could tell from her expression that she wasn't much impressed. She was, however, quite interested in what Sarah Brown was wearing and whispered slightly too loudly that she looked like, 'a lady with a good eye for a nice outfit'. This was high praise indeed and I was considering encouraging her to strike up a conversation with the Chanceller's wife about what she should wear to her friend's daughter's wedding the following month when there was a noticeable change in the mood of the room as though people were excited but desperately trying to hide it.

'It's Tony Blair!' said Mum with genuine surprise in her voice. 'It's Tony Blair!'

I was too busy taking in the big grin on Mum's face even to look around.

'Didn't you hear me?' she said. 'It's Tony Blair, he's in the garden!'

I was tempted to raise an indifferent eyebrow and look in the opposite direction just to let my mum know that I had finally beaten her at her own game, but the truth was I was just as excited as she was. Looking through the large window at the back of the room into what was to all intents and purposes Downing Street's back garden, I saw a jacketless Tony Blair on the patio of the adjacent building gazing into the mid-distance as though he was taking a moment's break from a long afternoon of meetings.

Once the event was all over and we were collecting our coats and preparing to make our way outside, I took out my camera and asked Mum if she fancied having her photograph taken in front of one of the most famous front doors in the world.

'Oh, Michael!' she said, as though I wasn't being serious.

'No really, you should do it.'

I practically had to lift her up and place her bodily in front of the door. My mum, a woman who arrived in this country with only a single suitcase and eleven pounds to her name, was standing outside the front door of the Prime Minister of England. This constituted the best tick on my To-Do List so far and seemed like the perfect end to a perfect week.

Chapter 12: 'Tidy home so that when people visit you no longer have to wear the shroud of shame.'

There was one item on my To-Do List that I would bet good money would be a universal entry on any To-Do List the world over: 'Tidy home so that when people visit you no longer have to wear a shroud of shame.' The only exceptions being those hallowed few who have a cleaner, live with their parents or have too much time on their hands. As I had a small baby, a three-year-old daughter and a wife who insisted on leaving half-drunk cups of tea around the house as though she was a tom cat marking his territory, this latter group was never going to include me.

Like most normal members of society, Claire and I did the once-a-week cursory clean so that Social Services didn't take our children away, but the kind of cleaning that would merit this week's tick wasn't the superficial calming down of chaos conducted in the few hours while the baby was asleep and our first-born was at pre-school. No, this was going to involve the hiring of skips, the moving of furniture, the implementation of Oprah-endorsed organisational systems, the use of industrial-strength cleaning products *and* the wearing of the kind of special suits and breathing apparatus normally reserved for council workmen clearing up the homes of deceased 'cat ladies'.

With the children out of the house (Maisie was at my

mum's and Lydia was at nursery) and a whole week set aside to earn these cleaning-related ticks, Claire and I decided to focus our attention for the first day of the five-stage process forthwith affectionately referred to as 'Operation Hose-down' to general household cleaning. Anything that hadn't had a good scrub, wipe, polish or scrape in the last year was going to get our fullest attention.

'Where do we start?' I said to Claire as we began unloading from the car the best part of fifty pounds' worth of Sainsbury's finest cleaning products. 'Down in the cellar, up in the loft or somewhere in between?'

'The kitchen,' said Claire a desperately shameful expression on her face. 'It's got to be the kitchen.'

Just as Dorian Gray had the picture in his attic, Claire and I (an outwardly respectable middle-class professional couple) had more than a few dirty secrets of our own most of which, as we pulled our five-burner Smeg cooker away from the wall and peered down at the tiled floor below, were currently staring right at us.

'What's that?' I pointed at a small dark-brown mass on the floor.

Claire swallowed. 'I think it's a Swedish meatball.'

'How long has it been down there?'

'When was it that we had Helena and Dan over to stay?'

I racked my brains for a few moments. 'Last February.'

'Oh,' said Claire despondently. 'So that'll be about a year then.'

'And what about those?' I pointed to a group of golden-brown discs.

'They're homemade biscuits. I was baking some a few months ago for Lydia's pre-school and they fell off the tray as

I was checking them. Anyway,' she added indignantly, 'enough about my misdemeanours, what's that about?'

I followed her finger to two shrivelled grey lumps.

'That was me,' I admit, 'and I'm pretty sure they used to be chips. They were on a plate. I lost control. I kept telling myself I'd—'

'And the other thing?'

'You mean the fork?'

'No, not that, the other thing.'

'The salt grinder?'

She shook her head. 'I mean the other thing.'

'Oh, that's an organic pork sausage.'

Claire hung her head in dismay.

'How long?'

'When did we get the cooker?'

'Three years ago.'

'That will be it then.'

There was a silence.

'We're pretty disgusting, aren't we?' said Claire, sadly.

'Yeah.' I put my arm around her and kissed her on the cheek. 'That's why we are made for each other. We appear to disgust each other in equal measure.'

Clearing the space behind the cooker of its rotting remains, kitchen equipment and cutlery wasn't the last grisly deed for the day. We moved the fridge to reveal lost grapes, a tangerine and an inordinate amount of dust and general debris. Venturing outside I removed the plastic drain cover that's supposed to keep leaves out but actually does the reverse and attracts them: I shoved my arms inside the stagnant water and fished out half a bucketful of rotting leaves and organic matter decaying slowly in the drain. As Claire remained in the kitchen scrubbing floors, wiping down walls and cooker hoods, I headed up to the bathroom to tackle the U-bend under the sink. For weeks now water had been going down the plughole at a much slower rate than usual and when I dismantled the U-bend I could see why. It was caked in toothpaste and general yuck, some of which flicked up into my open mouth and landed on my tongue, whereupon I'm not ashamed to say that I screamed like a girl, frantically scoured my tongue with a hand towel, rinsed it out about a million times with mouthwash, scoured again with a fresh hand towel and then went and lay down in a darkened room until I felt calmer.

The following day we failed to finish off the remaining cleaning and tidying chores and three days later (we had utterly misjudged how long it was all going to take) we finally finished and were free to tackle the next big job: throwing stuff out and reorganising the stuff that we were going to keep.

In preparation Claire suggested I consult a book that she had borrowed from Alexa but never actually read called *Organising From The Inside Out* by a professional organiser and de-clutter person called Julie Morgenstern who used to be a contributor to *Oprah* magazine (hence Alexa's endorsement). While it probably would have been a good idea to read the book, it wasn't on my To-Do List, so I couldn't do anything other than skim the blurb on the back. According to this there were three basic steps to being organised:

1. Analyse
2. Strategise
3. Attack

This was good stuff. We'd do it!

The analysis element was dealt with by Claire: 'I hate this house and everything in it.'

The strategy part came later: 'You start in the basement and I'll take the bedrooms because I don't want you buzzing round me while I'm listening to the afternoon play.'

Then we attacked.

My attacking wasn't what you might call focused. Assigned to the basement I soon grew bored and moved to: the living room where I partially alphabetised my CDs; the car where I cleaned out the boot; the bit at the top of the cellar where I cleared out all the coats and then (having panicked at the thought of Claire finding out how many jobs I had started and failed to finish) I crept upstairs to discover that the space that I had once known and loved as 'our bedroom' had become a breeding ground for very large, very full bin bags.

'What's all this then?' I sounded inexplicably like a 1950s' policeman. 'Are we having a jumble sale?'

'I have had enough.' Claire spoke through gritted teeth. 'This time, this lot is going for good.'

Claire and I had been in this position before, namely in the Great Bin Bag Wars of 1996 (when we got married); and again in 2000 (when we moved to our present house); and once again in 2003 (when the builders who had been occupying our home while they renovated it for eight months finally left) and it always went the same way. Under the guise of thinning out our wardrobes Claire would attempt to take every single item of clothing we owned (bar the ones we were wearing) to Oxfam. Her bizarre logic was always the same: 'But you don't wear any of this stuff!' And I would always reply: 'And I won't be able to if you're always giving it all away!' or the more sardonic, 'Who are you? The Clothes Wearing Enforcement Agency?' or my favourite: 'I'm saving them for the right occasion!' (This always made us laugh because I really would hate any occasion to arise when the only suitable outfit would be a purple lumberjack shirt teamed with an orange waistcoat.) This wouldn't have been so bad had it just been *my* clothes but I had to worry about hers too. I admit that some of my concern was the pain it caused me that she was giving away a top from Reiss that she had only worn twice even though it had cost over sixty quid; but I also had a sentimental attachment to some of her wardrobe. The checked shirt that she'd worn on our first date, the Bloc Party band T-shirt that I'd bought her two years ago and the Chinese silk pyjamas that she had wanted for so long that I was convinced I would earn enough good husband brownie points to be able to bank the lot and live off the interest. These were all clothes that I had loved and she was intent on binning them!

'But I don't wear them,' she predictably complained.

'And you never will if you keep giving them away!' I was equally predictable.

'Why don't you change the record! You say that whenever I try to thin out our wardrobes.'

'That's because you always misinterpret the words "thin out" to mean throw away everything we've ever owned,' I reasoned. 'I'll tell you what, why don't we just cut out the middleman and whenever we go shopping take the new clothes straight to Oxfam? It'll save a fortune in bin bags!'

'Fine, if you're so brilliant at sorting things out you can do this lot on your own!' snapped Claire as she threw the roll of bin bags in the direction of my head and stormed out.

*　　　*　　　*

Thankfully, as with the Great Bin Bag Wars of 1996, 2000 and 2003, this year's battle ended with the same face-saving result: a draw. Once Claire and I had made up following our row (which after ten years of marriage we found ludicrously easy) we went through the bin bags item by item and with a sparing use of veto agreed to give to Oxfam the stuff that I genuinely had no interest in. In return I got to keep some of Claire's clothes that I had various degrees of emotional or fiscal attachment to. After a week of disposing of ancient meatballs, tasting U-bend gunge and arguing with my wife, as To-Do-List ticks went this had definitely been of the 'hard won' variety.

Excerpt from Mike's To-Do-List Diary (Part 3)

Thursday 1 March

8.55 a.m. The good news: I've just set in motion the first part of Item 408: 'Go and see a doctor about the knee you injured playing football three years ago.' I have made an appointment for 5.00 p.m. tomorrow! The bad news: my childhood is still riding around in the back of the car.

2.55 p.m. I am in a plane on my way to Glasgow for an event that my publishers are throwing to promote various books to the trade. I had planned to watch the rest of *The Wire* on my computer as part of Item 813: 'Finish off the rest of Season One of *The Wire*' but as soon as I get on the plane I fall asleep instead. I suspect all this extra activity is beginning to take its toll.

Friday 2 March

19.55 p.m. I am back from Glasgow having managed to watch roughly ten minutes of the second episode of *The Wire* before falling asleep. Now it is Friday night and the kids are asleep, so Claire and I are letting our hair down and tackling Items 978–983: 'Drink up all the old duty-free spirits that you've bought over the years because you hate to miss a bargain'. In fact, while Claire only drinks wine and I prefer lager, none of our family or friends drinks spirits at all. Despite this we still have:

1 bottle of Peach Schnapps (Innsbruck Airport, Austria)
2 bottles of Dream Island Cocktail mix (Seychelles International Airport)
1 bottle of Mount Gay rum (Grantley Adams International Airport, Barbados)
1 bottle of Ouzo (Larnaca Airport, Cyprus)
1 bottle of Tequila (Mexico City International Airport)
1 bottle of Banana liqueur (Birmingham International Airport)

8.00 p.m. Claire and I have our first drink of the evening: two shots of ouzo each. It tastes just as vile now as it did when we first tried it on holiday in Cyprus five years ago. Age has not mellowed this drink at all. Why we bought it I'll never know.

8.05 p.m. Claire and I are making cocktails with the Dream Island Cocktail mix and some leftover lemonade. It tastes ace. 'This is like melted ice cream with a kick,' says Claire. 'We should've started drinking this a lot earlier.'

8.20 p.m. Three drinks in and we are on the peach schnapps. With lemonade. It tastes so sweet that I fear my teeth falling out and the immediate onset of type two diabetes.

9.33 p.m. Claire has opted out of the evening's experiment on the grounds that at least one of us should be legally sober should one of the kids wake up. Emboldened by flying solo I am mixing my drinks big time. In front of me is a highball glass filled with ouzo, Dream Island Cocktail mix, Banana liqueur, rum, the last bit of the lemonade and a fistful of ice. I've dubbed it the Dirty Duty. It looks slightly radioactive. Claire asks me if I think that Derek and Jessica would ever drink a Dirty Duty. I tell her they would if it came in a fancy glass and cost £16.00 a go.

10.31 p.m. I have had to stop drinking. My stomach is churning like a washing machine on spin cycle. I ask Claire if it might have been something I ate. She just raises her eyebrows and sighs.

Saturday 3 March
2.23 a.m. I am being sick.
2.53 a.m. I am being even more sick.
3.02 a.m. I am being sick again even though there is nothing left to throw up other than my kidneys.

Sunday 4 March
7.00 a.m. Claire is letting me have a lie-in as I still feel a bit fragile after my efforts on Friday night. With so much alcohol left over even after my valiant attempts with the Dirty Duty, I have decided to put this particular tick on pause and move on to something more edifying. Item 345 is: 'Have a go at those learn-to-speak-Italian CDs'. I'd bought the CDs five years ago when Claire and I were planning a holiday to the Italian Lakes but had never even opened them. Every couple of years Claire would threaten to take them to Oxfam. Wresting them from her grip I would swear that one day I would indeed learn Italian and then she would end up *ridere* on the other side of her *faccia*.

7.23 a.m. After spending the best part of twenty minutes turning my office upside down I eventually locate the CDs underneath a pile of old newspapers. I eagerly tear the Cellophane off, look at the CDs and read the labels. Each one lasts seventy minutes. One hundred and forty minutes is quite a long time to spend trying to learn another language. I imagine myself sitting in front of my computer practising Italian. One hundred and forty minutes is definitely too long. Perhaps, given that it's a Sunday and that I've been quite ill, I should try one CD to start with.

Monday 5 March
4.33 p.m. *'A che ora e servita la colazione?'* says the voice on the CD. 'Arrh key ohr-ahur eee sehr-vee-taher lah koh-laht-zee-oh-nehay,' I repeat, putting my heart into making my version of 'What time is breakfast?' sound authentically Italian. Sadly, I'm about as close to sounding authentically Italian as Peter Sellers' Inspector Clouseau is authentically French. My irreducible Brummie inflections and terrible grasp of pronunciation are not so much mangling this beautiful language as battering it to death with a sledgehammer and then running it over several times with a 4×4.

Tuesday 6 March
4.48 p.m. Having opted to put learning Italian on hold I'm trying to decide whether to tackle Item 412: 'Become a blood donor', or Item 328: 'Speak to a financial advisor about investing for the future so that you don't have to spend your dotage in penury', when I remember that I'm supposed to be at my local GP's surgery showing them my knee.
5.10 p.m. I am trying to explain to my doctor why I have waited until now to bring a three-year-old injury to the attention of a medical professional. 'It was always on my To Do List but I could never find the time,' I explain. He seems unimpressed. 'By waiting this long you've probably made the situation a lot worse.' He writes a letter of referral to a clinic for some physiotherapy.

Wednesday 7 March
9.55 a.m. I'm looking at the car boot filled with my child-hood and wondering how I'm to transport the pram and travel cot in my hands over to my parents' house so they can look after Maisie for a couple of hours. Claire says I should just bite the bullet and bin all the childhood stuff. I know she is right but I am still conflicted.

Chapter 13: 'Now you're well into your thirties start taking your health seriously.'

When people feel pain in their sinuses they think, 'Oh, I've got sinusitis.' When people get an unexplained spot on their hand they think, 'I'm sure it's nothing.' And when people start coughing and spluttering they think, 'I'm coming down with a bad cold, I'll get some Lemsip.' But when these things happen to me I don't think like other people. I think like me. Hence sinusitis becomes a potential brain tumour, a spot is the beginning of necrotising fasciitis disease and seasonal coughing and spluttering is down to a local park encounter with a dodgy-looking mallard – before you can say 'avian bird flu' I'm Googling the nearest supplier of Tamiflu. This pretty much tells you all you need to know about why Item 772: 'Make a decision about private health care', made it on to the To-Do List. But there was a second reason.

The week before I began writing the To-Do List, mail belonging to my arch nemesis and next-door neighbour, Derek, had mistakenly been delivered to us and among it was a BUPA renewal form. At the time I thought, 'Typical! He's so grown up that he's even doing stuff to make him live longer!' and I determined that looking after my health would be something that I did too.

Uninterested in joining BUPA I opted instead to find a way

of getting a complete health check that would allay my burgeoning hypochondria. Typing 'Body MOT' and 'Birmingham' into Google led within a few short minutes to my credit-card details and an online booking form to secure the next available appointment for the Health First Institute's Silver grade 'Health and Wellness Examination'. The gold was too pricey and involved needlessly scary MRI scans. Verily I was about to join the ranks of the media phenomenon known as 'the worried well'.

On the morning of my examination I felt distinctly agitated. So far, much that I'd attempted on my list had been frustrating, wearisome or even plain boring, but at least never life threatening. As I was forever pointing out to anyone who asked, the List wasn't a 'parachute out of a plane' kind of affair and I certainly wasn't a 'parachuting out of a plane' kind of guy. Life-threatening activities just weren't me. In fact I was the polar opposite of an adrenaline junkie. My stimulant of choice was Ovaltine. Therefore if there were any life-threatening activities to be had I preferred to experience them third hand, ideally within the pages of a good book or on a TV screen. But this was different. I was voluntarily pushing myself to the very outer edges of my comfort zone by submitting to an unwarranted medical examination that could result in me discovering I'VE ONLY GOT SIX MONTHS TO LIVE.

'But wouldn't you want to know if you'd only got six months to live?' asked Claire as I explained my fears.

I looked at her as though she were mad. 'Of course not.'

'Why not?'

'Because when you're a man, ignorance isn't just bliss. It's also the stuff that keeps the walls from falling down.'

'I'm sure you'll be fine,' said Claire kissing me on the cheek and handing me a plastic bag.

'What's this?'

'Something to eat after the examination because, in case you've forgotten, you can't eat anything until after your blood test.'

My heart sank. I'd been really looking forward to breakfast and now even that small delight had been snatched from me.

'I might as well go,' I sighed. 'Maybe if I get there earlier they'll see me earlier which will mean that I'll get to eat a bit earlier too!'

From the outside, the Health First Institute had something of the air of an upmarket dental surgery, with its frosted window and official-looking logo of an eagle perching on an outstretched hand. Buzzed in through the large black front door I entered a reception/waiting room where the dentist theme continued with pale cream walls, framed arty prints and comfortable seating.

The receptionist smiled warmly and took my name and credit card details in case I died during the examination. I sat down and waited to be collected.

In her uniform Tracy resembled a small child playing dress-up rather than a fully qualified medical professional. Were private medical care centres governed by the same rules as public ones? Did the nurses have to have training or would anybody do? I needn't have worried. In a quiet yet forceful tone she demanded that I provide her with a 'mid stream urine sample'. You don't get much more professional than that.

I took the container into the loo but wasn't one hundred per cent sure what she meant. Common sense suggested she was referring to the bit that was not the beginning or the end but not knowing how full my bladder was might make it difficult to tell. I opted to leave a couple of seconds before starting my collection and then, displaying hitherto un-dreamt-of skills in bladder control, provided intermittent blasts of what I hoped to be quality stuff.

Next Tracy introduced me to nurse practitioner Alison who would be conducting my initial examination.

'Right,' she began. 'I'm going to take a few measurements, collect a few samples, conduct a few tests and then once we're done I'll take you upstairs for something to eat before your consultation with Dr Anwar. He'll take you through the results of your examination.' She paused. 'How does that sound?'

'Great.' What else to say?

Alison measured my weight and height then got out a device that she informed me was a more accurate way of measuring my body mass index. A cursory glance at the chart showed that my body and I were quite clearly in the 'need-to-lose-some-weight zone', although this news was somewhat tempered by the fact that I had a relatively high muscle ratio. It was all I could do not to punch the air and whoop like a game-show contestant. I might be overweight but I was officially deemed muscularly well endowed.

With the tests over, Alison pointed me in the direction of the upstairs waiting room and said Dr Anwar would come and collect me when he was ready. The upstairs waiting room was nothing like an upmarket dental surgery; it was more like an upmarket snack bar. There wasn't just one kind of breakfast moment on offer on the counter that spanned an entire wall, there were dozens of items: fruit, mineral water, cereal, muesli, pastries, croissants, milk, tea, coffee, fruit juice and all free! I was more than a bit peckish and tempted to have a go at pretty much all of it. But mindful of where I was and what for, I restrained myself and selected a cereal bar. No sooner had I taken the wrapper off and jammed the whole thing into my mouth when a tall man in a white coat entered the room.

'Mr Michael Gayle?'

I nodded, frantically trying to swallow my cereal bar.

'I'm Dr Anwar. Please follow me to my office whenever you are ready.'

At this point my heart really was racing. Even if you manage to convince yourself that everything will be okay, there's always a small part of you that's ready for bad news. In my case, that small pessimistic/terrified/worried part is actually quite big and it's the reason why I don't smoke or take drugs, jump out of planes or snowboard, play the stock market, walk across train tracks at level crossings unless the lights are green even if there isn't a train for miles. Because when it comes to bad news I don't think, 'Why me?' No, when bad news comes my way the first words out of my mouth are invariably, 'Gah! I knew it!'

'So,' said Dr Anwar, opening my notes, 'before we take a look at your earlier examination results I will finish off this part of the morning with a physical exam. Just slip off your trousers and lie on the examination table.'

I nervously did as instructed. Dr Anwar fixed me with a firm stare and asked: 'Mr Gayle, do you check yourself?'

Although this was a euphemism with which I wasn't familiar, his deep, doctoral tones left me in no doubt as to what he was referring to.

'As part of today's examination, we like to show clients how to check correctly for testicular cancer. May I have your permission to proceed?'

'Yeah, fine,' I said in squeaky voice. This was possibly the most bizarre interaction that I'd had in a very long time.

Dr Anwar nodded and took some rubber gloves from a box on his desk. I hopped off the table and dropped my underwear. Ever the professional, Dr Anwar turned his head slightly so that we weren't making eye contact, then reached down to my groin area and began gently rolling first my left and then my right testicle between his fingers.

My mind during this whole process was a blank; I knew that if I entertained a single thought I'd end up collapsed on the floor laughing uncontrollably like an overgrown school boy. So I thought about nothing. Zero. Not a thing. Once it was over, I slipped my pants back on and got dressed. I probably would've given myself a round of applause for the amount of restraint that I had shown but then I remembered that there could still be some bad news coming my way and sobered up in a flash.

The best of the good news was that my HDL cholesterol count (that's the 'good' cholesterol to you and me) was way above normal and I wasn't dying of anything horrible. In fact my overall risk of coronary heart disease in the next decade was just two per cent compared with an average of five per cent for a man of my age.

Before I could give myself a high five, however, he gave me the bad news: my Body Mass Index, body fat percentage and waist–height ratio were all too high; on top of that my lung function wasn't great (although this was to be expected with my asthma); my triglyceride count was quite high; and there was a trace amount of blood in my urine indicating a mild kidney infection.

In short, if I wasn't going to fall apart in the near future I would have to do the following:

The To-Do List

1. Reduce my calorie intake.
2. Maintain healthy eating patterns.
3. Increase aerobic exercise.
4. Reduce my saturated fat intake.
5. Reduce my intake of refined simple sugars.

I left the Institute somewhat stunned by how unfit I was. Making my way to the car park, I reached for my car keys and discovered the packed lunch Claire had made for me in lieu of breakfast. Under normal circumstances I would've wolfed the whole lot down in a second but I barely glanced at it. Instead, I started up the car and told myself that this time things really were going to change. Fortunately for me Item 70 on the To-Do List was 'Start losing weight before you end up in a Channel Five documentary about fat people so huge that they have to be winched out of bed by helicopter'.

Chapter 14: 'Go on a diet . . . because at the rate you're chowing down extra large Mars bars, mate, you'll be in trousers with elasticated waistbands before the year is out.'

Before turning thirty I had been something of a beanpole. There are pictures of me in my early twenties where I had real cheekbones despite the fact that I'd think nothing of inhaling a family pack of crisps for breakfast, cracking open a Pot Noodle for lunch, chowing through a plate of pasta around tea time and polishing off a post-pub bag of chips on the way home. Blessed with a metabolism that appeared to burn off pretty much everything that I shovelled in meant that I never had to fear the consequences of my eating actions.

Cut to a decade later and things couldn't have been more different. Having bagged myself a lifetime commitment from a member of the opposite sex ('for better or worse' should have been exchanged for the words 'for thicker and chunkier') I got very comfortable very quickly ('Shall we go out and meet up with friends or stay in, phone up for a takeaway and watch this brand new TV series called *Property Ladder*?'). This, combined with a sharp turn-down in my metabolism, soon meant that my body, instead of burning off that second helping of Wall's Viennetta, was turning it directly into fat and gluing itself to my midriff.

Getting rid of those extra pounds I'd been carrying around for the past four years called for a two-pronged attack involving both eating less and regular physical exertion but I decided to concentrate my initial efforts on controlling my calorie intake. My first action under the new regime was to eliminate temptation by removing every last fattening item (chocolate, biscuits, cakes) from the house and dropping them all into a bin bag to take to my parents' house with the specific instruction not to release this food back to me even if I begged. My mum, as is her way, looked at me as though I was mad, mumbled something about not wanting 'fatty foods' in *her* house and handed me a leaflet for a local weight watchers group called FatBusters! taking place at the community centre.

'It doesn't look like my kind of thing,' I said.

'What does that mean?' tutted Mum. 'You should go if you're serious about losing some of this.' She patted my stomach and laughed. 'Look, it's wobbly just like a water bed.'

'Fine,' I snapped wondering why it was okay to give me a hard time about my weight. 'FatBusters! here I come.'

The following afternoon I picked up my mum for the afternoon FatBusters! session. I'd pictured a bunch of middle-aged women sitting on uncomfortable chairs in a draughty church hall extolling the virtues of cottage cheese and, although it was a draughty community centre rather than a church hall, pretty much everything else was spot on.

FatBusters! main clientele appeared to be retired women, middle-aged women and younger women with children.

As the only man in the room it was hard not to feel like some kind of an interloper. I could see from the looks I was getting that some of the other participants felt my presence was impinging on their freedom to express themselves as though fat really was a feminist issue.

Part of me wanted to lift my T-shirt thereby revealing that I too suffered from 'muffin top' but I feared that might create the wrong impression. So when it came to my turn to talk about myself, I decided to expose myself mentally instead.

'My name's Mike, I'm thirty-six years old and I've come to FatBusters! because I think I'm addicted to food.'

Linda, who was leading our course, nodded sympathetically. 'In what way do you think you're "addicted", Mike?'

'Well, put it this way, I've got this friend called Gary, who's a bit younger than me and is stick thin and sometimes when we go out for a drink I find myself fantasising about swapping bodies with him and then spending a whole day just eating and eating.'

I paused to gauge how I was doing with my fellow FatBusters!. They seemed more baffled than threatened by my presence.

'For instance, wearing my friend's body I imagine starting my day with a massive full English breakfast, followed by a couple of packets of crisps at around eleven, with maybe a spot of candy floss followed by a doughnut chaser around midday. Around one I'd probably have a pub lunch . . . something like steak and kidney pie and chips and then around three-ish I'd probably eat a bit more . . .'

I tailed off because Linda was staring at me intently. I briefly wondered if I'd over-egged it somewhat. I had indeed fantasised about swapping bodies with Gary but it wasn't as though I thought about it all day, every day.

'I'm going on a bit, aren't I?'

Linda shook her head. 'No, Mike, I'm sure we can all identify with those kinds of obsessive thoughts.'

'Great,' I replied. 'Should I carry on and tell you what I would have had for tea?'

'I think we've got the idea,' smiled Linda. 'Now moving on to Janet . . .'

After everyone had 'shared' with the group we were introduced to all the FatBusters! materials and products, the most important of which was the Star calculator. A handy reference guide on how to take the pleasure out of eating once and for all. The first meeting took just over three quarters of an hour and I still felt as though FatBusters! wasn't going to be for me.

'What did you think of that then?' I asked Mum as we filed out of the community hall.

'I don't think I'll be going back.' Mum shook her head and pulled a face. 'It wasn't really my kind of thing. I can't be bothered with all that faffing around with booklets and eating their special brands of foods. I'm going to follow my own diet.'

'Which is what exactly?'

'To eat less and exercise more.'

I had tried diets before. A few years earlier Claire and I had tried the Atkins diet for a month and then the South Beach Diet. And while Atkins worked for a while (I think I lost around half a stone) and to a degree South Beach did too (I lost a couple of pounds) they both ended up with me falling off the wagon. When I say falling, what I mean is crashing and burning to such an extent that I'd find myself walking, nay, sprinting up to the newsagents at the top of my road and then, confused by a flurry of red lights and white noise blocking out my senses and my conscience I'd eventually open my eyes to find myself back at home, lying naked from the waist up on my bed, with chocolate smeared across my face, empty crisp packets surrounding my body, and an intense feeling of self-loathing in my heart.

This time, however, with my mum's homespun philosophy of 'eat less and exercise more' still ringing in my ears I decided that I would find my own way of losing weight and began referring in public (without the faintest degree of irony) to the 'Mike Gayle Sensible Eating Diet Plan and Exercise Regime'. Better known by its snappy acronym MGSEDER this was my no-nonsense contribution to the world of diet and exercise and basically consisted of bits of well-known diet knowledge, a reduced alcohol intake, the bits of Atkins that I got on with best and a vague plan to 'walk more' and engage in 'other' physical activity.

Diary excerpts from the first ten days on the Mike Gayle Sensible Eating Diet and Exercise Regime (Part 4)

Sunday 1 April

First thing in the morning I make my way over to my local Marks and Spencer food hall and begin stocking up on 'healthy foods', which include the following: one tub of low fat macrobiotic yoghurt, five apples, five low GI ready meals and a two-litre bottle of mineral water. Standing in the queue I don't dare look to my right for fear of catching sight of rows of sweet-based impulse buys. Even with my eyes fixed firmly ahead I imagine that I can see packets of Red and Black gums just within range of my peripheral vision and I'm so distracted by this that I fail to see the grumpy-looking cashier scowling at me because I'm holding up the queue.

Monday 2 April

Although it's only day two of the diet I can already see that losing weight is going to be more difficult than I imagined. Yesterday I commenced my diet by consuming the first of my low GI ready meals in lieu of breakfast. How did it feel to be eating vegetable lasagne just before nine o'clock in the morning? Weird. Very weird. And around 11.00 a.m. (my usual snacking time) I was as hungry as ever.

Tuesday 3 April

The downside of having all this specific diet-related food in the house is that now I know it's in the fridge waiting to be eaten it's pretty much all I can think about. As I'm eating the GI meal for breakfast I'm already thinking about my first apple and when I finally eat the apple mid-morning it's all I can do to hold off on my 'handful of brazil nuts and raisin chaser'. Once I've scoffed those, I fantasise about the macrobiotic yoghurt that I'm having for lunch. Every now and again I find myself thinking, 'Surely I'm doing an awful lot of eating for someone who is trying to lose weight.'

Wednesday 4 April

Today I've decided that I'm focusing too much on food and too little on exercise. Having lost in my time enough money on unused gym memberships to actually buy my own gym, this time round my exercise regime is going to be a lot more straightforward. After work in the morning, armed only with an apple and half a bag of brazil nuts, I walked all the way into the centre of Birmingham. The good news is that this was forty minutes of low impact exercise that allowed me time for that 'personal reflection' and 'growth' type stuff that Mark Forster had spoken about. The bad news is that by the time I reach the city centre I've convinced myself that I've burned off the M&S low GI chicken and rice breakfast meal plus the apple and nuts too. Reasoning that I am now in some kind of calorie deficit I allow myself to have my MGSEDER treat of the month so head to Subway and order a six-inch meatball marinara sandwich on healthy Italian bread *without* cheese. Though sacrificing Subway's infamous processed cheese triangles makes me more than a little sad I have to say it still tastes utterly amazing.

Thursday 5 April

This walking thing isn't really working for me. Before I was halfway home from yesterday's city centre Subway excursion I was too knackered for words. After a short internal debate I hailed a taxi, planning to give the excuse, should the driver ask, that I was late for an important meeting. I needed to find a form of exercise that's even lower impact than walking. When I mention this to Claire, she suggests that I 'try limiting my exercise to breathing'. There is little doubt that she is being sarcastic.

Friday 6 April

I have just invested a considerable sum in a flash-looking Carrera mountain/road bike hybrid, along with a brand-new helmet, lights and yellow rain coat thing all from Halfords. Cycling, I have decided, is the answer to all my exercise needs. Buying a bike means sufficient financial outlay to guilt me into using it and should things not quite go to plan I will at least have something to sell on eBay. It's a win win situation.

Saturday 7 April

The bike is going on eBay. In a single journey to the centre of Birmingham I have been cut up, yelled at, beeped and nearly knocked over by a lorry and that was before I even left my own road! Having spent an afternoon getting to grips with how stupendously inconsiderate most car drivers are, I can't see how this cycling thing is going to work. Which would I rather be? Slightly cuddly with a limited life span? Or thin but only because I'd been flattened by a lorry driver who wasn't paying enough attention?

Sunday 8 April

I'm in Manchester for a work thing and being away from home is proving to be somewhat hazardous to my diet. Instead of my usual bio-yoghurt lunch I had an M&S cheese and carrot chutney sandwich and a bottle of water on the train. This wouldn't have been so bad had I not chosen to purchase a packet of Percy Pig sweets as a present for Lydia. Having consumed most of my lunch before my train had even left New Street station, I proceeded to inhale the entire bag of Percy Pig sweets before we'd reached Wolverhampton.

I resolve to get myself back on the straight and narrow and stay there during tonight's festivities.

Monday 9 April

Well, I'm back from Manchester and not only did I fail abysmally to recover from my Percy-Pig-inspired fall from grace, I have made things a lot worse. If I was the kind of bad workman who blamed his tools I'd put the blame for my downfall firmly at the feet of the people I work for. Having laid on a reception featuring free booze with mini fish and chips, they made matters worse by shepherding me into the hotel restaurant for a slap-up meal and bottle of wine. Now as the kind of man who can't resist the temptation of eating a whole bag of soft-fruit-gum-based confectionery that I'd bought *for my daughter*, what chance did I have of resisting this free booze 'n' food extravaganza?

Tuesday 10 April

I've just weighed myself. After ten days of suffering I have actually managed to lose three whole pounds! Expect my diet book and work-out video next January because I am a genius. This To-Do-list malarkey is a walk in the park.

Chapter 15: 'Now you've reached the halfway point see what the Sunday Night Pub Club think of what you've done so far.'

It was hard to describe just how good I felt when, on the last Sunday in April, I had reached the point designated by the Sunday Night Pub Club as halfway to my destination. The temptation to count up ticks as I went along was great, but I knew not to focus on the numbers but rather on getting things done. 'It's like birthday cards,' I explained to Claire one evening. 'They make your home look that bit more cheery on your big day but you mustn't take the number you get as an annual barometer of your popularity.'

Still, my mid-mission audit was a necessary evil if I was going to keep up the level of energy required to fulfil what remained of the To-Do List, so with great trepidation I made my way to the Queen's Head to stand up and be counted.

Ordering my usual pint, I waited for the other members of the Sunday Night Pub Club to turn up. Danby was first, quickly followed by Henshaw then Gary and by the time it got to half past nine Kaytee, Steve, Arthur and Jo had arrived too.

'So how's this all going to work then?' Jo pulled a hammer out of her bag.

We all looked at her as if she had lost the plot. She grinned and explained, 'We're judges aren't we? And it's the nearest thing I could find in the flat to a gavel.'

I took out the List, and explained how I thought the evening should go: 'I'll read out the items that I believe I've ticked off the List, and explain to you how I did them then you ask a few questions and agree whether I've actually achieved them or not.'

'What about appeal?' asked Jo. 'Are you allowed to appeal or is our word final?'

I thought for a moment. Danby and Arthur could both be pretty harsh judges so if something really was in doubt I needed to know that I'd get a fair deal. I looked at Jo and her lump hammer and smiled. She's from Tamworth. There are no fairer people in the nation than those from that area of the country. 'I'm making you the appeals judge, Jo. Please treat the responsibility of your position with the seriousness it deserves.'

'Buy me a pint and the decision is yours!' said Jo, banging her hammer on the table. The surrounding tables went silent. We were in for a long night.

'So, have you actually lost weight?'

It was just after ten and having managed to get them to agree to most of my ticks I was now locked in debate with Henshaw.

'Of course I've lost weight.'

'Yeah, but how much weight? An ounce? A couple of pounds? Three stone? What?'

I looked down at my pint. 'Okay, okay, here's the truth, I dropped a couple of pounds during the first couple of weeks of my diet but then I started getting busy, and the novelty started to wear off and . . .' I paused and gestured to the pint of Carling in front of me. 'This stuff doesn't exactly help the cause so the bottom line is, yes, I lost weight but I also put some on too.'

Henshaw shook his head mournfully. 'Mate, you know I'm on your side but there's no way that can constitute a tick.'

The others were shaking their heads too.

'He's right, Mike,' said Kaytee. 'To tick off "lose weight" I think you've got to lose weight and keep it off for at least a month.'

I looked pleadingly over at Jo.

'That look won't wash here, Gayle. I'm with Kaytee and Henshaw on this one.'

'Right,' I conceded, 'so I don't get the "lose weight" tick because I didn't keep it off or the "learn a new language tick", because I can't remember a single word of Italian?'

'That's right,' said Jo, rubbing her hands like a power-crazed loon. 'You haven't got any problems with that, have you? I wouldn't like to think that we weren't taking this seriously.'

'Of course not,' I replied dryly. 'So apart from those two things I can have all my ticks? Let's count them up then.'

I was more than a little nervous. A lot of this past month had been taken up by tasks that weren't exactly easy ticks and some ticks I expected to be easy ended up being almost impossible. For instance Item 977: 'Alphabetise CD collection', ended up taking me more than a week to complete because a) I'd neglected to factor in just how many CDs I owned and b) halfway through organising them it occurred to me that they needed to be sub-divided by genre.

I listened to my friends totting up the ticks, arguing about the total and then going back for a recount, before arriving at a different number altogether.

*   *   *

'Well, according to our stats,' began Jo, 'by this date in your mission you should be somewhere around the halfway mark and I can now reveal that even with your refused-tick total standing at two you've done better than expected and have completed a staggering six hundred and forty-one ticks!' She picked up her lump hammer and held it under my chin as though it was a microphone and I an Olympic athlete who'd just smashed a world record.

'So how do you feel right now, Mr Gayle?'

'Right now?' I couldn't prevent a cheesy grin attaching itself to my face. 'I feel on top of the world.'

In retrospect this was like waving a two-fingered salute in fortune's direction. And whether I believed in fate or not, fate appeared to believe in me enough to feel insulted by my big idea for To-Do-List success. As less than a week later the To-Do List came to a crashing halt.

PART FIVE

May–August

(During which I discover that this List thing isn't going to be an absolute walk in the park after all)

Chapter 16: 'Try your best not to die . . . or failing that at least do it quietly.'

The halting of the To-Do List occurred on the Sunday following my halfway audit. I returned home from the Sunday Night Pub Club just after midnight and slowly made my way to bed. Claire would normally be lying on her side with Maisie next to her in her Moses basket, but although Maisie was fast asleep Claire was nowhere to be seen.

I stuck my head out of the door and noticed that Lydia's bedroom light was on.

'Babe?' I called out in a stage whisper. 'Everything okay?'

'Sort of.'

I was confused. What exactly did 'sort of' mean? Had her mother come to stay unannounced? Had we got mice? Had our elder daughter just announced that she sees dead people?

With much trepidation I gingerly entered Lydia's bedroom prepared to avert my eyes, leap on a chair or scream (or some combination of all three) should the need arise. But Claire was sitting on the edge of our daughter's bed gently stroking Lydia's forehead.

'What's up? Is she ill?'

Claire nodded.

'What is it? The 'flu?'

She shook her head.

'A runny tummy?'

Another shake.

'So what then?'

'What's the single thing in the world that you're most afraid of?'

'Being convicted for a crime I haven't committed and spending the rest of my life in prison.'

'I mean other than that.'

'Okay, then it has to be receiving murderous phone calls on stormy nights only to call the operator and be told that they're coming from inside the house!'

Claire laughed. 'If you carry on like this I'm just going to have to come straight out with it.'

'Look, I'm a grown man, I've got a To-Do list and I'm doing it. Whatever it is I'm sure that it'll be—'

Finally the penny dropped and my frontal lobes began to throb with anxiety.

'You're . . . you're . . . you're not talking about what I think you're talking about, are you?'

Claire nodded.

'But how could this happen?'

'It's been floating around pre-school apparently.'

'Floating around pre-school? You make it sound like a fairy godmother. If there was an outbreak of typhoid at pre-school you wouldn't say it had been ''floating around'', would you?'

'You're being hysterical,' said Claire firmly.

'Too right I'm being hysterical,' I screeched. 'Our daughter has got chicken pox.'

Now chicken pox in a four year old is no big deal. Kids get it all the time. It's almost a rite of passage. And hey, don't some mums actually throw chicken pox parties so that they can get the whole experience out of the way as soon as possible? But my concern wasn't actually for my four-year-old daughter. My concern was one hundred and ten per cent for me, because at the age of thirty-six I was one of the few people I knew that had never had chicken pox.

Like any good borderline hypochondriac I'd skim-read enough self-diagnosing health-related web pages to know that chicken pox and adulthood were not a good combination. While in childhood the worst that could happen was you might end up with the odd scar, in adulthood there was a 1 in 100 chance of inflammation of the lung (pneumonia) plus the added (albeit very rare) complication of inflammation of the brain (encephalitis). The words from one particular website I once visited while convinced that I was showing symptoms of beri beri were burned into my mind: 'See a doctor urgently if you become breathless, confused, or if you have any unusual or severe symptoms.'

Given that both breathlessness and confusion were part of my everyday life (as a thirtysomething asthmatic writer who finds the ordering system at Nandos Chicken way too complicated), I had been in a state of alert for the onset of chicken pox ever since.

I couldn't even take solace in the fact that there was a high chance, statistically speaking, that it wouldn't kill me because the other fact I knew about chicken pox in adults was that it was painful. And not just, 'Ooh, that's a bit uncomfortable,' but the kind of pain which, when my wife's friend Heather came down with it at the age of thirty-four, she described as being '. . . *easily* worse than childbirth'.

Now, while I'd never actually given birth I had seen the process up close and personal twice now, and the thought that I might have to endure something described as . . . '*easily* worse than child birth', terrified me. To go through something that's '. . . *easily* worse than child birth', and not even get a lifetime's supply of decent father's day presents in return seemed to be very wrong indeed.

'You're sure it's chicken pox?' I asked as I slowly edged out of the room.

'She's got the spots. She's got the high temperature. And I've had texts from some of the pre-school mums and a couple of their kids have got it too.'

I felt my throat tighten. I'd always known this day would come once we had kids but I'd never imagined it would happen so soon.

'And there's no way you could have made a mistake?' I asked. 'You know, mistaken some finger-painting splatters for a sore?'

'Babe, there's no two ways about it, Lydia's got chicken pox.'

I glanced at my daughter lying quietly on her bed, looking incredibly sorry for herself. I took a deep breath and took a couple of steps closer.

'How are you feeling, sweetie?'

'Okay, Daddy. Can I have a kiss please?'

I looked over at Claire, then back to Lydia. I was being thrown a challenge by the gods of good parenting: deny my poorly child a kiss versus saving myself from a pain easily worse than childbirth. It was like *Sophie's Choice* only without the Nazis.

'It's nothing like *Sophie's Choice*,' snorted Claire as I made my literary allusion aloud. She threw me a lifeline.

'Daddy's got to go and do something important, sweetie,' she explained to our daughter. 'Maybe he'll come and kiss you when you've managed to get to sleep.'

'But I want a kiss from Daddy now!' wailed Lydia her face crumpling.

Before I knew it the words: 'Of course Daddy will kiss you, sweetie,' had left my lips. I held my breath and strode purposefully into the contamination zone. I gave her a big hug and kissed her on the cheek.

'Thank you, Daddy,' she said looking up at me. 'I feel much better already.'

'No problem, sweetie.' I exhaled the last remnants of my oxygen reserve. 'But Daddy's got to go now.' Trying my best not to faint, I left the room, shed my clothes in the hallway and informing Claire that nothing less than a boil wash would do, strode naked to the bathroom for a hundred-degree-Celsius shower.

A week passed and I convinced myself that after all my fussing and whining I had natural inbuilt immunity to the dreaded pox. Perhaps I'd already had it before and both my parents and I had forgotten about it.

Lydia had been fine once her temperature had come down and was stir crazy after her brief spell in quarantine. Today was the end of all that. Having fully scabbed over she was to be allowed out and was going to make the most of it all. We lay in bed contemplating plans for the day. I was going to do a few List things in the morning, at midday we'd meet up with our friends John and Sue for lunch, then we'd go to the cinema for the first time since Maisie had been born.

It was going to be a good day.

My hand casually brushed against my bare chest. My fingertips felt wet. I tried to locate the source of the wetness and found a tiny burst pustule. My brain went into denial. 'It's just a spot,' I told myself, going into the bathroom and looking in the mirror over the sink. But it wasn't just a single spot. There were two on my scalp, three on my face, one on my chest and a couple of others on my legs and shoulders.

I let out a small scream of anguish.

'What's the matter?' Claire found me curled up in a foetal position on the floor next to the sink. 'Are you all right? Have you hurt yourself?'

'I've got the pox,' I whispered pathetically. 'Listen,' I choked back man tears, 'I think you should leave now and take the children with you. I don't want them to see their old dad sobbing like a schoolgirl before he passes to the other side.'

'It's chicken pox, not smallpox,' said Claire briskly. 'And I don't expect you'll be passing anywhere for a while yet.' She bundled me back into bed, and left me trying to imagine what A PAIN EASILY WORSE THAN CHILDBIRTH would be like. I'd broken my leg once playing football and it had killed. Would it be worse than that? Or how about the time that I had gastric flu? The pain in my stomach had seemed unbearable. Would it be worse than that? And what about when I cut my shoulder open falling off my bike when I was five? I'd howled for days after that at the very thought of all the pain I'd been through. Just as I was beginning to whip myself up into a real frenzy Claire returned wielding a posh electronic thermometer, which she jabbed into my ear. When it made a loud beeping noise she examined the screen.

'You've got a temperature,' she said with all the authority of an especially grumpy Hugh Laurie. 'I'm going to call the out-of-hours doctor, tell them that you're an asthmatic and insist that they give you the anti-viral medicine to reduce the effects of the pox.'

I sat bolt upright. 'There's anti-viral medicine?'

Claire nodded sagely. 'Apparently as long as you take it within twenty-four hours of the first spot appearing it can reduce the effects of the virus quite considerably.'

I looked at my wife with newly acquired admiration.

'How do you know all this stuff?' I asked.

'Google,' she replied. 'The second I realised Lydia had got it I knew you'd somehow end up getting it too.' She shook her head. 'Right, you start getting dressed, I'll take the kids to your mum's and when we get back we'll head out to the doctor's.'

Not only did the nice doctor sympathise with my affliction, he also gave me a course of Acyclovir and informed me that if I felt even the slightest bit worried I should return without hesitation.

I returned to my bed, took the tablets and waited for full health to return. It didn't happen. Instead, I suddenly went very cold, and then I went very hot and then I started coughing a lot while drifting in and out of a feverish sleep. When I woke up a few hours later I tried to call Claire and discovered two things: first, my vocal chords had completely stopped functioning and second, by process of deduction (the newspaper with Monday's date on it gave the game away) I had been asleep a lot longer than a few hours. I tried to get up but my legs wouldn't follow my commands and so I had no choice but to wait patiently for someone to discover me. It didn't take long. First on the scene was Lydia, long since recovered from her own encounter with the pox and now standing in the bedroom doorway considering me with a watchful gaze.

'You're awake, Daddy.' She climbed up onto the bed next to me. I nodded as enthusiastically as I could.

'You've been asleep a long time.'

I nodded again.

'Daddy? Why aren't you talking? Are you being silly?'

I shook my head but she clearly didn't believe me because in a perfect replication of her mother, she rolled her eyes and then bellowed at the top of her lungs: ''MUMMY! DADDY'S BEING SILLY AND PRETENDING THAT HE CAN'T TALK!'

Duly summoned, Claire came up the stairs carrying Maisie and joined Lydia in staring at me.

'I thought you were never going to wake up,' she said.

'I can't speak,' I mouthed silently. 'Voice gone.'

'I told you, Mummy. I told you he was pretending that he couldn't speak.'

'I really can't speak,' I mouthed in the hope that they might be able to lip-read. 'I really have lost my voice.'

Claire rolled her eyes. 'Come on, Mike! Enough's enough!'

There was a loud thump. A loud thump that happened to be me falling out of bed as I'd reached for a pen in order to write, 'I'm not joking'. Normally, falling out of bed onto my head would have resulted in a modicum of yelling and shouting. Voiceless, all I could do was open and close my mouth like a flailing goldfish on dry land.

'You really have lost your voice, haven't you?' Claire apologised profusely as she helped me back into bed. She handed me a pen and notebook on which I wrote, 'Don't worry about not believing me, don't worry about the fact that I've been asleep for the best part of twenty-four hours . . . now that I know that Acyclovir isn't working just call the doctor again and make sure he gives me something . . . anything at all . . . to stop A PAIN EASILY WORSE THAN CHILDBIRTH.'

In the end, somewhat disappointingly (given the amount of time and effort I had expended trying to avoid it) the Acyclovir must have worked because THE PAIN EASILY WORSE THAN CHILDBIRTH never materialised. Instead, I suffered a smattering of blisters, some mild itching, a raised temperature and a comedy lost voice. It did take it out of me physically though and for days after the fever had gone and the blisters were on the way to healing themselves, all I felt up to was lying on the sofa watching various repeats of *Murder She Wrote* on TV.

It was a week and a half before I was back to normal and at least another couple of days before the To-Do List got any kind of serious consideration. Even without counting up all the ticks it was clear I was getting behind and needed to get back on track as soon as possible.

Chapter 17: 'Find out if you really are related to Abraham Lincoln.'

A couple of days later having thrown myself into activities as diverse as re-seeding the lawn (18), using a UV pen to mark valuables with postcode (144), and having had a go at learning basic HTML (832), Claire and I were settled down on the sofa in preparation for an evening of top televisual entertainment: Item 14: Season One of *The O.C.*

'So how are things going so far?' Claire asked as she skipped through the DVD menu.

'Just look at me, I'm practically svelte.'

'Indeed you are, but other than the diet, how is the whole List thing going?'

I shrugged. 'It's okay, I suppose.'

'Only okay?'

'I knew it would be hard but not actually *this* hard. Even the easy ticks aren't that easy and the difficult ticks are even more difficult than you think they will be. As time goes on and I start more things, I'm running around frantically spinning plates like a circus act in an effort to keep all these things going at once.'

'Are you going to carry on with it?'

'I know it sounds mad given everything that I've just said, but even though it is really difficult, it is already paying dividends. I've got more energy and when I'm working on

160

the book I'm more focused because I know I haven't got all day to mess about it with it.'

'So what's next for you To Do?'

'I'm tracing my family tree.'

Claire looked perplexed. 'Mike, your family are from the West Indies. How are you going to do that from Birmingham?'

I shrugged and turned off the TV. 'I don't know really. But it's a good job I sorted out Item 611 back in January.'

'What was Item 611?'

I paused, reluctant to continue because I knew that Claire would blow a fuse.

'Come on, what is it?'

'"Renew passport because you never know when you might need to leave the country in a hurry."'

Before I could even form a defence, steam was coming out of my wife's ears.

'I can't believe you're planning to fly off round the world and leave me to cope with the kids on my own!'

'Not necessarily, babe,' I tried my best to calm her down. 'Only if the need arises.'

'How long for?'

I faked confusion to buy myself a few blissful moments of calm. 'What do you mean?'

'Exactly what I said,' she snapped. 'Should you go gallivanting around the world for this part of your To-Do List, how long would you go for?'

There was nowhere left to hide. It wasn't as though flying to Jamaica was like getting the train to London. At best it was a twenty-odd-hour flight each way and with all the various bits of research I'd need to do I'd be pushing it to be done in less than a week and a half.

'How does a couple of days sound?' I trimmed a few days off the total in the hope of softening the blow.

'And who's going to look after *your* children while you're away in the sunshine?'

Claire referring to *our* children as *my* children was a bad sign. I was in big trouble. For a second I contemplated suggesting that she recruited both mums to help out but then it occurred to me that Claire may well have meant the question rhetorically. Given that since Maisie was born I'd had sole responsibility for the girls for approximately three hours while Claire had her hair cut and had been so traumatised that I had had to take the day off from all To-Do-list-related activities to recover, I understood her fury.

'Look, I'll start the research and we can deal with whatever happens when it happens, can't we?'

'Don't you mean that *I* can deal with whatever happens when it happens?'

'No,' I replied. 'Whatever happens we'll deal with it to-gether.' I presented her with my best sad face (capturing the very essence of contrition) quickly followed by a kiss and big cuddle, I added as some extra neck-nuzzling time for luck. Slowly but surely I felt my wife's body go from rigid and unyielding to 'slightly melty'. Only when it had concluded its transition to 'warm putty', did I allow myself to relax.

'I love you, you know,' I whispered in her ear. 'A lot of women would make a big deal about their husbands clear-ing off around the world at the drop of a hat so it's really cool that you're being so understanding.'

'Fine,' said Claire rolling her eyes (a clear indicator that I had laid it on a little too thick.) 'We'll deal with it when we deal with it but I'm making no promises that it will be okay.'

'That's all I'm asking for. Anyway, chances are I won't need to go so this will all just be a storm over nothing.'

The following afternoon, in an effort to be more green and lose some weight I jumped on my bike (no takers on eBay yet!) and rode to Mum and Dad's house. A journey that would have taken less than seven minutes by car actually took three quarters of an hour and I arrived looking like I was seconds away from cardiac arrest.

When my mum opened the door she looked me up and down and asked if I'd been swimming. 'I've heard it's good for getting rid of all that belly fat,' she said patting my stomach. 'Still, it'll take a few more laps before you start to see the difference.'

There was little point in informing my mum that I was just sweating profusely, so I followed her into the kitchen for a drink of water.

'Where's Dad?'

'He's gone into town. Why, did you want to speak to him?'

'I actually wanted to speak to both of you.'

'Why?' There was hopeful inflection in her voice and a glint in her eye. 'Have you got some news? Claire's not pregnant again, is she?'

I couldn't believe it. It had only been a couple of months since I'd made her a grandmother for the second time and she was already holding out for more? Was no number of grandchildren enough to sate this woman?

'Of course not.'

Mum looked disappointed. 'I've got a couple of balls of wool upstairs that could do with using up and I found a lovely pattern for a hat and booties.'

'So you were hoping Claire and I would have another baby just so that they didn't go to waste?'

Mum laughed. 'The more the merrier – that's what I always say. So what do you want me for anyway?'

'I need you to tell me everything you know about the Gayles because I've decided that I'm going to trace our family tree.'

The main reason why Item 190: 'Trace family tree' was on the To-Do List was because I didn't know a great deal about either side of my family beyond my grandparents whereas Claire knew pretty much everything there was to know about hers. Prompted by the birth of Lydia, Claire had done some in-depth investigations and traced a distant branch of the family to Hereford, a census entry featuring her great-great-grandmother and, through conversations with her grand-mother, discovered that in addition to being part Irish, as she had always known, she was also part Jewish and 'so rumour had it' had a bit of gypsy in her too. The Richards side of her family sounded like a game lot and I didn't want our children to think of the Gayles as being the boring bunch in the gene pool. This was pretty much the explanation that I gave to my mum.

'Michael,' she sighed, 'there's nothing much to tell.'

'Let me be the judge of that.'

'Well, I'm the eldest, and then there's your three uncles and your auntie. Then there was my father Edward and my mother Gwendolyn and her mother . . . a lovely woman we used to call Juju and that's pretty much it.'

'What do you mean that's pretty much it? What about your other grandparents?'

'My father's father had died long before I remember and so had my mother's father.'

'What about their names or when they were born or where they got married?'

'Michael, it was a long time ago.'

My mum had a point. She was seventy-one and having left her native country all those years ago had packed more into her time on this earth than most people would have if they lived twice as long. It was no wonder that a few key names had been forgotten along the way.

Over the next hour or so I got a few more details, like where she was born and the district that my grandmother had originated from in Jamaica (along with some great anecdotes that I'd never heard before about her childhood) but I still only had enough for a family twig. The success or failure of this particular tick now rested squarely on the shoulders of my dad. When I finally sat him down and grilled him too, he knew no more than my mum.

'What were you hoping for?'

'I dunno,' I sighed. 'A few more names and a bit more detail would have been useful.'

'People didn't really pay much attention to that kind of thing back in those days,' explained Dad. 'I bet you didn't know that my birthday isn't the one on my birth certificate.'

I was flabbergasted. 'How come?'

'It was the law that a birth had to be registered within four months of it happening. People were too busy farming to find the time so when they did they'd always change the date to within four months so they didn't get fined.'

That explained a lot about the Gayle trait for ignoring or bending any rules that they didn't see the point of (a trait that I possessed in abundance), but it didn't get me any closer to a more extensive family tree. The only way I was going to get more information was by taking myself off to Jamaica – a trip that would cost me a fortune, reduce my daily tick count and seriously annoy my wife.

Just then my mobile rang. It was Claire.

'You've drawn a blank with your parents and you're thinking about going to Jamaica, aren't you?'

'How do you know?' I looked around the room for a hidden camera. 'You're not watching me are you?'

Claire laughed. 'No, I just guessed. I've talked family trees with your mum before now and never got very far myself, so I took matters into my own hands.'

'What have you done?'

'I've been on the internet and found a lovely lady called Mrs Bleether who is the answer to all your problems.'

'And Mrs Bleether is what exactly?'

'A Kingston-based genealogist who, charging by the hour, will get you your family tree thereby saving you having to fly off to the West Indies and saving me having to explain to our kids why I had to strangle you, their father, with my bare hands. How does that sound?'

A Jamaican-based genealogist who spent all day tracing family trees versus me, a three week stay in a country I hadn't been to for over twenty years attempting to achieve something that I'd never done before. It was, to quote my agent, 'a no brainer'. Such a no brainer that I felt like a bit of an idiot for not coming up with it myself. I emailed an enquiry to Mrs Bleether and she wrote back that although it would take a number of months given her current workload she would be more than happy to take on my case.

Turning on my computer a few weeks later to send an email to my accountant in a bid to fulfil To-Do List Item 98: 'Sit down with your accountant and don't stand up again until you understand the basics of how he works out your tax bill') I discovered an email from Mrs Bleether.

I felt sure that she had succeeded in tracking down all the various branches of my family tree and that her email would contain names and dates of my long-dead ancestors whom I would be in a sense 'meeting' for the first time. *How far back had she managed to get?* I wondered. Would there be any surprises? Did my dad's side of the family, as my mother always said, really originate from the 'runaway slaves' known as the Maroon people? And would this explain why we Gayles were all born with a stroppy rule-breaking streak a mile wide? And what about the rumour (possibly started by my middle brother) that we were related to Abraham Lincoln?

I was seconds away from finding out the truth.

Dear Mr Gayle,

Unfortunately it has not been possible to trace your family tree with the limited amount of information that you were able to provide. Should you find yourself able to provide a greater wealth of information at some future date please do not hesitate to contact me.

Yours sincerely

Mrs C. Bleether

'Are you disappointed?' asked Claire after she read the email.

'I suppose so. Not because of the missed tick. I was actually interested in finding out a bit more about the Gayles of the past.'

'Well, you still can.' Claire reached across to type 'Genealogy DNA testing' into Google. 'I saw an article in *The Times* a while back about various companies who have set up businesses to analyse people's DNA and work out their genetic heritage. It's not as good as a big sheet of paper with a bunch of names on it but it has to be better than nothing. What do you think? Shall we order you a test?'

I thought for a moment. Did I really want to have my DNA tested to determine my genetic heritage? Of course I did! It was so wonderfully *CSI* that it was all I could do to stop myself swabbing the inside of my mouth with a couple of cotton buds that very moment. We decided on a DNA testing company and ordered its 'Gold Heritage package' for £299 which would be delivered in five to ten working days and would tell me loads more about my genetic make-up than the £199 silver package and the £150 bronze package which, as far as I could gather, would only determine whether or not you were human.

'How do you feel now?' asked Claire as I closed down the computer.

'Pretty good, actually. Okay, so after all this work I've put in I still haven't ended up with a full tick but do you know what? That's okay. The important thing is to keep going no matter what.'

Excerpt from Mike's To-Do-List Diary (Part 5)

Monday 21 May

3.44 p.m. I am on the internet looking at a report which states that since the introduction of decimal currency in 1971 over 6 billion one-penny coins (that's a staggering £60,000,000) have been lost, never to be seen again. I'm guessing some of them are currently in my house annoying my wife which is why Item 857: 'Collect together all the loose change in the house and do something useful with it' made it on to the List. On this particular task I have to hold my hands up and admit that the only person who leaves loose change around the house is me. I lose money all the time. I get sick of change loading down my pockets so I take it out and put it somewhere handy, like the mantelpiece. Then Claire comes along and says, 'That doesn't live there,' and puts it somewhere else and before you know it money is everywhere.

3.51 p.m. I have just checked the sofa and found £3.63 and two cashew nuts.

4.03 p.m. I have just checked the kitchen drawer by the back door and found £5.22.

4.20 p.m. I have just checked under our bed and found £1.89, a missing library book, three hairgrips and a year-old copy of *Mother and Baby Monthly*.

4.37 p.m. I have just checked both cars and found £8.44, a mouldy tangerine, sixteen sweet wrappers and Lydia's toy baby's knitted underpants.

4.48 p.m. I have just emptied the two pint glasses of change that have been sitting on the shelf in my office, the mug of change from our bedroom and the jug of change from the counter by the sink in the bathroom into a very large plastic carrier bag.

5.01 p.m. I'm at Sainsbury's and with Lydia's help am pouring all the money that I've found into the change-sorting machine that stands in the lobby. It's actually quite exciting. The loose change makes a terrific sound and I feel as though I've just won big on a Las Vegas slot machine only in reverse. As the machine sorts out the cascade of coins the numbers on the front of the machine quickly rack up: £1.21 . . . £3.44 . . . £6.21 . . . £8.95 . . . £12.31 . . . £16.87 . . . £19.51 . . . £23.40 . . . and then finally, following a series of deep clanks and screeches that make me worry that I have broken the machine (and after spitting out €3.30, a one-peseta coin, sixteen Greek drachmas, five German Deutschmarks, two parking tokens and eleven screws) it stops at a staggering £31.02. 'What shall we do with all that money, Daddy?' asks Lydia. I deliberate, my finger hovering above the 'cash now' button, and then having pictured all of the useless tat I might buy with £31.02, I press the 'donate to charity' button and head home.

Tuesday 22 May
2.22 p.m. So that I can tick off Item 413: 'Wear hats more because you look good in them' I am on my way into town in search of headgear whilst sporting a light-brown Kangol hat that, along with my olive-green army hat

and grey Nike baseball cap, was already part of my small but perfectly formed, admittedly vanilla hat collection. Today I am looking for a hat that is a little more off the hat beaten track – something with a bit of attitude that says to anyone who looks at it: 'Yeah, that's right, I'm a hat, what of it?' I want the kind of hat most men would think twice about even trying on let alone walking out of the shop with, which I'm sure will be pretty easy because most men I know wouldn't be seen dead in a hat, vanilla or otherwise.

2.44 p.m. I enter Selfridges in search of man hats.

2.54 p.m. Man hats appear to be thin on the ground. I think about asking one of the trendy assistants if they have a hat department but fear coming across like a slightly overweight confused thirtysomething trying to claw back what little cool he once possessed.

3.03 p.m. Success! Apparently Top Man is *the* place to go for man hats. I pick up a black pork pie hat but am overcome by self-consciousness. Is there any act more embarrassing than trying on a hat in public? What if it looks rubbish? What if I think it looks great but other people think it looks rubbish? What if it actually looks great but I'm just too self-conscious to realise this? I try it on. It looks rubbish. I try to work out if it really looks rubbish or just a bit unusual. In the mirror I spot two girls looking at me. Their expressions say: 'Look! A man trying on a hat! How silly!' I wish I was a pensioner. No one mocks old people in hats! Too embarrassed to continue I put the man hat down and leave the shop but vow that once I've recovered my composure (possibly in a month or so) I will be back and a man hat will be mine!

Saturday 26 May

9.38 a.m. I am on my way into town with Claire and the kids and we are talking about mental blocks. Ten years ago Claire's 'auntie' Margaret gave us two £5 Debenhams gift vouchers as a wedding present, which was very kind of her, and we really did appreciate them. Unfortunately for the last decade – that's right, a whole decade – we haven't managed to spend them. For the first year they used to go with us everywhere as they lived in Claire's purse. Following the great purse purge of '98 they were moved to a drawer in the hallway for a couple of years until we moved house when they seemingly disappeared until, while clearing out the drawer of my office desk, they miraculously emerged sandwiched between an ancient Nectar points card and Lydia's birth certificate. It was like accidentally coming across the treasure of the Sierra Madre. I was unsure what to spend them on, so they had sat in my drawer long enough to merit inclusion on the List (Item 967). And today we are going to spend them.

10.05 a.m. Claire and I are having an argument.

Claire: I don't understand why I've got to ask if these things are still valid. It's not even my list!

Me: Because it was your auntie.

Claire: Auntie Margaret wasn't even my real auntie.

Me: But she loved you just like any real auntie would.

Claire: You only want me to do this because you're scared of asking someone yourself.

Me: And?

Claire: Fine, I'll do it! But next time one of us has to do something embarrassing in public it'll be your job!

10.08 a.m. Claire has just got the green light from a Debenhams lady of advanced years that the vouchers are legal tender! 'Great,' says Claire, 'we have ten pounds to spend which probably would've bought us a lot more ten years ago.'

10.27 a.m. After much toing and froing we have finally settled on what we are going to spend our vouchers on: a pair of swimming costumes for the kids. Cheers, Auntie Margaret, you're a star!

Chapter 18: 'Go green because it's not just about plastic bags.'

It was just after ten o'clock in the morning of the first Sunday in June and I was standing on the muddy verge of a small 'A' road located on the edge of an East Midlands village.

'So what exactly am I looking at?' I asked my friend Dave.

'A mound,' replied Dave.

I blinked hard. Dave was right. The thing in front of us was indeed a mound. Not big enough to be a hill and too small to be a gentle rise in the landscape. It could only be described as a mound. A very large mound.

'I'm lost. Are you telling me that you drove me all the way out here from Birmingham when I could be doing To-Do-List stuff just to show me a mound? I don't want to be rude, mate, but I've got proper hills a lot closer to me and, to be frank, a lot more impressive than this. I thought you were going to show me some kind of environmental horror that was going to shock me into becoming a plastic bag-hating, 4 × 4-baiting, organic mung bean-munching eco-warrior.'

'I just did,' said Dave. 'You see, mate, roughly twenty-five years ago this hill was a clay mine that was sold off to the local council as a landfill site. The council then filled it full of rubbish, chucked a load of dirt over it and left it to grass over. They probably would have forgotten all about it had methane from a landfill site in Loscoe in Derbyshire not exploded in

March 1986 destroying a bungalow and rendering two other houses unfit for habitation. Ever since then it's been the job of people like me to keep an eye on sites like this.'

'How long for?' I asked. 'Ten years, twenty years, forever?'

'Put it this way,' said Dave dolefully, 'the likes of you, me and probably our children will be long gone before we can stop having to deal with the consequences of this particular pile of rubbish. Now multiply this one mound from twenty-five years ago by the number of councils there are nationally and multiply that number by the millions of tonnes of rubbish we've been burying in landfill sites every subsequent year in the UK alone and you can see that we've got a big problem. So how's that for a horror story then? Good enough for you?'

'It really is time I went green then, isn't it?'

'Probably.'

'Right then.' I pulled the List from my bag and flicked through to the appropriate page. 'You can now consider Item 166 on the To-Do List: "Go green because you know you really ought to", officially kick-started.'

Going green had been on my unwritten To-Do List for so long it had ceased to be funny. Like most people my age I'd paid lip service to the idea of being greener but apart from newspaper, bottle and plastic recycling that had pretty much been it. It probably would've stayed that way too had it not been for the imminent arrival of Lydia. That made me consider what the world might be like as she grew up. Once she'd been born, I had no time for anything that wasn't going to happen in the next ten minutes; and the idea of being more green got pushed to the back of the queue somewhere behind 'clear leaves out of gutter' and 'remember to put preservative on the shed'. It was only when we knew Maisie was on her way that I suddenly recalled in an 'Oh, yeah, I was going to do that wasn't I?' kind of way my mission to save the planet. I needed inspiration and that was when I put the call in to my friend Dave, an environmental officer, hoping that he might show me something that would inspire me to earn my Go Green tick.

Returning home from Dave's mound I searched out Claire and sat her down.

She eyed me suspiciously. 'You've got that look in your eye.'

'Which look?'

'That "I'm going to change the world" look. The last time I saw it was when you started this list of yours, the time before that was when we got that huge electricity bill and you turned the heating off and insisted that we walk round with our coats on all the time. The time before that was when you read that article about that couple who didn't have TV and you took the plug off ours and made us play Scrabble day in day out. And then the time before that . . .'

'Yes . . . yes,' I replied dismissively, 'I get it, "Mike's a bit faddy and gets a bee in his bonnet about stuff sometimes", but this is different.'

'Aha! So you admit this is another one of your mad fads then?'

'No . . . yes . . . maybe. Look, I've just seen something that has convinced me that we can't carry on the way we're going.'

'We who?'

'You, me, and the rest of the human race.'

Claire offered me her best eyes-closed-this-will-all-end-in-tears shaky head. 'So what is it now?'

I said, 'We're going green, babe,' and then explained how Dave had opened my eyes to the ways of green.

'Okay,' she said slowly. 'That all sounds reasonable enough. So where's the catch?'

'There is no catch. We're just going green.'

'How green is green? Are we talking lime green, pea green or an emerald green?'

I thought for a moment. The purchasing of a wind turbine, the banning of all chemicals from the house, the recycling of our own waste, the purchasing of only organic produce, the boycotting of multinational companies, the bringing to an end of all non-domestic holidays, the disposal of both cars and the end of all new clothes purchases . . . and the changing of my name to something a touch more eco-warrior. Exactly what shade of green would all that be?

'How does Militant Green sound?'

Claire put on her very best 'this had better be a joke' face. 'Look, Mike,' she began, 'I was up with Maisie and her colic at 2.30 a.m. for twenty minutes, then 2.55 a.m. for half an hour and then finally 4.20 a.m. for the best part of forty minutes and I'm in no mood to be trifled with . . . so whatever big ideas you've got . . .' she squinted as though trying to read my mind, '. . . for wind turbines, the boycotting of multinationals and getting rid of both the cars, you can think again.'

'Fine,' I replied reeling at her stupendous psychic abilities. 'Let's aim for pea green and then see how we feel when we get there, okay?'

'Fine.' I could tell from her face that she was already regretting her decision.

So as not to alienate Claire too much during the initial stages of the greening of the Gayle household I started off quite gently, using the internet to search for ideas and order one or two purchases along the way to help our greenification. Some three and half hours later those one or two purchases had swollen to just under two dozen. I ordered a water butt that fits straight onto the guttering downpipe; an electronic gizmo that can tell you how much energy you're using in each individual room; a water purifier so that we could finally renounce all those evil food miles involved in importing Evian from the French Alps; and a weekly delivery of locally grown organic vegetables. It felt good to have bought all of these things. It was as though each time I whipped out my credit card and tapped in my details I was chipping a little bit of Dave's mound away and simultaneously saving planet earth for my children. But of all the purchases that I made that day it wasn't the supply of natural cleaning products, the solar-powered iPod charger or the Standby Buster (that will mean I'll never have to feel bad about turning a TV on with a remote control again) that made me happiest. It was a simple black plastic box, a tray arrangement and a bag of worms that really did the trick.

My eco-wormery arrived late in the afternoon on day six of my greenification effort and by then the novelty of being the greenest people on our street was already beginning to wear thin. The cleaning products were okay but not great, Claire was getting sick of me telling her how much money we were wasting having the lights on while watching TV and, despite forking out the best part of £150 on them, the reusable nappies had been an unmitigated failure. It wasn't that they didn't work (they actually did the job very well indeed), more that neither Claire nor I could face the job of scraping Maisie's poo off the inside bit of the nappy on a regular basis. Maisie made things extra difficult by offering us a delivery of such combined liquidity and stench that all we wanted to do was burn the nappies in the hope of destroying

the smell. The wormery was a different kettle of fish altogether. On the website it had looked revolutionary and
exciting; surely it wouldn't disappoint?

The idea was this: in exchange for forking out the best part
of fifty quid for a worm house plus worms I would get a
completely organic food and paper waste-crunching machine that could allegedly consume up to 4 kilograms of
food per week and churn out in return 'a full tray of worm
castings' aka 'Black Gold' compost. The fact that I still had
two bags of ordinary Homebase compost left over from an
all too brief gardening spurt last summer didn't dampen my
enthusiasm one iota. Having grown up in a family that had
never had an animal of any kind in the house (nearly everyone in the Gayle household had an allergy to something or
other) after thirty-six years I was finally getting not just one,
but several hundred pets of my own.

Claire, Lydia and I sorted through all of the bits that made
up the wormery to get to the exciting bit, the worms. All day
we'd been imagining how a company might go about sending 2,000 worms through the post. Lydia, being four, imagined that they would probably come wrapped in cotton
wool. Claire, somewhat older, guessed they'd be in some
kind of pot with holes in. As for me, I secretly hoped they
would be dried out in temporary suspended animation and
would re-animate the moment I added water. We were all
wrong. There were only thirty or forty worms at most, and
rather disappointingly they were stuffed in a plastic bag with
a bit of compost and appeared not to be moving.

'They're dead, Daddy,' said Lydia gravely.

Claire and I exchanged worried glances. Hers said: 'They
are, aren't they?' while mine said, 'How long is our daughter's obsession with death going to last?'

'No they're not,' I declared eventually. 'They're just resting.' I flicked through the wormery booklet and was relieved to see that the worms' immobility appeared to be a natural reaction to the stress of the journey.

'See,' I said, pointing out the relevant section to Lydia even though she couldn't read, 'the worms are just suffering from jet lag like we do when we take a plane to go on holiday.'

Lydia nodded thoughtfully. 'But that's not two thousand worms is it, Daddy?'

I shook my head. 'No, sweetie, I don't think so.' I checked the instruction manual and the receipt that came with it. There in the small print was the reason why we only had thirty worms: we have ordered the wormery starter pack. For an extra £24.99 we can order another kilogram of tiger worms or we can wait for two years for the worms to get their breeding up to full speed. I was loath to spend any more money on worm recruits so made the decision to set up the wormery, give the worms we'd got some leftover food and hope that with a bit of luck and the occasional blast of Barry White every now and again, they'll somehow get their numbers up.

As we set the worms loose in their home for the first time, added some damp newspaper and allowed Lydia to wish them good night, I couldn't help but feel smug. This was me and my family going green and saving planet earth one step at a time. How could I not feel smug? It probably would have been a very good To-Do-List day all round had I not checked my emails half an hour later and discovered something that once again would force me to take my eyes off the To-Do List ball.

Chapter 19: 'Have a quiet (but forceful) word with the Indian film industry about some of their dubious business practices.'

It started with an email:

> Hey, Mike,
>
> I'm a fan of yours from Mumbai and I loved, loved, loved your book *Mr Commitment* but did you know that this book has been turned into an Indian movie as well? The film, *Pyaar Ke Side Effects*, has been out for about a year now so I'm sure someone must have told you but in case they haven't I'm writing to you as what's really angered me is that they didn't even bother giving you credit! The book was much better anyway.
>
> Have a great day
>
> Preti

I was curious. Was this person really saying that someone in India had made a film based on my second book without asking my permission? It seemed ridiculous. I cut and pasted the name of the film into Google and pressed return. Nothing happened. I pressed return again. Still nothing happened. I pressed return one last time and still nothing: my modem was completely dead. Having called up my ISP I established that 'due to unforeseen technical difficulties' my internet connection was dead.

While half of me was curious about the alleged Bollywoodification of one of my novels the other half suspected it was some kind of prank carried out in the name of humour. Steve from the Sunday Night Pub Club once turned up with his coat zipped up to his neck even though it was a warm summer's day. Halfway through the evening he announced that he was 'hot' and took off his coat to reveal a T-shirt with a huge picture of my face on it; another trickster friend, Danny, unbeknownst to me once sent me home wearing a badge bearing the legend: 'Bobby Davro for UN Secretary General'. It could have been either one or even both working together because when it came to Steve and Danny anything was possible.

By the time my internet was back on the following day, my mind had moved to the List and Item 900: 'Get the city council's building regulations people in to finally check all of the changes we've made to the house like we should have done four years ago'. I'd spent most of the afternoon searching out the original paperwork and just needed to arrange for them to come out to the house. Having finally ticked off something that had been kicking around my guilty conscience for so long, I'd celebrated by spending what was left of the day playing with Maisie, so it wasn't until the following morning that I fired up the computer and checked my email. Amongst various notifications from Facebook and MySpace and Amazon were a few emails from my website:

Hi, Mike,

My name is Reyhaneh and I'm based in Chicago. Recently I picked up *Mr Commitment* and I have to tell you that I haven't laughed so hard in a long time!!! I'm writing you now because tonight I rented a Hindi DVD of a new Bollywood movie entitled *Pyaar Ke Side Effects* – translated as 'The Side Effects of Love', which to all intents and purposes is your book! Not only was the movie an 'Indianised' version of your book but they've also literally used parts of it scene for scene (with only a minor diversion copying the movie *Meet the Parents*). I didn't see any mention of your book in the opening credits or on IMDB. I couldn't watch the whole thing without emailing you (not sure how it ends yet as I'm writing to you). Are you in the UK? You should have no trouble getting a copy of this movie. I'd love to hear your thoughts. Again, I have to say – thank you for the intense tickles from your hilarious book!

Best wishes,
Reyhaneh

This was getting weird. Either Danny and Steve were in cahoots or something was up again. I decided to test the theory by Googling the name of the film again. This time the first stop was IMDB where I discovered the name of the producer and that it had been given a user rating of 7.2 out of ten. Flicking through the next couple of entries and reading reviews, various things made it sound a little like *Mr Commitment* but only when I read the plot synopsis on Wikipedia did I discover how shamelessly close the plot was to my own book. Whoever had edited the film's entry agreed and had added the doleful comment: 'The plot shares many similarities with Mike Gayle's book, *Mr Commitment*.'

I couldn't believe it. It had got nothing to do with Steve or Danny. I really had been Bollywoodised!

'You've been what?' asked Claire in response to my news.

'I've been Bollywoodised.' My voice was full of indignation. 'Some bloke in India has taken one of my books and turned the whole thing into a two-hour film without paying me a red cent!'

I could see that Claire was finding it hard to be quite as outraged as I was, but for my sake she ruffled her eyebrows into a big frown.

'What can you do about it?'

'I don't know. Apparently the Indian film industry does this kind of thing all the time. In fact I'm pretty sure they did the same thing to Barbara Taylor Bradford a few years ago and she took them to court over it though I'm not sure that they won as Indian copyright law is pretty lax.'

'You should call Simon,' suggested Claire. 'He's your agent. That's what he's there for.'

'You're right, but before I do I want to make sure that I've got all my facts straight.'

'How are you going to do that?'

'Get hold of a copy of the film and watch it.'

Given that I knew next to nothing about the world of Bolly-wood films, it was hard to know where to begin my search. I thought about emailing the two people who had alerted me to its existence but as they were based in India and the US they would be of little help to me here in Birmingham. Instead I decided to contact my friend Hassan, a sports writer for the *Dalston Gazette*, because although he's only half Indian, I reasoned that half an insight into the Indian community was better than no insight at all. Plus, Hassan was on my To-Do List under Item 577: 'Catch up with Hassan as you've not caught up with him since he got married'.

I called Hassan's mobile number and waited.

'Is that you? Who's died?'

'No one, you old misery,' I replied. 'I'm just calling for a chat. How's the missus?'

'Good, thanks. How's yours?'

'Great. And we've got a new kid into the bargain too.'

'Congratulations. I must come up and see your brood sometime.'

'That would be lovely.' I paused wondering how to segue from come up and see me sometime to 'Come on, Hassan, give me the inside skinny on your people and the Bollywood film industry.' I decided to jump straight in with both feet. 'Mate,' I began, 'I've been Bollywoodised and I haven't the faintest clue how to get hold of a copy. Can you help me?'

'Of course, mate. What's it called?'

I told him the title and listened as he tapped his computer keyboard. Was he accessing some secret Indian website that only people from the south Asian sub-continent knew about?

'There you go, mate,' he said after a few moments. '£14.99 from Amazon or £6.00 second-hand.'

I shuddered with embarrassment. Still, at least I had earned another tick and caught up with an old friend.

'Thanks, mate, you're a lifesaver. As soon as I get off the phone I'll order it second hand. At least that way I'll be getting one up on them rather them getting another one up on me.'

The DVD arrived two days later in a small brown padded envelope. On the cover of the box was a woman on a moped, with a guy with a black eye riding pillion on the back. According to India FM the film is 'A MASTERSTROKE!!! An Ideal date Flick that will Appeal to everyone in Love!' Subhash K Jha (whoever s/he might be) is in agreement proclaiming it to be 'the one romantic comedy which could equal Hollywood's *When Harry Met Sally*.' I am now completely and utterly captivated. Here I was standing in my office in Birmingham holding a DVD of a film that some guy in India had based on one of my books without even telling me! I didn't know whether to laugh, cry, or book a flight to New Delhi to sort this out man to man.

I took the DVD out of its case and slipped it into the slot on the side of my computer but had a change of heart and pressed eject. I wasn't sure I could face watching the premiere of my book turned into a film on my own without dying inside. I needed help and support. I needed the Sunday Night Pub Club.

Several hours later they were sitting in front of my TV, bowls of freshly made popcorn in their hands and a look of disbelief on their faces.

'I can't believe they did that and thought they could get away with it,' said Amanda as the end credits rolled.

'I thought it was quite funny.' Gary grabbed a handful of popcorn from the bowl in front of him. 'And surprisingly watchable. Granted it's no *Seven Samurai* but it's no *Deuce Bigalow: European Gigolo* either. A solid three out of ten I think.'

I smiled weakly at Gary who was clearly just trying to wind me up and looked down at the notepad on which I'd made a list of similarities in character, plot or dialogue. After scribbling down over sixteen pages of notes in the film's first forty-five minutes I gave up. Tearing my own hair out seemed less painful.

'So what are you going to do?' asked Amanda stifling a laugh as Gary began singing one of the film's many dreadful songs. 'You're not really going to fly over to New Delhi and poke the guy in the eye are you?'

'No,' I replied, 'I'm going to do what I should have done when I first heard about this. I'm going to call my agent.'

*   *   *

'Mike,' boomed Simon. 'How are you? How's that list thing of yours going?'

'Great,' I replied instinctively, before remembering why I'd called and that I was very, very angry. 'Actually, scrap that, Simon, I'm not great at all . . . I've been Bollywoodised!'

I told Simon the story and rather than laughing he boomed that he would get on the case with the legal department. I imagined him putting down his phone and running down the corridor turning over secretaries and tea trolleys as he made his way towards legal at full pelt.

Two days later I got the following email from Simon:

> Hi, Mike, have talked with legal and it looks like given the way Indian copyright law is we'd stand little to no chance of winning a case.
> Have a great day,
> Simon.
> PS. Don't let all this stuff distract you from the To-Do List!

At this prompting I looked over the To-Do List lying underneath a large pile of books. It had been sitting there unopened and un-loved now for the best part of a working week. Simon was right; as annoyed as I was about this liberty that had been taken with my work I shouldn't let anything take me off task. Picking up the DVD case of my dodgy adaptation I smiled. Legal issues aside it was quite flattering that they liked my book enough to rip it off. I reached for the To-Do List and scanned its pages. It felt good to be back here again in a world where things were more straightforward. My eyes locked onto one particular item and refused to budge. I'd found my next tick and I vowed once again to myself that nothing, least of all dodgy unauthorised adaptations of my work, was going to come between me and the List.

Excerpt from Mike's To-Do-List Diary (Part 6)

Friday 23 June

3.22 p.m. I am just about to make an appointment for Claire and me to make our wills at the solicitors on the High Street so that I can tick off Item 20: 'Make a Will because having twice sliced through the cable while trimming the hedge with the electric hedge cutters I believe my time here might well be limited.'

3.34 p.m. The deed is done. We've got an appointment for Monday morning.

3.45 p.m. I feel a little bit weird about what I've done and tell myself not to dwell on mortality. I think I'll go and do some gardening.

3.51 p.m. Claire is asking me if I'll remarry if she were to die tomorrow. I tell her no. I will mourn her death forever. She studies me carefully and tells me that she reckons that I'll be remarried within six months because I don't like being alone.

4.02 p.m. Claire is asking me whether I'd like to be buried or cremated. I tell her I prefer to be buried.

4.03 p.m. No cremated.

4.04 p.m. No buried. Definitely.

4.15 p.m. Claire asks me what music I'd like played at my funeral. I ask her if we can stop talking about death because it's putting me off my hedge trimming.

4.20 p.m. 'Okay,' I say putting down the trimmers, 'since you ask I think I'd like "Tonight" by Richard Hawley as that always makes me feel a bit emotional.'

4.21 p.m. 'Actually I think I'd like "All Flowers in Time" by Liz Fraser and Jeff Buckley because it's a cracking song.'

4.22 p.m. 'Or maybe "The Anchor Song" by Bjork because that's really sad but quite life affirming too but not the studio version, it has to be the live version recorded in Union Chapel.'

4.30 p.m. 'Do you know what?' I sigh. 'I don't really care what music I have at my funeral so you choose. Just no Abba, okay?'

Saturday 24 June

4.55 a.m. I am lying in bed thinking about the Will when Claire turns to me and whispers: 'Are you awake?' 'No, I'm fast asleep.' She asks me if I'm thinking about the Will, and I tell her, 'No, I'm thinking about sleeping.'

4.59 a.m. 'Who do you want to leave your stuff to?' asks Claire who patently doesn't believe that I am asleep or thinking about sleep. 'You can have all of it,' I reply. 'But I don't want all of it,' she says. 'If you leave me all of it I'll feel obliged to keep all of it which is unfair. You can't clutter up this house in death as well as life you know. I don't mind having the good stuff that reminds me of you but the rest of it either has to go to Oxfam or your mates: you decide.' 'Fine,' I reply. 'I'll sort it out.'

Sunday 25 June

9.00 a.m. I'm on the phone to my old school friend John. 'All right, mate,' I say. 'Just to let you know that should I kick the bucket any time soon the fifteen boxes of Scalectrix that I bought off eBay are yours.'

9.35 a.m. I'm on the phone with my friend Jackie who was best man at my wedding: '. . . and to you I'm leaving all my vinyl and a couple of books.'

10.35 a.m. I'm on the phone to Arthur from the Sunday Night Pub Club: '. . . and to you and the rest of the Sunday Night Pub Club I'm leaving all my CDs.'

12.01 p.m. I'm on the phone with my brother Andy. 'If I die which things of mine do you fancy?' I ask him. 'I'll have your DVDs and your bike.' 'Consider them yours,' I reply magnanimously.

12.32 p.m. My phone is ringing. It is my middle brother Phil. 'Andy says that you're making a Will,' he says. 'What am I getting?' 'What do you want?' 'I'll have your computer if no one's got dibs on it.' 'I think I'm leaving that to Claire. No one's got dibs on my 1977 Shogun Warriors toy Godzilla,' I tell him. 'It's really cool. It's about a foot and a half tall and it's on wheels and when you waggle the button on the back of his head fire comes out of his tongue.' 'Nah,' says Phil. 'Fine,' I reply. 'You can have my fax machine then.'

1.03 p.m. I text my friend Richard: 'Should I die I'm leaving you my 1977 Shogun Warriors toy Godzilla. When you waggle the button on the back of his head fire comes out of his mouth.'

1.05 p.m. A text from Richard: 'Lovely thought, mate. But no thanks.'

1.06 p.m. Me: 'What about if I throw in a brown ceramic Mr T money box too?'

1.03 p.m. Richard: 'Now you're talking! Cheers, mate!'

Monday 26 June

4.08 p.m. Claire and I are dropping the kids round at my mum's before heading to the solicitor to make our Wills. We're both feeling more than a little unnerved. 'What if we die in a car crash on the way to the solicitor's?' asks Claire. 'Who will look after the kids?' I'm guessing that's one of the many questions we'll have to sort out on the way.

4.35 p.m. We're sitting waiting for our meeting with Brian the solicitor. Neither of us is saying much but I sense that Claire wants to cry.

5.12 p.m. I am exhausted and emotionally drained. 'It's very depressing making plans for your own death,' says Claire as we head home with the draft Wills in our hands. 'You're not wrong there.' I reach over to give her hand a little squeeze. Claire is not in the right frame of mind for tender moments: 'Keep your hands on the wheel,' she screams. 'What are you trying to do, make our kids orphans?'

5.35 p.m. We pull up outside my parents' house and practically race to the door. The kids are playing in the garden and we pick them up and give them a big hug. Lydia is more than a little bewildered by her parents' sudden rush of affection but decides to enjoy the moment without any further questioning.

8.55 p.m. We've drawn up a list of people who love our kids nearly as much as we do and once we get over ten we start to relax. 'No matter what happens to us,' I tell Claire, 'they'll be all right.' So we sign the papers, put a stamp on the envelope and put it in the post box at the end of our road. Next week some time the papers will be fully drawn up and we'll have to go in once again and sign them in front of witnesses but as far as I'm concerned this is one To-Do-List item that has been fully ticked off.

Chapter 20: 'Beware invitations from strangers.'

It was just coming up to seven on the first Monday in July and I was sitting at breakfast watching my elder daughter slurping up spilt milk from the table while her baby sister looked on in wonderment from the comfort of her mother's lap when Claire turned to me and asked the one question that I was hoping she wouldn't ask: 'So what have you got planned for the day? Anything exciting?'

'Oh, nothing much,' I tried to sound casual. 'You know, just a kind of ad hoc arrangement that I made with Danby last night.'

'Oh, that's good, what are you doing?'

'Well last night he was telling me how he'd booked the week off but had nothing to do and so he's sort of helping me out this week.'

'How?'

'Tomorrow we're going to London to the Tate Modern to see some art exhibition he's been raving about because Item number 121 is: "Do more cultural stuff . . ." '

'And today? What are you doing today?'

There was no way out; I was going to have to tell her the truth. 'I'm . . . I'm . . . I'm going to have a facial.'

There was a long silence.

'You're going to have a facial?'

'Yes, a facial.'

Claire rolled her eyes *and* shook her head. I was in trouble.

'Why?'

'Because it's on the List, Item 579: "Get yourself a skin care regime because you're not getting any younger".'

'But what about "Keeping it real"?'

'Having a skin care regime *is* keeping it real. Think about when I'm sixty. Would you rather be married to a sixty-year-old man with the face of a bulldog or a sixty-year-old man with the face of an angel because he started a skin care regime at the age of thirty-six? This is the twenty-first century, babe. Real men moisturise.'

'And Danby's having one because . . .?'

'He's had them before apparently. He's quite the regular.'

Claire looked forlorn and I realised I was being slightly insensitive. 'Is this because you want to have a facial too?'

'I'm thirty-four,' a double revolution of eye rolling in my direction, 'I'm still trying to shake my baby weight and this morning I was up at 4.00 a.m. with *your* youngest daughter, why would I like a facial?'

I think she was being sarcastic.

'Do you want me to book you one?' I asked even though I hadn't planned on ticking off Item 12 again: 'Be nicer to wife because it'll only be a matter of time before she compares notes with her mates and finally works out what kind of a rough deal she's on', quite yet.

'No.'

'Are you sure? Because I'll book you one if you want one.'

'I said I don't want one.'

'Fine, I won't book you one then.'

In the end I felt so guilty about my day out with relaxed and toned facial skin that I not only booked her in for a facial

193

but also booked her in at Nicky Clarke's to get her hair done. It wasn't technically on my list but in a bid to stockpile Brownie points, I briefly considered getting her hair cut by Clarke himself. But after finding out how much this would cost I reasoned that it would be cheaper and more useful to buy a small family car instead.

It was just after nine when I arrived at the salon for my appointment and Danby looked as though he had been *in situ* for some time.

'Mike, mate how are you?'

'All right.' I eyed him carefully. 'You've made yourself at home.'

'Indeed,' he replied. 'I'm going to make the most of this.' He raised the glass of orange juice in his hand. 'This is my second, and I've got a cappuccino on its way too. Do you want one?'

'Nah, I'm fine.'

Danby looked at me.

'What's on your mind? You look like you're about to face a firing squad.'

'I feel a bit weird.'

'Weird? Why?'

'Well you know . . . You and me sitting here first thing on a Monday morning in some swanky salon about to have a facial.'

'And?'

I blurted out, 'It feels a bit girlie. I told Claire that real men moisturise but I'm pretty sure they don't. Other than shower gel, deodorant, aftershave and a bit of toothpaste, real men don't do toiletries.'

'You're just nervous because it's your first time,' said

Danby. 'Trust me, once you've had it done once you'll love it forever.'

We were no longer alone.

'Hi, I'm Jasmine,' said the girl on the left of Danby. 'And I'll be taking you through your treatments today.'

'And I'm Keeley,' said the girl on the right of me. 'And I'll be taking you through your treatments today.'

Keeley was beautiful. Somewhere between a young Sophia Loren and Jennifer Lopez's better-looking kid sister. In a matter of minutes I was going to be entering a darkened room with a beautiful woman who was not my wife who would then close the door behind her and ask me to partially disrobe. Now this might not be a big deal to swanky, single, metrosexual London types but to not so swanky married men living in the West Midlands it was definitely disconcerting. It wasn't that she was suddenly going to offer 'extra services' or even that she'd become so overawed by my Adonis-like body that she wouldn't be able to keep things professional. The problem was simply that: beautiful women make me nervous.

'Have you done this before?' asked Keeley.

Suddenly I was unable to produce saliva.

'No,' I croaked eventually. 'It's all new to me.'

'Right then, if you'd like to slip your top off and put on the gown over there I'll wait outside and come back in when you're ready.'

In spite of my nervousness as new experiences with incredibly beautiful women go it was pretty good. There was a fair bit of rubbing of my temples and shoulders (despite the tenuous connection they have to my actual face) but I did quite enjoy it and at the end when Keeley half-heartedly tried to sell me a ludicrously expensive collection of lotions and potions that she had used on my 'combination skin' I was so relieved that I agreed to take the lot.

The feeling of 'lightness and well being' that Keeley claimed to have instilled in me lasted for the rest of the week. I felt full of lightness and wellbeing when Danby and I headed off to the Tate Gallery. I felt full of lightness and wellbeing the day after that as I ticked off 'Watch *A Clockwork Orange*' (Item 590) and 'The first *Godfather* film' (591) and still felt reasonably floaty the day after that when I bought a new lawn mower in preparation for an assault on my garden. In fact I was fairly steaming through the To-Do List. I was beginning to think to myself that I'd more than likely have the lot ticked off by the middle of the summer when on the following Sunday morning Claire turned to me and whispered something that diminished any trace of lightness and wellbeing that might have been lingering: 'Oh, I forgot to tell you, Derek and Jessica have invited us for dinner tonight.'

I sat bolt upright in bed. 'They did what?'

'Invited us to dinner.'

I was unable to fully comprehend what I was hearing. 'Is this a joke?'

'No.'

'Because if it is it's not funny.'

'Good,' replied Claire, 'because it isn't a joke.'

'But they don't like us. We don't like them. Why would they want to offer us an evening of food and polite conversation?'

Claire shrugged. 'Look, it was as much a surprise to me as it is to you. Yesterday afternoon I took the kids up to the shops and bumped into Jessica. Normally she lets me get away with an energetic hello and a big smile but for some reason she drew to a halt and launched into a conversation about pre-schools that lasted the best part of an hour and culminated in the dinner invitation. And before you ask, yes I did try to change dates, in fact I tried every trick in the book to make out that we were busy but Jessica came back with so many alternatives that I had to give in and agree that tonight was the best bet.'

'So that's it then? Tonight, when I should be with my beloved Sunday Night Pub Club I'll be making chit chat with our next-door neighbours? I can't believe it.'

'Well, you'd better suck it up and move on because to-night we're going round to their place.'

With this unwelcome news still ringing in my ears I got out of bed to start To-Do Listing but found it hard to concentrate. Even later in the day having worked on my book, set the ground work for tackling Item 397: 'Start a pension', collected my mum for baby-sitting duties and put the kids to bed, the very idea of eating with our neighbours felt wrong. At seven o'clock as I was supposed to be getting ready, I was lying on the bed drawing up a list of the reasons why I really, really didn't want to go around to Derek and Jessica's for dinner:

1. Because it would involve making small talk.
2. Because at some point I would be left alone with Derek and we'd be forced to talk about cars, work, sport or the weather.
3. Because at some point I would be left alone with Jessica and we would be forced to talk about children, the weather or our other neighbours.
4. Because at some point they would ask me what I

was currently working on and I would have to explain and then they would nod and say something like, 'I must apologise I haven't read any of your work. With so many books and so little time I tend to just concentrate on the classics.'

5. Because at some point during the evening Claire would end up running out of conversation and would ask me to tell them about the To-Do List.

6. Because the temptation to drink too much might result in my lips loosening enough to tell them both that Claire and I were semi-stalking weirdoes and that the idea for the To-Do List in part, came from us wanting to be more like them.

7. Because no matter how the evening went, at some point Claire and I would have to return the favour and cook for them and then they would eventually feel obliged to invite us round again and the self-perpetuating nightmare would never come to an end.

8. Because the temptation to drink too much might also result in my lips loosening enough to tell them that we once heard Derek shout at Jessica: 'That's it! I'm sick to the back teeth of your mother!' and how we listened to the subsequent argument with the aid of a glass to the wall.

9. Because I was afraid that they might ask me questions about things they hear from our side of the shared wall like: 'Why is it, Mike, that whenever you're in the kitchen the only song you ever sing is "Move Close" by Phyllis Nelson?' 'Why do neither of you ever conduct a conversation with each other while you're in the same room?' and finally, 'Why is

it that as you're coming through your front door and turning off the burglar alarm I hear Claire scream with laughter while you bellow in a spooky voice, 'I'm going to goose you!'
10. Because despite my all-singing all-dancing outer persona, inside I am actually quite shy and terrible at delivering funny anecdotes.

'Do you think there's any way to get out of this?' I asked Claire as I emerged from the bathroom having just brushed my teeth. 'Maybe one of the kids could start throwing up and we could tell them we're worried about leaving them. Our kids are always randomly throwing up, you'd think the least they could do is throw up the one time when we really needed them to.'

'No, Mike,' replied Claire firmly, 'we are not going to make one of the kids throw up just so that you can get out of going next door.'

'But I don't know what to wear,' I countered. 'Do I put on a suit or go round in jeans. I don't think I've ever seen Derek in a pair of jeans.'

'No, you're right,' said Claire slipping on her posh dress. 'Off duty Derek is definitely more of a chinos and button-down shirt kind of man.'

'Exactly,' I replied. 'And I'm so not a chinos and button-down shirt kind of man. I'm a T-shirt, jeans and, at a push, jacket man.'

'Then wear that, then. Derek and Jessica know that you're a writer and so therefore a bit "arty" and they know how you normally dress when you're off to Imran's to get your paper, so . . .' Claire paused to snigger, 'I'm guessing that as long as you don't turn up wearing a waistcoat, tie and tailored shorts matched with knee-length argyle socks and burgundy brogues you'll be all right.'

The outfit referred to here was a real one that I used to wear around the age of eighteen when I was going through an experimental fashion stage. With the exception of another at university that saw me attend an Inspiral Carpets gig wearing the bottom half of a pair of M&S pyjamas, my fashion rebellion never happened again.

There was no getting out of this. I decided on the following outfit for the evening ahead: pin-striped jacket, red T-shirt with a photo of a burger and fries on it, jeans and white Converse. It said, I can do smart or casual but I'm happiest when I get to do both at the same time.

With half an hour to go I left my wife putting on her make-up and was about to head upstairs when the phone rang. In olden times I would've rushed to answer it, viewing phone calls as a welcome diversion from real life, but these days I barely raise an eyebrow when the handset trills because no one rings me on the landline. As I was musing on whether I missed old-fashioned phone calls or not, Claire stuck her half made-up head round the door, a puzzled expression on her face.

'That was next door. Their youngest has apparently been throwing up like billy-o since about five this afternoon and so they've asked if it's okay if we cancel tonight.'

I punched the air and let out a muted, but nonetheless heartfelt, 'Result!' I was about to head upstairs to lose myself for several hours on the internet when I stopped and turned around.

'Do you believe them?'

'What do you mean?'

'Do you believe that their kid really is chucking up like they're saying?'

'Why, do you think they're making it up?'

'Well isn't that exactly the excuse that I was suggesting that we should pull on them?'

'But why would they invite us if it was always their intention to cancel?'

'Maybe it's Derek. You said yourself that Jessica did it off her own bat. Maybe when she told Derek he was like, "No, I can't stand them! Tell them our kids are sick or I'm leaving you!"'

'Yeah,' jeered Claire. 'Like that's true. And anyway, so what? You didn't want to go anyway.'

'But that was before I knew that Derek didn't want us to come around. Who does he think he is making us get a baby-sitter, preventing us eating tea at our usual time and then taking the invitation away at the last minute. Call them back and tell them that we're really sorry that their child is sick and that we'd love to rearrange for next month and instead of us coming to them, they can come to us. Go on, babe, ring and tell them that.'

'You do realise that you're insane, don't you?'

'Yes,' I replied. 'Now will you do it?'

Claire shook her head. 'No way! I absolutely refuse to be dragged into your deluded world. If you want to invite them round then be my guest.'

'Right then,' I said haughtily, 'I'll do it myself.'

'I'll get you the phone.'

'You do that.'

She handed me the phone and I stared at it blankly.

'You're not going to do it, are you?'

'I would do. But it's getting late and their kid's sick plus

201

I've got to take into account that I can't really afford the time to do anything that's not on the List right now. July and August are going to be very busy months List-wise. I really don't think I can take any time off.'

'Not even for a holiday?'

'Especially not for a holiday.'

'Really?'

'Well, not right now . . . maybe the month after next?'

'Or maybe even this one.'

I frowned at Claire. 'What's that supposed to mean?'

'It means that I've already booked a holiday, and whether you like it or not, you're coming. And before you start moaning about how I haven't consulted you, let me refer you to the contents of exhibit "A": my daily diary.' Claire began reading extracts from the diary that I had bought her for Christmas: 'January 3rd: Suggested to Mike that we book a holiday because we always leave it until the last minute. Mike said, "It's on my list, babe." February 8th: On the train up from London I looked out at the snow and suggested to Mike that we book a summer holiday. Mike replied, "Of course, babe, it's on the List." April 10th: Mike and I are walking past a travel agent on our way out for a coffee. Suggested to Mike that we nip in and get some brochures. Mike said, "It's on the List, babe. I'm on it." May 5th, May 18th and May 28th: Mentioned to Mike that June was just round the corner and that if we didn't book a holiday soon there would be little or no choice. Every single occasion Mike was like a broken record insisting that booking a holiday is, "next on the List". Will I therefore give him three weeks to get it sorted before I take the whole thing into my own hands?' She paused dramatically and fixed me with a hard stare. 'And guess what? Those three weeks are up.'

The To-Do List

I found myself bizarrely attracted to this new, more assertive version of my formerly happy-go-lucky wife. She had well and truly got me and I didn't have a leg to stand on. And she had saved me from hours of dithering, as there are few things I loathe more than booking holidays.

I looked at Claire and grinned. After the exhausting year she had had so far she deserved a break, and for that matter, To-Do List or not, I was more than a little knackered thanks to my current heightened pace of life. Even so, a holiday needn't mean a holiday from the List.

'Great,' I pronounced as a plan began to hatch at the back of my mind. 'Let's go on holiday.'

Chapter 21: 'When on holiday make sure to pack some light reading.'

Claire had chosen the holiday well. Very well indeed. Fully accommodating a young baby and a four year old who had occasional trouble sleeping, Claire had booked us a holiday not only in the same country that we had visited the year before but also in the very same hotel. Thus just after three p.m., having left our home eight hours earlier, we arrived at the Intercontinental Hotel in Malta knowing exactly what to expect. Once we had checked in and unpacked it was only a matter of a quick change of clothes before we were making our way up to the hotel's roof-top swimming pool and the glorious Mediterranean sun.

Settling ourselves on sun loungers underneath an umbrella, we grabbed a child each, slathered them both in sun-block and began earnestly getting into the holiday spirit. As Lydia played in the water by our feet, Maisie napped in my arms and, liberated, Claire delved into her bag and pulled out a copy of *Heat* magazine. Reasoning that there was nothing to stop me joining her in a little light holiday reading I pulled out Leo Tolstoy's one thousand three hundred and fifteen page epic *War and Peace*.

War and Peace (Item 1021) had been on my mental To-Do List for some years now. Having first been introduced to the novel by my secondary school English teacher, Mrs Parker, who hailed it as a 'must read classic', at the age of thirteen I had searched it out from my local library and had been stunned to discover that it was roughly the same size and density as a house brick. Having read the back of it, I concluded it was marginally less interesting than one too. Phrases like 'gossip-filled rooms of a St Petersburg party', 'fortunes of the aristocratic Bolkonsky and Rostov families' and 'epic sweep of national events and the private experience of individuals during the Napoleonic Wars', were more than enough to make it clear that this wasn't going to be my kind of thing, especially given that the other reading material in my hands at the time were books one and two in the *Grange Hill* novelisation series.

Since those heady days I was reminded of it every once in a while by watching Woody Allen's magnificent pastiche, *Love and Death*, or at university hearing it name-dropped by people who wanted to show they were serious students of the classics. On such occasions I'd think to myself, one day I really must get around to reading that and while novels that I had previously put into that category, like *Slaughter House Five* and *On The Road*, got read, when it came to *War and Peace* I always seemed to find something more pressing to do. This time was going to be different. This time I was going to give Tolstoy my very best shot.

**Excerpt from Mike's To Do List Diary (Part 7);
Tolstoy Do List Diary**

Monday 16 July

Today is the first full day of our holiday. Yesterday, in the late afternoon Maltese sunshine I opened my copy of *War and Peace*. Handily, the Oxford World Classics edition begins with a breakdown of the contents of each chapter. It is over fifteen pages long and is in really small writing. I get as far as reading about Book Three, Part Two before admitting I have no idea who anyone is or what any of them are doing and have to go back to the beginning. I reach the same point some time later and remain just as clueless. I decide to give up and concentrate on the book itself.

Tuesday 17 July

The novel kicks off with someone called Anna Pavlona Scherer throwing a party although, having read the opening few pages several times now I'm still not sure why. I don't think it's her birthday but I could be wrong.

Later, in need of a break, I take Maisie for a stroll around the roof whilst conducting a quick survey of poolside reading material. The results are as follows:

Books by Dan Brown: 11
Books by J.K.Rowling: 20

Books by Leo Tolstoy: 1
Books by maverick economists: 2

While obviously disappointed by the lack of Gayle on the roof top I can't help but feel pleased that I am the one person 'doing' Tolstoy and award myself several house points.

Wednesday 18 July

I have now reached page 146, which pleases me no end. The downside is that I still can't work out what's going on. People are walking in and out of rooms. There's someone called Anna Mikhaylovna who seems to have a problem with someone called Catiche. I'm pretty sure there's a Prince Andrew and someone called Mary but I wouldn't stake my life on it. Claire thinks that I should read around the events of the book to put it into some kind of context. I can't help but wonder if Tolstoy was a great writer who, like artists who aren't very good at drawing noses, was just rubbish at writing endings because even though I'm only on page 146 I know this book needs to be a lot shorter.

Thursday 19 July

It's just after midday and my family and I have switched locations to the beach near the hotel. Claire is on child-watch duty and I am supposed to be continuing with *War and Peace*. Instead I am assembling a mental list of all the famous classics that I have read and *understood* without recourse to other books to explain them, because *War and Peace* is making me feel like a bit of a thicko. 'I've read *Finnegan's Wake*,' I tell Claire, '*The Electric Kool-Aid Acid Test* and the Bible but compared to this, even the third book of *The Lord of the Rings* is starting to look like a walk in the park.'

Friday 20 July

We're back at the pool for a change of pace and although I feel guilty about it I have left *War and Peace* back in our hotel room and have brought instead my old friend, Time Coach Mark Forster's book *Get Everything Done and Still Have Time To Play* along with me, as it too is on my To-Do List (Item 1000). I read the back cover and the introduction and then Lydia asks me to go for a swim. When I return I end up reading Claire's *Heat* magazine from cover to cover and falling asleep.

Saturday 21 July

My family and I are dining at the hotel's swanky outdoor restaurant. Maisie is asleep in her pram, Lydia is throwing bread into the sea and Claire and I are in deep discussion about *War and Peace.*

'I think deep down you don't want to read it.'

'What makes you say that?'

'Because you haven't read it.'

'But I do want to read it.'

'Why?'

I think for a moment. 'Because it's the kind of book that you're supposed to have read.'

'Says who?'

I shrug. 'People.'

I don't know how but I can tell that even from behind her sunglasses Claire is rolling her eyes.

'I think that it's probably an okay book if you're into Russian literature but most people read *War and Peace* because it's a big fat book that gets name dropped a lot as a shorthand signifier of supposed intellectual greatness. In my position as a former English student at one of the UK's premier redbrick educational institutions, I can tell you first hand that it's not all that.'

I can hardly believe my ears. 'So you've read it then?'

'Years ago at university.'

'So what happens in the end?'

Claire shrugs as Lydia crawls in to her lap. 'I have no idea.'

Sunday 22 July

It's the last day of the holiday. Not only am I back at the beach but I'm back reading *War and Peace*. Despite agreeing with most of Claire's speech yesterday I think that I probably should carry on reading not because it will make me any wiser (the words fall out of my head the second after they enter), and not because I need the tick (though I do) but for the same reason that George Leigh Mallory wanted to climb Mount Everest: 'Because it's there.'

Refreshed from the holiday, I felt ready to throw myself into To-Do Listing again and I attacked the List with everything I'd got. I started getting up half an hour earlier every day and the ticks started coming, if not thick and fast, then at least reasonably regularly and far from slow. The eclectic nature of some of the things I was tackling were startling and heartening at the same time. One day I would be knee deep in ancient bank statements attempting to address Item 356: 'Shred all old bank, credit card statements and letters from financial institutions so that you don't end up having your identity stolen', and the next I would be staring at my younger daughter in wonderment at her new-found smiling skills in a bid to fulfil Item 426: 'Spend a whole day with your new kid trying to make her laugh.' Later I'd lurch from a day on Item 843: 'Find out what the big fuss is about Bob Dylan', to an afternoon in Cannon Hill Park attempting to undertake Item 1005: 'Learn to catch a fish so that I will have all the skills I need to live off the land (or water)'. It was like that maxim of Karl Marx that a man should be able to hunt in the morning, fish in the afternoon, rear cattle in the evening and criticise after dinner without permanently becoming hunter, fisherman, cowherd or critic. This was me. I was getting a million and one different things done every day. It felt great.

But at the same time the List was taking its toll not necessarily on me but on Claire. Any time that I wasn't working was shared between To-Do Listing or playing with the kids or getting extra sleep. I was in danger of neglecting my wife and undoing all my good work earlier in the year. I needed to do something special for her. Something to demonstrate that I really did think she was the best woman in the world. Three days later I hit the jackpot.

Ever since she turned thirteen Claire has been a fan of the artist Prince. When we first got together she would regale me with tales of how she would buy Prince's new albums on the day they came out and spend hours locked in her bedroom studiously attempting to learn the lyrics whilst dreaming of the day she would get to see him in the flesh. Unfortunately she was thwarted in the one opportunity that did present itself by her mother who thought that Prince's stage show contained sufficient 'adult' material to render it inappropriate for a fifteen-year-old schoolgirl from Leicester. Unable or unwilling to run away and see him against her mother's wishes, Claire had missed out on her chance to see Prince. Until now.

Surfing the web I came across an announcement that Prince was going to be playing what I thought was a one-off concert at the 02 Arena in London. 'Great,' I thought. 'I'll keep Claire in the dark, get tickets, book a hotel, book my mum in to babysit and one evening I'll spring the whole lot on her and in one fell swoop grab the coveted "Best husband in the world award".' It was a no brainer.

The tickets were being released for sale at 10.00 a.m. on the following Tuesday. At 9.55 a.m. I sat glued to my computer refreshing the Ticketmaster website every five seconds with my credit-card details at the ready so that I could be first in the queue. At 10.00 a.m. on the dot nothing happened. At 10.05 a.m. still nothing. And when still nothing was happening at 10.10 a.m. I started to panic, imagining that thousands of Prince fans were getting in ahead of me.

I went to The Prince website and was puzzled to discover a notice advertising advance tickets for a secret Prince gig at Koko in Camden starting at 11.00 p.m. and going on to the early hours. I assumed that the tickets were for an after-show party following on from his 02 Arena concert and so I clicked on the link which took me to the Ticketmaster website. Grateful that it now appeared to be working I bought the after-show tickets and tickets for the best seats I could find for the actual gig.

Thoroughly pleased with myself at having pulled off a Prince double whammy, I booked a hotel and my mother and headed down to the living room where Claire was playing with Maisie.

'Just so that you know,' I began casually, 'it's official: I am indeed the best husband in the world.'

Claire laughed. 'As if there was any doubt.'

'No, I mean it. I'm the best. Who's the one recording artist in the world that you'd most like to see play live?'

She didn't miss a beat. 'Prince!'

'And guess who's going to see him in August?'

Claire's jaw dropped. 'Are you saying that you've got tickets to see Prince? I didn't even know he was playing! That's brilliant. I love you so much right now!'

'And there's more.'

'More than Prince tickets? We're not going to meet him are we?'

'No, but what would be the next best thing?'

She shrugged.

'Well, how does an exclusive secret Prince aftershow party sound? Because we've got tickets to that too.'

It was minutes before I could stop her jumping up and down and running around screaming, 'I'm going to a Prince aftershow party!' And then she only stopped to ask me what she should wear and how long Prince might play for and whether we might meet him? It was as though the fifteen-year-old Claire had had her all-time top dream come true. It was great. I really was the best husband in the world.

When Claire had calmed down I returned to the loft to check my emails and discovered I'd got two messages. The first was from Ticketmaster telling me that they would email me my ticket for tonight's secret concert later that afternoon. I was confused. The concerts weren't until August so why were they going on about tonight? I opened the second email. It was from my friend Matt, a huge Prince fan whom I'd emailed earlier to let him know about the tickets.

> Hi Mike, great news that you've got the tickets. I've been lurking on some Prince fan sites and word is that he's going to do something really special. See you tonight!

212

I double-checked Matt's email, no, I hadn't misread his message. It definitely did say: 'See you tonight.' I had an awful sinking feeling in my stomach. The sinking feeling was right. The secret Prince party was for that night in London.

The list of reasons why we couldn't go was long and tedious. Lydia had a pre-school play that we'd promised to go to, Maisie was teething and wasn't sleeping very well, I had a newspaper article that needed to be in first thing, Claire was supposed to be seeing a friend who she had already cancelled on three times, Claire didn't want to go without me, I didn't want to go without Claire and on and on. How something so great turned into something so awful so quickly I'll never understand.

In the end I gave the tickets to my brother Phil and over breakfast the following morning Claire and I read about it in the Bizarre column in *The Sun*. Touts were asking hundreds of pounds for tickets. The venue was really small. Prince played loads of his hit songs. There were tonnes of celebrities in the audience. Prince didn't leave the stage until three in the morning.

In contrast Claire and I had watched a repeat of *CSI: Miami* and gone to bed only to be woken up by Maisie (at 11.05 p.m., 1.05 a.m. and 3.23 a.m.) and Lydia (complaining of foxes in the garden at 4.12 a.m. and 4.32 a.m.).

Of course we loved our kids and would never have been without them for a single second. But this was a pretty brutal demonstration of the difference between a life with kids and one without. The following night, as we consoled ourselves with a Chinese takeaway Claire said ruefully, 'Perhaps we are proper grown-ups after all.'

Excerpt from Mike's To-Do-List Diary (Part 8)

Monday 6 August

1.22 p.m. I have had enough of driving around with all my childhood belongings in the back of the car. I have to do something.

1.32 p.m. I have dumped all my old school exercise books in the paper-recycling box.

2.34 p.m. I have taken my junior microscope to the Cancer Research shop on the High Street. Maybe it will inspire some kid who might have gone into a life of crime to become a doctor or a scientist instead.

Tuesday 7 August

9.01 a.m. I have taken all my old school exercise books out of the recycling because I can't bear to part with them. My next stop is the Cancer Research Shop on the High Street to get my microscope back. Claire tells me that I am a hoarder. 'Tell me something I don't know,' I yell as I close the door.

9.45 p.m. The microscope is mine although it cost me £4.99 which is roughly £4.98 more than it is worth.

10.00 a.m. I feel bad about this but have no choice than to move everything that was living in the boot of my car into the boot of Claire's car on the grounds that she hardly ever uses her car and so won't miss the space.

Wednesday 8 August

5.50 a.m. I have got up early in order to tackle Item 120: 'Print out all the digital photographs that you've never got round to printing off.'

6.00 a.m. I have just opened my computer's digital photo software to assess the size of the problem. I have a staggering 3,483 pictures of which roughly 94% are of Lydia and Maisie, 3% are pictures of other people's kids, 2% are of sunsets on holiday and 1% of me and Claire. This is going to be tougher than I thought.

10.32 a.m. I am in PC World looking for a colour printer. I flirt with the idea of asking one of their staff for advice but quickly give it up when I'm unable to find anyone who actually works there. I end up asking a middle-aged customer lingering in computer cabling because he looks like he knows what he's doing. He suggests a flash-looking printer that doubles up as a fax machine and a scanner as he's got one at home. I thank him, grab one from the display and head for the check out.

11.12 a.m. I have downloaded the latest printer drivers, I have double checked the cartridges and plug and unplugged the USB cable more times than I care to remember and I cannot get the printer to work for love nor money.

11.15 a.m. I call the printer manufacturer's helpline and anticipate AOL-style service. The first question is have I set it up correctly and I tell them that I have. The second is if I'm sure that it's actually switched on and of course I want to curse them for asking such blindingly obvious questions but then I look over at the printer and notice that the little 'on' light is actually off.

11.16 a.m. The printer is working.

12.18 p.m. It has taken me the best part of an hour to print out a single decent photo. The first one came out looking like an X-ray, the second made my daughter look like a junior version of the Incredible Hulk and the third and fourth ones were ruined because I'd put the paper in the wrong way.

1.34 p.m. Of the 3,483 photos on my computer I have so far managed to print out six, two of which are of sunsets. This is trying my patience to the extent that I am verbally abusing both the computer and the printer with the threat of violence.

2.02 p.m. I am wishing that someone would invent a machine that would just do the things that you want it to do without you having to get involved with any of it.

2.05 p.m. I've just repeated my invention wish to Claire. She tells me I've already got one: 'It's called a wife and it's how ninety per cent of the things that need doing in our house actually get done.'

2.10 p.m. I ask Claire if we really need hard copies of the photos of our kids. She doesn't reply. This can be interpreted as: 'You already know the answer to that question so don't even bother trying it on, pal.'

3.10 p.m. I have filled up five and a half CDs with the best images from my computer (roughly 1,540 pictures) and am taking them down to Boots to get them printed out.

3.42 p.m. The woman in Boots wants to know how many photos I've got to print. I tell her 1,540 and she laughs and tells me to stop joking around. I'm forced to explain that I'm not joking around so she gets out her calculator and does the sums: 'That'll be £ 231,' she says.

4.11 p.m. In a bid to drive the cost down the lovely woman from Boots and I have gone through all five and a half CDs and picked out what we think are the best images. Given the wealth to choose from and the fact that we're basically trying to represent the last four years of Gayle history we find it hard to narrow it down to anything fewer than 150 photos which she works out will cost roughly £22.50. A bargain!

Thursday 9 August
4.55 p.m. I am sitting in a coffee shop on the High Street watching my wife weeping as she looks through the edited version of the last four years of our lives: anniversaries, get togethers, barbecues, birthday parties, family holidays and new babies galore. In a masterstroke I have not only earned this tick but gone some way towards being the best husband in the world. I share my observation with Claire. She just smiles and carries on looking through the photographs.

Chapter 22: 'Appreciate your mates because without them the highlight of your Sunday nights would probably be *Songs of Praise*.'

It was the second Sunday in August and I was in the Queen's with the Sunday Night Pub Club, catching up with each other's news. Steve and Kaytee were considering a career change and buying the lease on a shop on Moseley High Street; Amanda had won a cruise to the Canary Islands by completing one of those 'This product is so wonderful because . . .' competitions promoting a new line of wholemeal bread; Gary had been out two nights on the trot and hadn't been to sleep for thirty-six hours; Arthur had bought some more Dr Who figures; Jo was going off to Norwich at the weekend to see her old flatmate; and Henshaw and Danby had spent the weekend at various kids' birthday parties. As well as this we'd also discussed who (sitting around the table) we'd most like to be trapped in a room with; why it would be virtually impossible for Oasis to ever make another decent album; and voted for our top three vegetables to complement the perfect Sunday roast. All in all it was shaping up to be another sterling Sunday Night Pub Club night.

Afterwards, Henshaw and I made our way along Moseley High Street to the minicab office on St Mary's Row.

Henshaw turned to me. 'So are you pleased with how your list thing is going?'

'Yeah really pleased. I feel like I'm finally getting things done.'

'Good, I'm chuffed for you, mate. So, what do you think you've learned so far?'

'About what?'

'About your To-Do List. I'm curious to know what insights you've had frantically doing all this extra stuff.'

'I dunno,' I replied eventually. 'I haven't really had the time to do much reflection.'

'None of us do these days,' he said laughing. 'But since you're doing this and it may at some point turn into a book, don't you think you ought to?'

In the back of the cab I reflected on Henshaw's question. He was right, I had been doing the List off and on for some eight months now, which in terms of the time I'd allotted to the project was two thirds of the way to my goal. I should be well on the way to learning a few things about life. What was the point otherwise? A quotation that I'd read when I was seventeen and thought meaningful enough to inscribe in ballpoint pen on my army issue rucksack sprang into my head: 'The unexamined life isn't worth living.'

It was late on a Sunday night; I was in the back of a mini-cab listening to an Asian version of Simon Bates' *Our Tune* while quotations from long-dead Greek philosophers randomly popped into my head.

When I reached home all I wanted to do was crawl into bed but my thoughts were urgent enough to make me grab a piece of paper and a pen. I wrote:

Things I have learned from the To-Do List so far

1. I have good friends.
2. I miss some of my old friends.
3. Everything takes longer than you think it should.
4. Some things that you think are going to be hard are pretty easy.
5. Some things that you think are going to be easy are pretty hard.
6. There is no such thing as enough time.
7. Sometimes doing stuff makes life easy.
8. Sometimes doing stuff makes life a lot harder.
9. Seeing my mum's face when she saw Tony Blair was priceless.
10. As hard as it is, being a dad is the best job in the world.

I looked at the pad in front of me. As lessons acquired over the past eight months they didn't seem too bad. Yawning, I put down the pen and was about to start getting ready for bed when it occurred to me that I hadn't made my mind up about what my next big list thing was going to be.

I scanned the entries looking for something to grab my attention but nothing sprang to mind. As a diversionary tactic I opened my laptop and saw that I had an email. A big smile broke out and got bigger as I read the contents of the message.

The email was from Susie Dent, one of the co-stars of Channel Four's long-running quiz series *Countdown* telling me that, yes, it would be okay if my friend Arthur had his photo taken in front of the show's *Countdown* Conundrum Board.

My next big tick was here.

*   *   *

All of the Sunday Night Pub Club were on the To-Do List in the form of 'Do something nice for . . . (insert name of Sunday Night Pub Club member here) and some of them had already been ticked off. Steve had informed us all one night that he'd never had anyone send him flowers so I sent the largest bunch I could find to him at work; Gary had received his in February when during an attempt to come up with a definitive list of 'the most fanciable female singers of the Nineties Brit Pop era' Gary confessed to a not inconsiderable crush on a particular female lead singer. A few weeks later, having called in a few favours from some friends of friends who knew her, Gary's girl indie singer crush very kindly called him on his mobile while he was sitting round at Arthur's house playing *Vice City* on the PlayStation. And in March, following a discussion about toys we had all wanted when we were young, Jo revealed how she had dreamt of owning a *Girl's World*. Three days, a hotly contested auction on eBay and a not altogether insignificant amount of money later, and a pristine never-been-out-of-its-box-before *Girl's World* was winging its way to Jo.

Since then things had gone a bit quiet on the 'do nice things for the Sunday Night Pub Club' front. Not for lack of trying. I'd been struggling to find anything for either Kaytee or Henshaw and although Danby did mention something about his love of merino wool underwear I decided that was perhaps a step too far. But Arthur was going to be the most difficult to please as he only ever really got enthusiastic about *Dr Who* and Paul Weller and he already had pretty much every single Dr Who-related toy/DVD and the entire output of Paul Weller (even the really rubbish covers album). Or at least that was what I thought until his new girlfriend Amy revealed that in her spare time she travelled the country being in the audience for TV shows. So far she had ticked off *Trisha*, *The Wright Stuff*, *Dancing On Ice*, *Top of The Pops*, *Question Time*, *Blind Date*, *Play Your Cards Right*, *The Weakest Link* and *Can't Cook Won't Cook*. The only one that she hadn't been on was *Countdown*. Arthur piped up how he'd always wanted to have his photo taken in front of the *Countdown* conundrum in a 'Sir Edmund Hillary planting a flag on Everest kind of way' as he had only ever missed two episodes of *Countdown* in the last three years. Suddenly I had a way to make his dream happen and add a little something extra into the bargain.

About a year ago I was invited to be a judge on the Best Novel section of a well-known book award. My fellow judges were Kate Adie and *Countdown*'s Susie Dent and, following a summer of reading, we all met up to discuss who we were going to put forward as the winner of the award. I'd felt a little out of my depth given that Kate was famous for reporting the news while being shot at and Susie was famous for knowing the Oxford English Dictionary inside out. Fortunately both were exceptionally nice people and for a short while they were candidates for Item 364 on my To-Do List: 'Try to make friends with new and interesting people so that you don't spend your whole life talking about films, music and last week's episode of *Dr Who*.' Just imagining the look of surprise on the Sunday Night Pub Club faces if I turned up at the Queen's with Kate Adie in tow was enough to make me smile.

I made sure that my first email to Susie was chirpy and not at all stalkerish:

Dear Susie,

It's Mike Gayle here. I was a judge with you on the Book Awards. I was just wondering whether it would be okay to bring a couple of mates up to Leeds to watch *Countdown* being filmed. Hope you're well!

Mike x

Dear Mike,

Do come to *Countdown* and bring some friends! Just let me know when you have in mind.

Hope you're well.

Susie x

Great, I thought to myself, another tick. But then I realised I could kill two birds with one stone and follow up on a promise that I had made earlier in the year and before I knew it I was writing another email.

Dear Sam,

Remember how I said that now that we were friends again that we shouldn't lose touch? Well me and Arthur and his bird are coming up to Leeds. How do you fancy meeting up and coming to see *Countdown* being filmed?

Less than a minute later I received the following reply:

Wahey! Do I ever! I love, love, love *Countdown*! Let me know the dates and I'll book the day off work.

Sam x

So, suddenly it was on. Me, Arthur, Amy and Sam were heading over to Yorkshire TV to watch *Countdown* being filmed.

Sam looked well and happy and was overjoyed at seeing Arthur for the first time in a decade. I introduced her to Amy and they exchanged comments about how much they loved *Countdown* and how excited they were at the thought that they might get to meet the show's main presenter, Des O'Connor.

We were all laughing and joking so much that we didn't pay much attention to the huge coaches lined up on the double yellow lines outside the studios. Had we been paying attention we would have gleaned an early indication of our fellow audience: a sea of old people. One hundred and twenty of them covering every shape and size. There were tall old people and small old people. Old people in wheelchairs and old people on crutches. Old people who looked like old people versions of Hollywood stars (Danny De Vito, Will Smith and Nicole Kidman) and old people who looked as though they were seconds away from taking their last breath. All we could see was old people.

And then there was us. Four youngish-looking people dressed like students.

'It's like being in the nursing home in *Cocoon*,' said Arthur. 'I'd guessed that old people were into *Countdown* because my mum loves it but this is ridiculous.'

'Do you think they'll turn on us?' grinned Amy. 'You know, start a fight because we're on their turf?'

'They'll be fine,' I replied, 'I've got an affinity with old people because like them I enjoy moaning, hate being cold and am partial to the occasional Werther's Original.'

Realising that we were blocking the only door into the foyer and risked being tutted into oblivion we tried to make ourselves as inconspicuous as possible, a task not helped by Arthur gleefully taking photos of us against an octogen-arian background.

After half an hour or so some trendy-looking twentysome-things wearing headset microphones and carrying clip-boards appeared as if from nowhere and began their spiel about the dos and don'ts of watching *Countdown*. The old people 'oooohhhed' and 'aaahhhed' at all the right moments while Sam, Arthur, Amy and I looked on in a mealy-mouthed fashion as we tried to hide our resentment at no longer being the youngest people in the building.

The lead youngster-with-head-mic clapped his hands to get our attention.

'Right, we're going to go into the studio now so could we have anyone in a wheelchair or with a physical disability going in first, then the following guests: Mike Gayle, Arthur Tapp, Samantha Campbell-Midford and Amy Langham.'

If it had been a competition to find the best way to embarrass four thirtysomethings in front of a crowd of old age pensioners, the youngster-with-head-mic would have won hands down. As we joined the queue behind the extra elderly and infirm and ahead of people some forty years older than us, we could feel the eyes of every pensioner in the room boring into the back of our skulls, as they silently asked themselves, 'What's so special about that lot that they get to go in front of us? We fought world wars and made this nation great. All they've done is leech off the government, listened to loud rock music and taken drugs.'

It was the very definition of the walk of shame.

The stress and strain we had endured was worth it to see Arthur's face light up when the production assistants handed him an official *Countdown* notepad and pen. We got to have our photos taken on the podium in front of the *Countdown* Conundrum. Even I was aware that we were standing on hallowed ground. All in all it was everything that we'd hoped would be.

It was just after eleven by the time Amy's Fiat Punto pulled into my road. Climbing out of the car Arthur thanked me for sorting everything out.

'You should get your own TV show called *Mike'll Fix it*,' said Arthur.

'I'm already working on it.'

As I scrambled around in my bag for my front door keys and Amy beeped her car horn goodbye, I thought to myself that this was what the List was all about. Making things happen that wouldn't have happened if I hadn't pulled my finger out. My head suddenly flooded with things I was desperate to do. Heading inside I made my way upstairs and went to my desk to find the List and work out which particular item would make the most sense for me to do next but when I opened the drawer I was shocked to discover that it wasn't there. I checked all the drawers, the top of my desk, my shelves, the bed, my bag and my coat but to no avail. Panicking, I turned the entire room upside down before acknowledging that somehow, somewhere, I'd lost the List.

PART Six

September – The End

**(During which I mostly try to fill
the huge empty void caused
by the absence of the List)**

Chapter 23: 'Learn to look after your things.'

As a child how many times had my mum told me to take better care of my things, otherwise I'd 'live to regret it'? A hundred? A thousand? Probably more like ten thousand. And now here I was, alive and regretting it. Big time. And if my mother had been right about this, what else might she have been right about? Would my finger get stuck up my nose if I carried on picking it? Would I catch a cold if I went out in winter without a vest? Would I not feel the benefit if I kept my coat on indoors? And though these thoughts raised a small smile, it faded all too quickly once I recalled what had led to them in the first place. I went downstairs to enlist Claire's help.

'It's got to be here somewhere,' she reasoned. 'You're never without it. It'll be in your office somewhere.'

'I've already checked.'

'But how well did you check? Remember that time when you were completely convinced that you'd lost that £500 that you'd taken out to pay the builder and how you got me and my mum to scour the streets for it while you turned the house upside down looking for it? Where was it in the end?'

'On my desk.'

'And was it even hidden under anything?'

'No,' I sighed. 'It was just sort of sitting there.'

'And what about the time we were supposed to be going out for an anniversary meal and you thought you'd lost the car keys somewhere between the car park and the restaurant? We spent the entire night walking backwards and forwards looking for them – with me in my heels! – and where were they in the end? Inside your suit jacket where you insisted you'd checked a million times. I couldn't look at you for days without wanting to throttle you. See? There's hope yet. More than likely it's somewhere obvious just waiting to be found.'

'Okay, you've made a pretty good point,' I conceded, wondering why these things always happened to me. 'I'll check again.'

I spent until just after midnight going through my office, the bedrooms, the kitchen, the living room, the bathroom, the conservatory and even the cellar. I checked inside cupboards, toy boxes, the oven (even I thought that was a long shot); underneath beds, duvets, sofas, tables and small children. I went through the newspaper and magazine stack, my record collection, the food cupboards, our wardrobes and the drawer by the back door (noticing en route that it was fast on its way to becoming repopulated with takeaway menus). I then checked the roof area next to the skylights, the garden shed, the newsagents up the road, the lining of my black suit jacket, underneath the front wheel of the car, the bath, inside my printer's paper drawer and between the pages of my copy of *War and Peace*. It wasn't there.

Thoroughly dejected I returned to the bedroom where Claire was giving Maisie her midnight feed.

'I can't find it anywhere,' I said flopping down on the end of the bed.

'Didn't you make a copy of it?'

'Of course I didn't,' I snapped. 'It was a handwritten To-Do List, why would I bother making a copy of it?'

Claire glared. 'Well I can think of at least *one* good reason.'

'I'm going to have to try to remember every single thing that was on the list aren't I?' This was going to be like that time that I'd deleted three weeks' worth of work by accident and all anyone would say by way of sympathy was: 'Ooh, you should have backed it up on one of those little memory stick things, shouldn't you?' I dropped my head into my hands. 'It'll take me weeks to remember and copy all that out again – weeks that I should be spending actually doing the List instead of trying to re-create it.'

'Look, Mike, you're being hysterical,' said Claire. 'You're not thinking properly. Wherever it is it can't be that far if you're referring to it every five seconds. Now think: where is the last place that you can remember having it?'

'I don't know,' I cried hopelessly.

'Did you take it with you to Leeds?'

I shook my head. 'There was no need.'

'So it was something that you did before you headed off for *Countdown*?'

'I did quite a few things in the days before I went to *Countdown*.'

'Okay, well, in the morning take the last three and start there and see what happens.'

While I considered this advice, I sat watching Maisie have her feed. She looked so relaxed, so at peace with the world that I wondered what was the point of growing up if it's only to find yourself thirty-six years old with a 1,277-item To-Do List. Maisie had nothing to do but finish her midnight snack and get back to the business of sleeping. An ideal world if ever there was one.

'Fine,' I said. 'I'll come to bed now and start retracing my steps in the morning.'

It was just after nine when I turned up on Danby's doorstep.

'You've lost your list?'

'Exactly.'

'So what are you doing here?'

'Retracing my steps.'

The reason I'd started with Danby's house was because the day before I headed off to Leeds Danby and I (from nine in the morning to five when his wife got back from work) were attempting to break a world record. Not any specific world record you understand but any world record able to be broken in a two-bedroom terrace in Kings Heath with the minimum amount of props or expenditure of cash.

Item 862: 'Break a world record just to see if you can', was on the To-Do List because there had always been a small part of me that suspected it wouldn't be that hard to do as long as you applied yourself and chose a relatively straightforward record with which to do battle. Given its borderline silliness I had run this idea past Alexa, who reassured me that she had had various thoughts along similar lines. With the thumbs-up from the List's official moral compass, I'd recruited Danby and divided the day into seven-hour-long 'Record Breaking slots' (with an hour off for lunch) and drew up a list of seven records to attempt. Despite a valiant effort on both our parts (especially when it came to catching stacks of coins from the end of our elbows and eating baked beans with cocktail sticks) we failed to get anywhere close to a world record, let alone breaking one.

*　　*　　*

With no luck at Danby's, I returned home and got on the phone to my brother Phil as the second step to finding the List. Earlier in the year he had been a contestant on ITV's *Dancing On Ice* and that, combined with his being on my list at Item 61: 'Spend more time with middle brother', I had decided he should teach me how to ice skate. I'd met up with Phil at Hammersmith Ice Rink where he was hailed as some kind of skating hero. Sadly, despite my brother's skills I soon realised that I hated ice skating at thirty-six just as much as I'd hated it at fifteen and our afternoon of ice bonding was little more than me falling flat on my face and vowing never to put on a pair of skates again.

Phil hadn't got the faintest clue where my To-Do List might be and though I pleaded with him to trek over to Hammersmith to check the rink, I could tell by his laughter that he wasn't taking my desperation seriously. I was running out of options. Everything, and I do mean *everything*, was riding on the List being at my final destination: the Birmingham National Indoor Arena.

I'd gone there to take Lydia to see the Wiggles – four wholesome-looking Australian men, who wear brightly coloured jumpers, sing joyously silly sing-a-long songs and have their own programme on Nickelodeon. The Wiggles are Lydia's favourite people on Earth by a long way. And so when we heard that they were touring it was a foregone conclusion that we'd buy tickets to see them.

As I headed down to the NIA I tried to think as many positive thoughts as I could. Yes, the people at the NIA would have found the list. Or if they hadn't then I would find it on the floor in the car park. Or if not there then in the hands of a mysterious bearded man with a beatific smile who would approach me and say in a deep voice, 'Michael, I believe this is yours.' I'd take it from him and look up to thank him only to discover that he'd disappeared into thin air. To no avail. When I finally got to speak to one of the security guards he told me, somewhat firmly, that no red notebook with the words 'To-Do List' scrawled across it in marker pen had been handed in.

Back home I sat in the car outside the front door with the engine switched off. Should I carry on looking for the list or try to replicate it from memory? Had I really checked every-where? Could there be one place that I'd overlooked? An idea suddenly came to me. A couple of years ago a friend of mine nearly lost a £1200 watch when his three-year-old son picked it up from the dresser in his parents' bedroom, wrapped it up in loo roll and put it inside his toy castle. The three year old had denied being able to recall that his dad even had a watch let alone touching it and it probably would have never been seen again without nineteen rounds of 'Let's look in the last place that we would ever think to look'. Sure enough when 'Charlie's toy castle' became an option there it was lying inside the dungeon. Taking things without asking permission wasn't Lydia's style but even so . . .

Taking the stairs three at a time I went to Lydia's bedroom and found her sitting on the edge of her bed playing tea parties.

'Daddy, would you like to come for tea at my house?' she asked. 'We're having cream cakes and doughnuts.'

'Sorry, sweetie, Daddy can't have tea right now as he has to find something he's lost.' I kissed the top of her head and then kneeled down. 'Sweetie, I don't suppose you've seen Daddy's book, have you?'

'Which book, Daddy?'

'Daddy's List book, you know the one with the red cover?'

She shook her head. 'Haven't seen it.' Then added sweetly, 'Do you want me to help you find it?'

Staring into her big brown eyes it became obvious I was on my own with this one.

'No, sweetie,' I replied, ruffling her hair, 'Daddy will be fine on his own but pour him a quick cup of tea just in case.'

Heading back downstairs some fifteen minutes later I went to tell Claire and Maisie my bad news.

'Any luck?' asked Claire as I entered the kitchen.

I shook my head. 'How about you?'

'I've turned the place upside down and I can't find it anywhere.'

'So that's it then,' I said dejectedly. 'It's gone for good.' I sat down on the step.

'It's not the end of the world, Mike. I'm sure between the two of us we'll be able to remember everything you've done and fill in the gaps for the rest.'

'No, no, you're wrong. You can't replace the List. The List wasn't just a bunch of words on a piece of paper. It was more than that. It was hopes and dreams and me getting a life and being a proper grown-up.'

'And it still can be.'

'No, it can't. With the List gone I'm just going to have to accept that it's over, babe. I failed. I'm officially giving up on the To-Do List.'

Chapter 24: 'Don't mention the "F" word.'

It was kind of apt that my giving up on the To Do List coincided with the end of August, heralding as it does the death of summer. With all the bank holidays, the sunshine and the general sense of *'No one really does anything in August do they?'* mentality it was easy to forget about deadlines and that was what I had done. It wasn't so much that I'd forgotten I was supposed to be handing in my new book by the end of September, rather I'd decided to push it to one side. Yes, I'd been working on it but with the casualness of one who had all the time in the world. Now I had exactly one month. And given that it was writing novels rather than ticking items off a To-Do List that kept a roof over my family's heads I really did need to get *my* head down. I probably would have done so had the close of summer brought the one thing that I feared more than my impending novel deadline: Lydia starting 'big school'.

Talk of 'big school' had been dominating conversation in the Gayle household for some time. Plus Lydia had taken to trying on her brand-new school PE kit at every available opportunity. She'd slip into it after breakfast forcing us to peel it off her after lunch and all it took was a single visitor to our home (grandparents, neighbours and even the guy who came to read the gas meter) for her to shoot upstairs to her bedroom, returning moments later to casually parade

236

around the living room inviting admiration. It was great that she was so happy about going to school. We were over the moon that she was seeing it as the beginning of an exciting new chapter. But that didn't prevent Claire (and occasionally myself) as viewing it as the beginning of the end.

'She's my baby,' said Claire tearfully having just explained to Lydia at bedtime that there were only a few more sleeps left until big school. 'I don't want her to go to school. I want her to stay with me and be happy.'

'She will be happy,' I reasoned. 'She'll make new friends and she'll be learning fun new things just like she did at pre-school.'

'What if she doesn't like it?'

'What's not to like? Getting to hang out with a bunch of people your own age in a place where every afternoon you get "structured playtime" sounds brilliant. If she doesn't like it I'll go in her place.'

Claire didn't laugh. She just cried even harder.

'I tell you what,' I said giving her a big squeeze. 'Instead of thinking about what we're going to be missing why don't we concentrate on making the most of her last few days of freedom? You know, take Maisie over to my mum's and give Lydia a really good send-off.'

Claire nodded and sniffed. 'Okay,' she said. 'Let's give her the best send-off that we can.'

'You do realise that we're making it sound like she's just been sent down for a ten-year stretch at Her Majesty's pleasure?'

'Maybe we should stop watching so many court room dramas and give *The Vicar of Dibley* a spin instead.'

Claire and I really did make the most of Lydia's last days of freedom. We let her have an entire day of choosing what we did and where we did it on the first day of our long goodbye. She had us playing tea parties, babies and making dens underneath the dining table. After a lunch selected by Lydia of pasta, ham and cheese the action transferred to the nearby 'Fishy Park' (aka the Edgbaston Botanical Gardens) where she promptly ditched us in favour of her friend Tom from pre-school whom she had bumped into by the swings. Finally, as the sun began to set we headed over to my parents' house to pick up Maisie before making our way to Pizza Express, Lydia's final destination of choice.

Talking about the highlights of the day, I thought this could legitimately be construed as Item 3: 'Spend more quality time with number-one child so that she doesn't grow up attracted to emotionally distant men.' Once again as had happened at Christmas, the List was refusing to give up on me. Or perhaps this was an illustration of the upside of procrastination: if you put things off long enough eventually you'll get them done regardless.

On the morning of Lydia's first day at school it was hard to work out which of us was the most excited. For Claire and me half of the excitement came from remembering the highs and lows of our own first days at school; we felt as though we had inside knowledge not only of how she might be feeling but what she might remember too.

What Lydia will and won't remember of her first five years has been something of an obsession for us. Claire can remember various events that took place around the time when she was three while my memory seems to kick in more around the age of four. Previously I'd reasoned that if we split the difference we wouldn't have to do anything memorable until she was about three and a half and we could save ourselves a stack of cash by implanting false memories of flying to Disneyland for an afternoon or having tea with the Queen. Claire was having none of it and insisted that any memories had to be real. Despite outings to parks and zoos and soft play centres and the countryside, quite often the things that most stick in Lydia's mind are the everyday things like the time that she helped me put out the bin bags for the dustmen, or the day that we were gardening and she saw a worm for the first time. This must be what is making us sad about today, that having been present at so many different firsts we had to let her enter a stage where new things would be happening without us there to share them.

At twenty to nine, having finished off a 'first day at school' photo session (mostly featuring a smirking Lydia with her arms straight down at her sides as though standing to attention) a tearful Claire nodded that it was time to go. Having discussed in great detail what might be the best thing, we had decided that Claire would take Lydia up to school on her own and I would stay at home with Maisie. Giving Lydia a big kiss and a hug I watched her disappear out of my line of sight as she and Claire made their way to school. How did I feel? Okay, I suppose, a bit apprehensive but I was pretty convinced that she would take to it like a duck to water, and sure enough she did. She loved school. She loved her teacher. It was all going to turn out fine.

Later that evening, having listened to all of Lydia's first day at school stories and put both kids to bed, I wandered up to my office to do some work. I surfed the internet for a while seeing how the world had changed since I'd last checked before playing a couple of rounds of Scrabulous on Facebook, returning a few emails, checking MySpace and every other online time-wasting activity known to man.

As much as I loved the new book, the impending November deadline was causing me no end of stress and I couldn't see how I was ever going to make it even if I cut out non-essentials like eating and sleeping.

I was feeling more than a little overwhelmed when I heard the sound of footsteps and Claire burst through my office door screaming, 'I've found it!' As our habit is to walk around with pillows attached to our feet once we've put the kids to bed I knew that whatever it was had to be important.

'What?'

'It.' She kept her hands behind her back, hiding whatever 'it' might be from my line of vision. 'I've found it!'

It was weird seeing her bouncing up and down so joyously at the end of what had been a pretty exhausting day. 'A cure for cancer? A tenner down the back of the sofa? The Christmas chocolate that you hid so well that you forgot where you left it?'

Claire shook her head and grinned. 'It's the List, babe,' she said, presenting me with the object she'd been hiding behind her back, 'I've found the List.'

Chapter 25: 'Remember it's all Pink Floyd's fault.'

'It's like it's come back from the grave,' I said, opening it up and flicking through it. The pages seemed cold and damp, as if it had been left outside. Which as it turned out, it had been.

'You'll never believe where I found it,' said Claire. 'I was cleaning out the kitchen and listening to the radio when I heard the rumble of a diesel engine, which reminded me that I'd forgotten to put out the paper recycling for the bin men so I thought I'd better go and put the papers out. Anyway I dragged the recycling box to the front of the house and as I bent down to pick up a couple of newspapers that had blown off along the way I saw a headline on one of the supplements that caught my eye because it said: "Is your middle-class child eating too much veg?" Then I remembered that there had been another article in a different paper that same weekend that I had wanted to read so I started rummaging in the recycling like a mad old bag lady and there, sandwiched between two old magazines, was your To-Do-List book. How amazing is that?'

'That's incredible,' I said, partly in response to my wife's question but more in wonderment at her ability to add this level of detail to an anecdote that basically boiled down to: 'It was in the recycling bin.'

'How do you think it got in there?'

'Dunno, these things happen, don't they?'

'Do they?' Claire raised an eyebrow. 'Freud would say that there are no accidents and that it was probably your sub-conscious mind's way of saying you're getting sick of all this To-Do-List stuff.'

'Well, it's a good job that Freud isn't here otherwise I'd have to tell him he was quite wrong and the last thing I'd want to do is offend the father of modern psychoanalysis by telling him he was talking cobblers.'

'If you did he'd say that was exactly what he knew you'd say and that your aggression is indicative of a *guilty state of mind*.'

Ignoring the fact that Claire had spoken the last part of her sentence in a very bad Austrian accent I countered, 'Well if he was here I would tell him that what he said was exactly what I thought he would say in response to what I said.'

'Does that even make any sense?' asked Claire waggling her eyebrows at me in an accusatory fashion.

'It doesn't matter. As far as I'm concerned this conversation is over and I bid you, madam, a good day.'

As Claire went downstairs I wondered why I had come over all eighteenth century. Suddenly every last bit of en-thusiasm drained from me and I collapsed onto the bed.

Did Claire have a point?

Was it possible that I had subconsciously thrown away the To-Do List because I didn't want to carry on?

And if my subconscious was indeed trying to sabotage my efforts to defeat the List, what did this mean for the future?

I cast my mind back to the last time I had put the news-papers in the recycling box. It had been a Sunday evening, and, tellingly, it had been around the time that the List had gone missing, which ruled out my wife's involvement in its disappearance. I'd been attempting to plan my future week of To Doing before the Sunday Night Pub Club and not feeling too well disposed towards it. In a bid to kick-start Item 423: 'Find out what all the fuss is about Pink Floyd' (which I had been avoiding like the plague) I resolved that I was no longer allowed to listen to any non-Pink Floyd-related music until I had worked my way through all fourteen of the band's albums. This wouldn't have been so bad had it been a normal weekend but that Saturday in a bid to tick off Item 519: 'Buy more new music so that you don't end up one as one of those sad blokes who only listens to stuff that they liked when they were twenty', I'd spent well over a hundred quid in Polar Bear records in Kings Heath on CDs by The Hold Steady, Kate Nash, Richard Hawley, Amp Fiddler, Mice Parade, Iron and Wine, Calvin Harris, Ursula Rucker, Sammy Davis Jr, Laura Veirs, Mavis Staples and Beirut. Instead of listening to all this new music I was having to wade through Pink Floyd's *A Saucerful of Secrets* which, while I could see some people might like, I could never imagine, even with the doors of my mind wide open, ever voluntarily putting this CD on again. The list was ruining my evening and as *Take Up Thy Stethoscope and Walk* came on I'd had enough. Switching off the hi-fi and tidying up a bit, that must have been the moment when I'd scooped up the List with all the weekend newspapers littering the room and took the whole lot out to be recycled.

Maybe Claire's right, I thought, staring at the ceiling, maybe I was trying to sabotage myself.

I picked up the List and balanced it in my hand. Did I really want to carry on? And if I did, where to start? I needed a good place to get stuck in. Some ticks that were tough yet satisfying would put me and my subconscious back on the straight and narrow. For a moment or two nothing stood out and then suddenly it hit me. The items on the list with scribbled red question marks against them indicated tasks started but yet to be finished. This is where I would begin. My next course of action would be to visit the ghosts of tasks incomplete and try to exorcise them once and for all.

Starting with the previously abandoned Items 861 and 1277: 'Clean all downstairs windows so that you don't have to have the lights on in the middle of the day', I battled my way through a good dozen ticks like Item 588: 'Tell Dad that I love him while I still have the chance', (which from him prompted the anxious question from him, 'You're not dying, are you?'); and Items 555-560: 'Archive all the video of the kids onto DVD before you end up simultaneously losing a tape and their entire childhood in one go.'

Achieving these ticks had the effect of making me feel more positive about the List. This was no longer me cherry-picking the easiest ticks, no, this was me, head bowed, taking on the List like a raging rhinoceros. I was invincible. Or at least I was until I went for a mid-week drink with Danby and Henshaw who decided to take me down a peg or two by pointing out the one item on the List that I had attempted and failed at least twice.

'And it's not going to get any better with you drinking this stuff, is it?' Henshaw gestured to the pint in my hand. 'You must know that beer's full to the brim with calories, mate.'

'It's not that bad.'

'It's the diet equivalent of chocolate for blokes. If your Missus claimed she was on a diet and you caught her out snaffling a four-pack of Crunchies wouldn't you think that she wasn't taking her diet very seriously?'

'Claire doesn't need to diet,' I replied.

'Deviation!' crowed Danby. 'We're talking about you, not your Missus. So don't try getting off the subject.'

'Fine. Just tell me what the subject is and I'll stick to it like glue.'

'You don't really want us to spell it out to you do you, mate?'

'We could spell it out "Give us a Clue" style,' suggested Danby, and he stood up, with virtually everyone in the bar watching him, and proceeded to mime.

'One word,' said Henshaw barely able to breathe, he was laughing so hard.

Danby tugged his ear.

'Sounds like . . .'

Danby mimed a man putting on a hat.

'Sounds like . . . helmet,' offered Henshaw, giggling like a girl.

Danby shook his head.

'Sounds like cap,' wheezed Henshaw.

Danby shook his head again.

'Okay.' Henshaw attempted to recover his composure. 'Last try . . . sounds like hat.'

Danby touched his nose with his finger in affirmation.

'Okay,' said Henshaw. 'Let's gather together what we know. It's a single word that rhymes with "hat" that describes something obvious about our comrade here that he seems to need some help with. Could it possibly be described as a feminist issue?'

'Too right.' Danby spluttered into his Grolsch.

'Yeah, yeah, yeah,' I sighed. You've had your fun. Now let's move on.'

'But I thought you were tackling the List head on like a . . . what was it?'

'A "raging rhino",' I replied sheepishly, rueing my first and undoubtedly last mention of a horned animal as metaphor in the public arena.

'That's right,' said Henshaw. 'A "raging rhino," and yet so far you've tried to diet, bought a bike, joined FatBusters! and had an all-over-body MOT to scare yourself into getting fitter and how much weight have you lost?'

'None.'

'And how much have you gained?'

'I dunno, I don't weigh myself every five seconds, do I?'

Danby laughed. 'That sounds to me like the response of a bloke who has put on a pound or two since his last weigh-in.'

'Three, okay?' I could take no more. 'I've put on three pounds since I started dieting.' I looked at my pint and with more than a touch of remorse pushed it away.

Henshaw pushed my pint back towards me. 'Like the Garfield poster that my sister used to have on her bedroom door says: "The diet starts tomorrow so why bother messing up today?" '

'Maybe you're right. But I've had my fill of diets. I'm going to do something completely unrelated to the world of diet and exercise.'

'Like?'

'Like getting on a plane and taking myself off to the other side of the Atlantic,' I said triumphantly, picking up my pint. 'I, my friends, am going to New York.'

Chapter 26: 'Every once in a while do more of the things you do for love.'

'You're going where?' asked Claire the following day when I broke the news to her in the kitchen.

'To New York,' I replied. 'It's a List thing.'

'What kind of *list thing*? I thought your To-Do List was about you doing ordinary things.'

'It is.'

'So why has "Wind up wife by announcing that you've got to go to New York", suddenly appeared on it?'

'It hasn't, "Go to New York" has never been on the To-Do List.'

'So what possible reason could you have for going?'

'I can't tell you.'

'Why not?'

'Look, you'll just have to trust me. There's nothing dodgy going on. I'm not running away or trying to squeeze in a trip without you and the kids or get up to anything sneaky. But I do have to go and I do have to go quite soon.'

I attempted to give her a little hug but she went all stiff, wriggled free and fixed me with her sternest stare.

'Who else is going? Are you taking your Sunday night mates with you?'

'Nope, I'm flying solo on this one.'

'When would you go?'

'Towards the end of the month.'

'And how long for?'

'I'll be gone a day, two max.'

'Let me get this right. You're flying all the way to America just for a night or two?'

'I promise I'll explain everything when I get back.'

'And will I understand then?'

'Yes . . .' I suddenly felt slightly less sure of my answer, 'At least I think you will.'

'And this is really that important?'

'Absolutely. And, when this is all done and dusted I'll take you to New York whenever you like for as long as you like. But this thing . . . well it's really important.'

'Fine,' she replied. 'You go and do whatever it is that you've got to do. Just so long as you know . . .'

'What?'

'Me and the kids will miss you like crazy.'

Two weeks later just after eleven in the evening, local time, I found myself landing at Newark airport. On previous trips I'd managed to get through customs, jump in the back of a yellow cab to whichever hotel I was staying at, check myself in and, given that this was the city that supposedly never slept, still had plenty of time to indulge in my little I've-just-arrived-in-New-York ritual: CD shopping at the Virgin Mega-store near Times Square in the middle of the night.

Tonight was different. In a post 9/11 world it took three hours to make it through customs, by which time I'd lost the will to live, let alone the will to leave the safety and comfort of my hotel. So, following the ordering and polishing off of a quick room service minute steak sandwich and fries, I shed my clothes, crawled under the covers, flicked through a couple of pictures of Claire and the kids on my iPod, and fell into a jet-lagged sleep.

Five hours later a truck beeping loudly before bellowing in a Dalek voice: 'Warning! Vehicle Reversing!' dragged me from the depths of sleep. For a few moments I couldn't work out where I was. Thanks to the hotel's heavy curtains the room was pitch black and as my eyes adjusted I began to pick out the outline of various objects: a chair, my suitcase, the mirror on the wall. I wasn't at home. I was in a hotel. I looked at the clock next to the bed. It was just after seven in the morning. I closed my eyes then reopened them. I had a vague feeling that the hotel wasn't in London. It all came back to me. I was in New York City.

And suddenly I realised that it wasn't a dream. I really had flown all the way across the Atlantic just to buy my wife a $12 mug.

Six years earlier, around this very time of year Claire had taken me to New York for three days, as a surprise gift for my thirtieth birthday. We had done pretty much everything that you're supposed to do in New York. We went up to the top of the Empire State Building, visited the Museum of Modern Art, took walks through Central Park and visited Coney Island but most of all we shopped. And of all the shops we visited by far and away our favourite was the delicatessen-cum-homewares store, Dean and Deluca.

For those of you who have never been, Dean and Deluca is pretty much the delicatessen-cum-homewares store to end all delicatessen-cum-homewares stores. It's like a temple dedicated to the creation and consumption of food and is a wonderful way to kill an afternoon if all you want to do is stare and drool.

249

Staring and drooling is what Claire and I did over all of the amazing prepared food that they had on display. When we hit the homewares section Claire officially fell in love with a mug, a cream-coloured mug with thick contours and a solid-looking handle. Printed on the side of it in tasteful script were the words: Dean and Deluca.

I should point out here that Claire doesn't have many vices. She doesn't do expensive shoes or handbags. She doesn't really like shopping for clothes and has little to no interest in jewellery. With the exception of her hair (which she takes very seriously indeed) she is pretty much the definition of a cheap date. Her one Achilles heel, however, is mugs. She loves them. Claire's idea of a perfect day would be spent perusing the shelves of a shop called 'Mugs, Mugs, Mugs', while drinking from a mug only interrupting her perusing/drinking to look through the 'Mugs, Mugs, Mugs' catalogue for anything that they didn't have in store.

In the eleven years that we've been together I have seen Claire buy more mugs than any sane woman could want. She's bought tall mugs, small mugs, wide mugs and deep mugs; she's bought plain mugs and mugs with every kind of pattern. But I had never seen her look at a mug the way that she looked at that Dean and Deluca mug. It was mug at first sight. And unlike other mugs that, over time, tended to fall out of favour to be replaced by yet another of its kind, the Dean and Deluca mug was always number one. So when I managed to break it the summer before last by knocking it off the counter while making myself a cup of tea to go with my fried breakfast, Claire wasn't just saddened by its loss, she was devastated. And though I tried to find a replacement, purchasing several near-identical mugs from Heals, Habitat, the Conran Shop and John Lewis, to Claire's eyes none of them came close. I even scoured the internet but discovered the Dean and Deluca website didn't deliver to the UK. And that was when I realised that, excessive contributions to the world's carbon dioxide output notwithstanding, there was no option but to jump on a plane and get one in person.

Stepping out of the tranquil air-conditioned calm of the Muse hotel into the hustle and bustle of New York in the morning rush hour was like stepping from an old black and white movie into a full-on stereophonic Technicolor extravaganza. The yellow cabs, the skyscrapers, the pretzel sellers, the commuters dressed for business from the ankle up and for jogging from the ankle down – there was no doubt that I was in New York.

I opened my map of central Manhattan and tried to get my bearings. As far as I could remember there were only two Dean and Deluca stores in the area. The first was a smaller operation just off Rockefeller Plaza. Claire and I had visited it for lunch one afternoon and I had infuriated many busy office workers behind me in the queue by taking ages to formulate my order because I'd been distracted by the sight of Wesley Snipes walking past. It wasn't actually Wesley Snipes but just some random bloke who on closer inspection didn't even remotely resemble the actor in question, but it was enough to make me momentarily forget that I hardly ever imbibe hot drinks, let alone the tall skinny mochaccino that I seemed to be in the process of ordering. The second store, in SoHo, was the larger of the two and the one where Claire had bought the mug. Given that the Rockefeller centre was closer than SoHo I headed there first.

Walking through the busy New York Streets I tried to adopt

a confident strut as though I were a native and not a daft tourist with a funny walk. There's something about being in strange countries and not being sure of how things work that makes me self-conscious, so in a spot of reverse psychology I try to act the opposite of how I really feel.

My confident strut and I barely raised an eyebrow on my way to the Rockefeller centre, which I took as a good sign. Pausing outside the shop I peered in: they had mugs, but tall latte-types like the ones you get in Starbucks rather than the good solid diner-style mug that Claire loved so much. I thought about asking one of the girls at the tills, but even though it was only mid-morning there was a long queue and I didn't want a bunch of New Yorkers tutting at me for holding up the queue. My best bet was to head to SoHo and have done with it.

Although yellow cabs are a great way of getting around New York, nothing beats walking. The sights, the sounds, the tastes, the smells, they're all there to be witnessed first hand if you take to the streets. Heading down Sixth Avenue I made my way towards Broadway and then down into SoHo. On the way I passed a middle-aged woman in a fur coat and sunglasses walking six Yorkshire terriers, a group of school children heading into Madison Square Park and a man who may or may not have been the actor who used to play Dr Carter on *ER*.

It felt good to be here. Seeing the sights. Hearing the sounds. Walking the streets. And all for a good cause. Claire and I would definitely be back here soon, I told myself.

At the SoHo store, I took a deep breath and walked in. It had barely changed. There was still the café at the front and the amazing delicatessen counter to the right. Determined to claim my prize as soon as possible I headed to the rear of the store to the mug section and began scouring. I looked high and I looked low, repeating my actions several times over before throwing myself on the mercy of one of the store's assistants, giving her a detailed description of the mug. But to no avail.

It simply wasn't there.

Chapter 27: 'No matter how hard things get . . . no matter how fed up you are . . . make sure you don't give up.'

As dozens of New Yorkers buzzed around in my vicinity doing their shopping, the magnitude of my folly dawned on me: I'd flown over 17,000 miles in search of a mug that wasn't there in order to tick it off on a 1,277-item To-Do List that I now felt like ditching on the spot. Having overcome chicken pox, the Bollywoodisation of one of my novels, my wife booking random holidays without my knowledge, and losing the List, my mission was going to come to an end because of a simple $12 mug. It was more than I could take.

On the pavement outside Dean and Deluca I drew up a mental list of reasons why it would be completely okay for me to give up:

Reasons why it's completely okay for me to give up on the To-Do List this close to the end:

1. I'd given it my best shot.
2. I missed my kids.
3. The To-Do List had been a stupid idea from the very beginning.
4. I was on my own in New York.

5. It was practically my birthday (and no one should have to work this close to their birthday).
6. I'd almost reached the deadline anyway.
7. I could save myself the hassle of having to spend months on end turning the To-Do List into a book.
8. I wouldn't have to carry on pretending that I was getting anything out of *War and Peace.*
9. I'm already reasonably comfortable with the idea of failure so giving up on the List would be a great way of reacquainting myself with the notion.
10. I was tired. Really tired. Tired of trying. Tired of giving things my all. I wanted to stop racing round like a nutter trying to do everything and getting nowhere fast. I wanted to just stop and do a whole big hunk of nothing.

For balance, I then wrote a list of reasons why it *wasn't* okay to give up.

Reasons why it's not completely okay for me to give up on the To-Do List:

1. I've worked too hard to give up now.
2. One day my kids might read the To-Do List and be inspired.
3. The To-Do List is probably the best idea I've ever had.
4. So what if I'm on my own in New York? It's New York!
5. Why give up this close to my birthday and cast a shadow over something that should be fun?
6. I'd practically reached the deadline anyway.

7. The book version of the To-Do List could become a huge international bestseller and I could end up being endorsed by Oprah.
8. I'm already more than halfway through *War and Peace*.
9. I'd like to become reacquainted with the notion of perseverance.
10. Yes, I'm tired, but it was the good kind of tired. The kind of tired that you get from going the extra mile.

I weighed up my two lists in the hope that an answer might present itself to me. It didn't. And though I hoped that there might be a fortuitous conversation with a kind and mysterious beggar; or an inspirational inscription scribbled on the edge of a discarded newspaper; or even a well-timed transatlantic call from my wife telling me: 'This is what you should do.' The truth was there was none of the stuff of films and all of the stuff of regular old reality: a difficult decision to be made and a lack of certainty about the right course to take. And so without any help I made the decision myself. It could be right or wrong but it was mine and mine alone. A mature decision, dare I say it an adult decision: mug or no mug I was going to carry on to the bitter end.

What do you do when you've got six hours left in New York and a seven-hour plane ride ahead of you and not a single thing planned? Well, if you're me you walk across the road to a nearby coffee house, get in line, order yourself the largest fruit smoothie in the house, and once you've found yourself somewhere to sit you reach into your rucksack and pull out your brick-like copy of *War and Peace* and start reading.

*   *   *

It was just after seven in the morning when Continental Airlines landed at Birmingham International. I looked out of the window to see bright British sunlight sparkling over the wet tarmac. It looked like a cold but crisp day. The kind of day, especially when you've been away, that makes you appreciate the fact that you live in a country with distinct seasons.

As everyone around me began unbuckling their belts even though the seatbelt sign was still on, I reached over to the seat pouch in front of me, and plucked out *War and Peace*. Pausing only to smirk at the cover (a portrait of a camp-looking Colonel Yergraf Davydov, of the Household Troops, wearing a short red military jacket, ludicrously tight white leggings and calf-length boots) I used my thumb to flick rapidly and noisily through the pages then flipped it over and put it back again. This book, my sole companion for the last who knows how many hours, wasn't coming back home with me. I was done with it. I had conquered it by reading it from cover to cover and would now set it free in the hope that it would find a new home with someone who might love it more than I did. But the bottom line was this: this book had saved me in a way that a year ago I would never have thought possible.

From the moment that I opened up *War and Peace* in that Manhattan café right through to the concluding page of the second epilogue as the plane (according to the map on my mini TV screen) came in over Southampton, I had wanted to abandon it pretty much every hour on the hour. That wasn't to say that it was a bad book. There were some killer lines that I probably would have underlined with a pen had I not worried that I would then proceed to poke out my own eyes with it.

I got it, Tolstoy, I understood what you were trying to say and why. But the thing is, mate, having spread the whole story over the best part of 560,000 words, you'd made me cease to care what was happening to whom and why. Still, I'd got my *War and Peace* tick, and I felt good . . . in fact, I felt great. Part of that was that I'd just polished off a big fat book by a dead Russian bloke but mostly it was that I had defeated my demons and got through to the end. In personal terms this was my London Marathon, my journey to the South Pole. In fact, it was probably my Everest. And I'd conquered it. There wasn't anyone or anything that could take this achievement away from me. This brand-new tick had given me a new impetus, a new desire to conquer the To-Do List once and for all. But for the moment, all I had the strength to do was keep awake long enough to collect my bags, make it through customs and find a taxi. I barely remember the journey home, or even seeing Claire and the kids on the door step. The desire to crawl into bed and close my eyes was so powerful I couldn't resist.

'Dad! Wake up!' I opened my eyes and looked around. I was lying underneath a duvet. There was a picture of Audrey Hepburn on the wall. Two small children were bouncing on my chest and a woman was standing behind them smiling. Was I back in my New York hotel? I looked around at the room. The remnants of a slight damp patch over the chimney breast (Item 125: 'It's been three years since you got the damp in the chimney breast sorted so finish the job and re-paint.'); the eighties-style Chinese lantern light bulb cover (Item 918: 'Replace eighties-style Chinese lantern lampshade'); and rows of books lining the trio of IKEA bookshelves (Item 409: 'Take books that you've read and don't want, or haven't read and don't want, or even will never read and don't want, to Oxfam.'). If this was a New York hotel, I thought to myself, then it was a very poor one and I would be checking out as soon as possible.

I looked at my kids who were still bouncing up and down on my chest and I looked at my wife and smiled. This wasn't a New York hotel. This was home. The single best location in the entire world.

'How long have I been asleep?' I croaked.

'Pretty much since you arrived,' replied Claire. 'The cab driver said you were fast asleep from the minute you gave him the address and only woke up when he pulled up at the bottom of the road to ask which house number we lived at. Do you remember any of that?'

I shook my head. 'I don't even remember taking off my clothes and getting into bed.'

'Well, that would be because I helped you upstairs and you asked me to get your post and by the time I got back you were fast asleep on top of the duvet so I slipped your clothes off, tucked you in, closed the curtains and left you to it.'

'What time was that?'

'About half nine.'

'And what time is it now?'

'About quarter to six.'

'I've been asleep all this time?'

'Not a peep, not a word. I've never seen you this tired. Didn't you sleep on the plane?'

I shook my head.

'Something kept you awake?'

'Yeah, you could say that.'

'So did you get whatever it was that you wanted to do on the List done?'

I shook my head. 'Not exactly, but I'm still glad I did it.'

'Are you ever going to tell me what it was?'

'Of course, but how about we do it a bit later?' I sat up and gave her a kiss. 'The kids are going to bed in a bit so why don't we make the most of them now and then I'll nip out and get us a takeaway, crack open a bottle of wine and tell you everything.'

I headed downstairs with Claire and the kids for a 'dancing session' (a pre-bedtime ritual that Claire had invented in recent weeks to get rid of their last dregs of energy). Now that Maisie was walking by herself it was an absolute delight to watch her and her sister nodding their heads and bending their knees in time to Daft Punk, Bob Sinclair and any other bits of French House that we could lay our hands on.

Claire ran a bath and just as we were about to drop them both in the water Lydia asked me to get in too. I ummed and ahhed for a while because I was tired but then a second wind came from nowhere, and without pausing to think (or indeed take off my clothes) I climbed in the bath and joined them. Lydia thought this was the funniest thing in the world. Maisie was baffled. I was just glad to live in a world where all you needed to do in order to make someone's day was hop in a bath with your clothes on.

Bedtime stories were a medley of our all-time favourites that Lydia insisted on acting out as we read them aloud: *Cock-a-moo-moo* (a story about a cockerel that forgets how to crow), *Me Papa Tickle Me Feet* (a West Indian rhyme about the joys of tickling) and *Cluck-a-Clock* (a story about twenty-four hours in the life of the chickens on Farmer Brown's farm).

Bedtime drinks handed out and imbibed, we tucked the

girls up in bed, and following repeated cries for lost dummies and requests for visits to the loo, we finally managed to get them to sleep. True to my word I nipped out to our local Chinese takeaway, bought a Chicken Kung Po, Pad Thai and boiled rice, headed to the late-night garage for a bottle of their finest champagne, and headed home.

'I can't bear the suspense any more,' said Claire, setting down the remains of her Kung Po on the table next to her and pausing *Location, Location, Location* with the TV remote. 'You have to tell me why you went to New York and you have to tell me now.'

'What? Do you mean that you don't want to spend the night guessing? Because we could do that if you want.'

She attempted to hit me across the head with a cushion. I took that to mean she wasn't interested in guessing games.

'Okay, okay,' I said deflecting the blows, 'I'll tell you, just put down your weapon.'

'Right, weapons down and I'm all ears.'

'Okay . . . I went all the way to New York for you.'

'Why?'

'To see if I could get you a replacement for that Dean and Deluca mug that I broke. I knew how much you loved it. I scoured the internet without success so the best thing I could do was fly out there and get one.'

'You paid all that money for a flight and flew to the other side of the Atlantic just to get a replacement mug for me?'

I nodded. 'Plus, since I'm being green these days I've also had to cough up to offset my carbon emissions.'

Claire shook her head in dismay. 'How much?'

'Enough to have bought you at least a dozen of the mugs had they actually had them in stock.'

'They didn't have them in stock?'

'No. I suppose they must change designs all the time. It's just one of those things.'

'So you went all that way for nothing?'

'No, babe,' I replied. 'I went all that way for you.'

Claire stared at me with her mouth open for a minute. 'That has got to be the stupidest thing I've ever heard,' she said. 'It's just a mug. There'll be other mugs. And despite what you might think, Mr Michael "Big Gesture" Gayle, flying halfway round the world to buy your wife a mug isn't in the least bit romantic.'

'So why are you crying then?'

'I'm not,' she said, wiping her eyes. 'You must be seeing things.'

'Fine.' I gave her a big hug in the hope that it might mop up all the surplus emotion floating around the room.

I pulled her close, pressed the play button on the remote and carried on watching, laughing and occasionally hurling abuse at the people on *Location, Location, Location*.

Chapter 28: 'Do everything. I mean it. Absolutely everything.'

On the morning of the second Sunday in October, my first thought as my eyes adjusted to the light was that the day was finally here: my last day of To-Do Listing.

'How do you feel knowing that tomorrow it'll all be over?' asked Claire as we sat in the kitchen having breakfast with the kids.

'Great,' I pronounced. 'But a bit weird too. I can't really believe that I started with a list 1,277 items long and three hundred and sixty-five days later I've practically ticked everything off!'

'Isn't Daddy clever?' said Claire to the kids. She leaned across the table and kissed me. 'I'm proud of you, babe, I really am. How many things have you got to get done by the end of today?'

'Two.'

'Just two? Are you going to tell me what they are? Or are you going to be all mysterious again like you were over New York?'

'A bit of both,' I said airily. 'The first one is just for you and it's going to involve us taking a bit of a trip – but before you start panicking – no, it's not too far and yes, I've already arranged for Mum to come and babysit.'

Claire sat back in her chair. 'We're not parachute jumping,

sampling various different kinds of milks or reorganising your CD collection, are we?'

'No, we're going to Leicester.'

The few weeks since New York had been nothing short of mayhem. Still buzzing from the thrill of having travelled across the Atlantic for a mug that wasn't there only to conquer a big fat book by a dead Russian, I'd thrown myself back into the List with everything I had. It was hard to pinpoint a moment when I wasn't putting bank statements in folders, or photographs into frames, or watching DVD box sets, or painting window sills, or replacing every single missing light bulb in the house, or eating more fruit, or donating blood, or watching half a dozen of the TV cable channels that we never watch, or speaking to odd men in ill-fitting suits about invest-ments, or posting belated Christmas cards, or attending neighbourhood watch meetings or reading broadsheet news-papers cover to cover (even the really boring bits about political upheavals in countries that I can't pronounce), or finding lost things that I'd said I'd look for but never got round to finding, or reading the kind of literary novels that I'd bought because they were potential 'dinner party talking points' or trying to shop locally, or redeeming Tesco Club Card points, or attending Alexa's knitting club, or sewing buttons onto every single item of clothing that was missing a button, or correcting the date of birth on my driver's licence, or eating long-forgotten food from the depths of the freezer, or any of the other hundreds of items that had needed doing but that I'd been avoiding. Finally having just finished Item 972: 'Put preservative on shed', just after 5.00p.m. on the penultimate day of To-Do Listing I'd only got two things left, one of which, Item 12 ('Be nicer to wife because it'll only be a matter of time before she compares notes with her mates and finally works out what kind of a rough deal she's on'), I'd attempted several times but felt sure wasn't fully ticked off. I knew exactly what I was going to do to fully earn my tick.

'So, come on then,' said Claire as we sat down on the 10.15 Midland Line train to Leicester, 'how do you think that taking me back to my home town for the day is going to earn you a To-Do-List tick?'

The idea had arisen following a brief session of 'blue sky thinking' with Alexa which had resulted in the following:

1. A night at a posh hotel.
2. A trip on the Orient Express.
3. A weekend break in Paris.

'They're not quite right, are they? They're all a bit . . .'
   'Clichéd?'
   'No.'
   'Cheesy?'
   'No.'
   'Hackneyed?'
   I scowled in Alexa's direction. 'They're just not right, okay? I need something a bit more . . . you know . . . romantic and meaningful.'
   And then it hit me: I would re-create, down to the very last detail, my first date with Claire.
   To fully understand the ramifications of this, some background information might be of use. Claire and I first met at the wedding of some friends of ours, Vicky and Elton. And much as I'd like to say it was love at first sight I'm not sure it was, at least not for Claire. In talking to her at the wedding

265

reception I got the impression that she found me marginally annoying (this, I discovered later, was because at one point I'd asked her who was her favourite out of Starsky and Hutch – don't ask me why, it just happened – and she'd replied 'Hutch'. Seeing the disappointment writ large across my face she decided that I had lured her into a trap to make her look stupid and had taken against me). But on the dancefloor as we threw shapes to that all-time wedding reception classic, Motorhead's *Ace of Spades* I managed to redeem myself by making her laugh several times.

When Vicky and Elton returned from honeymoon I asked Vicky what Claire thought of me. Vicky told me she thought I was 'quite funny'. Vicky asked me what I thought of Claire. I told her I thought she was 'okay'.

'So why don't you ask her out?'

'I will do,' I replied decisively. 'Tell her I'll give her a ring.'

I'm guessing that when Vicky passed on this news she expected I'd call within a couple of days or a month at most. I am pretty sure she didn't think it would in fact be six months later . . .

What was I thinking? It wasn't as though I was seeing anyone else at the time. I was very much single. And yet . . . and yet I just couldn't make the call. At best I'd like to think that the romantic side of me had worked out that Claire was The One and was using this six-month period as a way of making sure (by what means I'm not too clear) that I didn't cock things up and at worst . . . well at worst I've a sneaking suspicion that I'd just added Claire to my already quite long twentysomething version of the To-Do List and hadn't quite got round to ticking her off.

Anyway, I did finally call her in the March of 1995, and our first date, the one I was about to attempt to re-create, took place, I kid you not, on 1st April. It was, as first dates go, quite romantic if a little twee. I bought her a balloon and some Space Dust because I was working the cute and quirky angle; she bought me a shortbread duck dipped in chocolate because people in Leicester tend to use the phrase 'me duck' as a term of endearment. I'm guessing we were both overthinking the whole situation.

We had coffee in her favourite café, Mrs Bridges, before wandering the shops around the Silver Arcade and making our way to Leicester's Museum and Art Gallery under the mistaken impression we were in a mid-period Woody Allen movie. We talked a lot about paintings we enjoyed and other cultural things but were both wishing that we could sit down and rest our aching feet.

Unwilling to give up the pretence that we could walk forever she took me to Castle Park where we killed time trailing around the gardens before making our way to the only film on at the cinema: *Natural Born Killers*.

It was, as first dates go, both eccentric and exhausting but it was also a lot of fun and well worth re-creating (with the exception of re-watching *Natural Born Killers* because once was more than enough).

'So what do you think?' I asked as we sat on the very bench in Castle Park where we'd shared our first kiss. 'Not bad, eh? Have I earned my tick for being the best husband in the world?'

'Yes,' she laughed. 'You can have your tick.'

On the train on the way back to Birmingham Claire looked round the carriage as though trying to summon the strength to say something that she had been stewing over for some time. 'I've got a bit of a confession about you and your To-Do List.'

'What about it?'

'I feel stupid because it happened ages ago and I should have said something at the time but I didn't want to seem petty, but the fact is you hurt my feelings and I think you ought to know why.'

This was something I hadn't been expecting.

'I hurt your feelings? How?'

'Do you remember back when you started the List and you asked Alexa's advice about being efficient and getting things done?'

'Yeah.'

'Well, you didn't ask me, did you?'

'But that's because you're not—' I bit my tongue.

It was too late.

'No, carry on. I'm not what?'

'Nothing.'

'I'm not efficient and I'm rubbish at getting things done? Is that what you're saying?'

'No, of course I'm not saying that. You're incredibly efficient. Like a well-oiled getting-things-done-machine. Not a millisecond of your time is wasted.'

'So why didn't you ask my advice?'

'Did you want me to?'

'Well, yes. It would've been nice to know that you thought of me first. That's not too much to ask is it?'

'No, of course not,' I replied, even though were Claire to want advice on buying a new car, putting up shelves, grilling meat, England's chances of winning the Rugby World Cup, constructing flat-pack furniture or how to kill a man with a single blow (should the need arise) the last person on the entire planet that she would come to would be me. 'You're right,' I said magnanimously. 'I should have come to you straight away. You're a qualified teacher of adult literacy skills, a mother of two and a wife of one, of course I should've picked your brains first.'

Claire smiled. I'd been forgiven. 'It's not like I was saying that I'm an expert, I just wanted you to ask me that's all,' she continued. 'Because even if I'm not the most efficient person in the world – which I admit I'm not – it would be nice if there were one person in the world who thinks I'm great at everything.'

'But you are great at everything,' I said giving her a big squeeze. 'I was there both times you gave birth so I've got first-hand evidence that you are indeed Wonder Woman. But don't worry, your secret identity is safe with me.' I paused and added a timely, 'I love you, you know.'

'Good,' she said grinning as she squeezed my hand, 'Don't you ever, ever forget it.'

It was two in the afternoon by the time we got home from our day out. Rushing into the living room we said hello to my mum and the kids before I delivered my next piece of news.

'Look,' I began, 'I'm going to have to ask you a favour. I know we normally spend Sundays together with the kids but I've just got one last To-Do-List tick to do and it's going to involve me being busy for pretty much the whole afternoon so I need you to mind the fort, is that okay?'

'Okay, what is it you've got to do?'

'Two things,' I replied. 'The first is to make a secret phone call and the second is Item 493: "Cook something out of all those posh-looking cook books that Claire keeps buying you for Christmas".'

Chapter 29: 'Learn from your mistakes.'

For as long as Claire and I have been together she has always bought me cookbooks for Christmas, presumably on the basis that, as I like eating food, it must follow that I like cooking it too. The first Christmas it was Delia Smith's *Complete Illustrated Cookery Course*; the Christmas that we got married it was Nigel Slater's *Real Fast Food*; the Christmas that Lydia was born it was Jamie Oliver's *The Return of The Naked Chef* and the Christmas after Maisie was born it was *The Wagamama Cookbook*.

I understood what lay behind her cookbook-based enthusiasm. The subconscious rationale of buying a celebrity chef's cookbook is, 'Look, for the price of a starter at a posh restaurant you can get access to the whole menu and will soon be living like Jamie and Jools Oliver.'

The flaw in Claire's seasoned gift-buying logic was that though I appreciated and often flicked through the pictures when I had a spare moment (the ones featuring raven-haired beauty Nigella Lawson being amongst my particular favourites) I had never actually cooked a recipe from any of them.

And it wasn't as though I didn't cook. For the first few years after we got married I cooked virtually all the time and not just stuff that needed to be microwaved or heated up in the oven either. I cooked shepherd's pies and chilli con carne and pasta dishes and fish dishes that I picked up from friends but for the most part I preferred to make stuff up, using whatever was hanging about the kitchen. While it occasionally ended in disaster (the vat of over-cooked sun-blushed tomato and Italian mushroom risotto lightly flavoured with the essence of burnt garlic being one such example) most of my experiments were among the best things that Claire ever tasted.

When I ended my mystery phone call I went into overdrive trying to come up with the perfect meal that would demonstrate that, thanks to the To-Do List, Mike and Claire Gayle had made some quite significant steps towards their goal of becoming 'proper adults'.

Leafing through all the cookery books I managed to narrow it down to a choice between Jamie Oliver's seafood pie and Nigella Lawson's cornbread-topped chilli con carne. I presented the two to Claire for a decision.

'I can see where you're going with the fish pie thing,' she said, looking through the list of ingredients, 'but seafood, plus you never having followed a recipe before, is going to equal food poisoning, so maybe you ought to go with the chilli.'

Claire had a point, especially as Oliver's recipe called for raw prawns, which I always found a bit intimidating whenever I passed them on the fish counter at my local supermarket.

'You're right,' I replied, 'It's got to be the chilli because a) it's less likely to kill us; and b) it can be jazzed up with a nice salad and posh bottle of wine. I'll do my work for today, stop around midday and then head to the supermarket to get all the ingredients.'

*   *   *

271

Ingredient shopping was a novelty, given my inexperience with the world of recipes. Well aware that most novice cooks usually dropped the ball at this stage, I wrote down the entire list of ingredients and the quantities required. As I wandered the aisles of my local supermarket it all appeared to be bog-standard stuff that I was putting into my trolley: onions, garlic, olive oil, crushed chillies, a whole bunch of spices, two large packs of minced beef and a couple of tins of kidney beans, but then I came across something that I couldn't find for love nor money: cornmeal.

Approaching a young man stacking shelves with tinned peas I attempted to overcome my unease by adopting the manner of a builder looking for a bag of Blue Circle cement. 'All right, mate. Any chance you could point me in the direction of cornmeal?'

'Cornmeal?' He looked blank.

'Yeah,' I replied, chewing imaginary gum. 'Cornmeal.'

'What's it for, a recipe?'

'Yeah,' I mumbled, looking at my shoes.

'What kind of thing is it?'

'That I'm cooking? It's a chilli.'

'No, what kind of thing is cornmeal?'

'I'm guessing it's like flour.'

'Right then, I'll take you to the flour aisle.'

Despite having spent a good ten minutes in the flour aisle I had no choice but to follow and watch him going through the pantomime of looking for something that I already knew wasn't there.

He eventually said: 'Looks like we're out of it,' and despite my unspoken love for the woman, I found myself inwardly cursing Ms Lawson and her recipes.

I called Claire and asked her to look up cornmeal on the internet.

'According to Wikipedia,' she began, 'cornmeal is flour ground from dried corn, is a common staple food and is different altogether from cornflour which is ground to a fine chalky white powder and is a valuable thickening agent in sauces.'

'I'm still none the wiser.'

'Maybe you should just leave out the cornbread-topping thing.'

'No chance,' I replied scanning the various bags of flour in front of me. 'What's gram flour when it's at home?'

Claire consulted Google and then came back with an answer: 'Flour made from ground chick peas. Why?'

'Do you reckon it's pretty much the same as cornmeal? I mean it's not like you'd be disgusted if someone presented you with a plate of chick peas rather than a plate of corn, would you?'

Claire, who doesn't like to deviate from the instructions for making instant coffee let alone an entire meal, didn't sound convinced. 'Maybe you should head out to Waitrose and see if they've got it.'

'Nah,' I replied feeling somewhat like a TV detective maverick, 'I'm going with gram flour and stuff the consequences.'

Later that evening as I observed the fruits of my labour, steaming and fresh from the oven, a perplexed-looking Claire entered the kitchen.

'I've just noticed that you've set the table for four people not two. Is there something going on that I should know about?'

'Yeah, there is sort of,' I replied guiltily. 'A couple of days ago I got to thinking about how all this To-Do-List stuff got started.'

'Didn't it start with our brand-new next-door neighbours and your arch-nemesis Derek?'

'Exactly,' I replied. 'Which looking back was really stupid. Which is why I've invited Derek and Jessica around for dinner – to make amends and see if we can be friends.'

Claire looked as though she was about to go nuclear. 'You've done *what*?'

'I've invited the nexties for dinner.'

'When?' she snapped.

'Tonight. They should be arriving in about half an hour.'

'You've invited our posh next-door neighbours round for dinner when the house is in a state, I haven't shaved my legs in a week, I haven't showered or got anything nice to wear that's ironed, and you're cooking from a cookbook for the very first time?'

'It'll be fine,' I said sternly.

'You can't just spring this on me! And anyway it's Sunday night. Shouldn't you be in the pub with your cronies?'

'That's all sorted. For the first time in its six-year history the Sunday Night Pub Club is becoming the Monday Night Pub Club.'

Claire nearly blew a gasket. 'And there's no way out of it?'

'None whatsoever.'

'Fine,' she spat. 'But I can guarantee you that it won't be me who's tidying up the house!'

By the time Derek and Jessica turned up just after eight, the house was tidy, Claire's legs were hair free and encased in 40-denier stockings, and I'd sampled enough of the cornbread to be assured that the consequences of going 'off recipe' and using gram flour were relatively mild.

Much to my surprise the meal itself went incredibly well. Not only did Derek and Jessica find my 'gram flour' story hilarious but they were a lot more human than I'd initially thought. Derek confessed to having spent most of his teen years in his bedroom playing his guitar and harbouring dreams of moving to London and joining a band; Jessica had revealed that having found out I was a writer she had initially felt too intimidated to talk to us because we might think that they were a bit 'square'.

'Can you believe it?' I said to Claire gleefully as we climbed into bed at midnight after a highly successful night. 'Derek and Jessica were actually intimidated by us! A man who used to have toothpaste encrusted on his T-shirts and a woman who used to wear furry tiger-claw slippers! How ace is that?'

'It's brilliant,' agreed Claire. 'But they're still way more grown up than we are. Did you notice Jessica's make up? I can tell you for nothing that wasn't Superdrugs own brand and as for all that stuff about it being so hard to find "a decent villa in Antibes to rent" at this time of year, I can guarantee that neither of them has ever been anywhere near the Butlins holiday camps I went to when I was a kid.'

'Still, none of that matters. Are we totally on top of everything? Probably not. But could we hold our own in a conversation about the war in Iraq, *Dr Who*, and the early singles of Take That without looking stupid? Yes, we could. And that can mean only one thing: we've arrived at the point we always wanted to reach. We are now fully fledged grown-ups.'

Chapter 30: 'Turn thirty-seven.'

The morning of my thirty-seventh birthday was near enough as good as a birthday morning can get. Following breakfast in bed (a good portion of which was polished off by the kids) I was made to open my presents. I say 'made' only because one of the best things about being a dad is getting the title 'Officially the grumpiest man in the house', and as such it was my duty to make out like I was completely not bothered by birthdays. The girls were having none of this, which was just as well. It's hard to be even remotely grumpy when your four-year-old daughter presents you with a painstakingly constructed homemade card in which she has written the legend: 'To the best daddy in the world.' You'd have to be in possession of a heart of stone not to be moved by that and given that my heart was made of ordinary flesh and blood I had a bit of a moment. Just as I was beginning to well up, Maisie, for reasons known only to herself, decided to throw up the bottle of milk she'd just polished off, and Claire and I went into wet-wipe-damage-limitation mode in a bid to save our bed from permanent sick penetration.

Once the commotion was over I continued with my present opening. Claire had excelled herself in making sure that every single present hit the spot and so as well as classic Gayle-friendly gifts like posh chocolate, jelly beans and those Lindt chocolate things with the melty stuff inside, taking pride of place atop my present mountain was a boxed reissue of the most desired toy of any boy born in the seventies: an Evel Knievel stuntman and bike.

'This is brilliant,' I gasped. 'Have you any idea how much I wanted one of these when I was a kid? I practically begged my mum for one every day for a year and I still ended up with a junior microscope!'

'I spotted it in a shop in the Bullring that's mostly full of tat, but the second I saw it on the shelf next to a box of inflatable sumo wrestling suits I knew straight away that you'd love it. Happy birthday, babe.' She leaned across the present pile and kissed me. 'And now the present unwrapping is all out of the way I'm going to make sure that you have the best day ever.'

And we did have the best day ever. It was faultless. After breakfast Lydia and I took it in turns to play Evel Knievel. For the uninitiated the Evel Knievel stunt set consists of Evel's bike, a toy Evel Knievel doll to go on the aforementioned bike and the futuristically monikered Evel Knievel 'Gyroscope' that you wind up as fast as you can before furiously launching Evel into whichever death-defying stunts you have laid on for him.

Starting out coyly with a few basic jumps utilising the Evel Knievel stunt ramp Lydia and I quickly graduated to increasingly dangerous stunts and culminated in the stunt of stunts (co-created with my daughter): the Evel Knievel Loft Jump. This involved Lydia and I lining up a couple of old shelves that we'd found in the basement, positioning Evel at the bottom of them, opening the window in the loft and then revving the gyroscope so quickly that when Evel made his way up the ramp and out of the window he was little more than a blur. Racing to the window we witnessed first-hand

Evel's rapid descent, and as he crashed through the bush opposite the kitchen window terrifying our neighbour's tabby into leaping several feet in the air we fell about laughing hysterically. We were unable to stop even when Claire was telling us off and later, at the restaurant over my birthday lunch, all one of us had to do was make a loud 'Vrooom!' and do an impression of the cat leaping in the air and we were both off in hysterics once more.

'So was that a good birthday then?' asked Claire as we stood in the bathroom brushing the kids' teeth.

'Brilliant,' I replied. 'Possibly the best ever. Evel Knievel really was a stroke of genius. It was like being ten again.'

'Good,' said Claire. 'Even though it will probably be me rather than you that will have to explain what happened to Oscar when next door complain that he's suffering from hypertension.'

'He always was a bit nervous. I just pushed him over the edge.'

'With a toy motorcycle.'

'He was in the wrong place at the wrong time.'

Claire rolled her eyes. It was the first time in a while. I had missed her constant exasperation. Getting a good eye roll made me feel that I was doing a decent job of being a husband. 'How are you feeling about tonight?'

'Okay,' I lied. All day I'd been having these moments of dread as though my unconscious mind was counting down to the evening's audit.

'Do you think you'll pass?'

I shrugged. 'I'm hoping so. Obviously it's not the end of the world if I don't but I'll be disappointed if I've failed. I really do want to beat the List, to feel like I took on the impossible and won. Let's face it, it's not like I'm ever going to climb Mount Everest or trek to the North Pole, and it's not like I'd want to either.'

'You hate being cold at the best of times.'

'Too right. But whatever it is that drives those guys or drives Richard Branson to do daft things with balloons . . . well it's the same thing that makes me want to conquer a 1,277-item-long list of everyday stuff.'

'I think they call it the right stuff,' said Claire.

'That's it,' I replied. 'All I want to know is that I'm made of the right stuff.'

Upstairs in the loft I sat down at my computer and wrote the following email to my entire address book:

> Dear all,
> This is a quick message for all of you that have been keeping tabs on my efforts with my 1,277-item To-Do List (and for the very few of you that haven't) just to let you know that a) It's my birthday today b) I had a very good day thank you for asking and c) I'm pretty sure that I've ticked everything off the list but I'll find out officially in an hour or so down the pub and once that's happened the tardy service for which I was previously world renowned will be resumed. Seriously though, it's all over in a bit so keep your fingers crossed for me that I hit my 99% target rate!
> Cheers
> Mike x

As I grabbed my coat and keys and kissed Claire goodbye I felt slightly odd. Events had taken on such a life of their own that it was hard to imagine any connection between the version of me that had started scribbling things down in his four-year-old daughter's notebook and the version that was feeling sick and nervous at the prospect of being audited by his friends. How had this happened? From my position on the doorstep I looked across at Derek and Jessica's down-stairs bay window. Though the curtains were closed a light was on and I could picture them sitting on their posh red velvet sofa, holding a glass of wine and watching TV on their flash-looking flat-screen TV (not just ordinary TV but 'proper grown-up TV' like, I don't know, *The South Bank Show* or a Channel Four documentary about Rwanda). This was what had started it off . . . not exactly keeping up with the Joneses but trying to *be* more like the Joneses. Had I achieved that? Did I project an air of maturity to the people I met? That was one of the big questions that would be answered tonight.

Turning from my moment of doorstep reflection, I made my way down the front path, hopped into the back of the cab and asked the driver to take me over to Moseley. No sooner had he pulled off when the phone in my inside pocket began to vibrate. It was my friend Sam from Leeds.

'All right, mate?'

'Yeah, I'm good thanks. I just thought I'd give you a little tinkle to wish you good luck for your list thing tonight and wish you a happy birthday for today.'

'Cheers, mate.' I was touched. 'It's really kind of you.'

'I wouldn't go that far,' replied Sam laughing. 'I'm just killing time before *Where The Heart Is*. Seriously though, I hope you had a great birthday today. Did you get anything nice?'

'You know, the usual: chocolate, socks and an Evel Knie-vel stunt bike.'

'I bet you love that, you always were a big kid even back when I first knew you. Anyway, I'd better be getting off because the ad break's nearly over. I wanted to let you know my news: I've started a To-Do List of my own.'

'You're kidding me?'

'Absolutely not! And before you ask I'm not giving myself any kind of deadline because . . . well, because I'm not a boy and I've got enough pressure in my life without adding to it. No, this is just between me and a small notebook.'

'I'm really chuffed for you, mate,' I replied. 'If you need any tips or just a simple pep talk you know who to come to.'

'Yeah right, Mike Gayle: the world's number-one expert on To-Do Lists!'

My cab pulled up outside the Queen's Head just after nine and I'd spent most of the journey fielding text messages of support from mates who had received my early email. It felt good that so many people were on my side; that collectively people from all around the country (and even a few outside of it) were projecting positive thoughts in my direction. I handed the cab driver a crisp ten-pound note and thought there was a slim chance things could go my way.

I made my way through to the bar on the lounge side and waited to be served.

'Are you the guy with the To-Do List?' asked the barmaid as she poured my pint.

'Yeah.' I was somewhat surprised given that in all the years I'd been going to the Queen's Head I'd never had a conversation with her about anything unconnected to the purchase of beer or possibly dry-roasted peanuts. 'How do you know about the List?'

'People talk,' she said laughing. 'I know it all: those audit things, your battle with your internet people and your jaunt up to Leeds to see *Countdown*. Some of the bar staff have been taking bets on whether you'll do it.'

'And what do they reckon?'

She pulled a face, which I took to mean, 'probably not'.

'And what do you reckon yourself?'

'Well,' she said, handing me my pint. 'I suppose it's like my mum used to say: "Strange things happen at sea".'

Refraining from the temptation to give too much thought to the barmaid's sea-faring mother I spotted my friends in the second of the pub's two lounges huddled around the tables next to the open fire, our favourite position.

'Here he is!' yelled Henshaw across the room. 'The birthday boy!' People not associated with the Sunday Night Pub Club turned briefly to look at me before returning to their own conversations. I sat down on a threadbare stool that had been saved for me and looked around at my friends. All the current Sunday Night Pub Club members were in attendance (Arthur, Amy, Danby, Steve, Kaytee, Henshaw, Amanda, Gary and Jo) but there were also a few extra faces who had made the effort to come out on this special Monday.

'Good to see you, mate,' said Jim, who hadn't been out with us on a Sunday night for at least two years. 'From what I gather you've been keeping yourself pretty busy.'

'Yeah,' I replied, thoroughly pleased to see him. 'You could say that.'

I caught up with all the other former members, Dave, Adam and Donna, before agreeing at the behest of the rest of the table to open all of my cards and presents before getting down to having the To-Do List audited.

It was great being amongst so many wonderful people, to find myself at the age of thirty-seven feeling like I was living out the lyrics of the *Cheers* theme tune. If I hadn't been so nervous about the audit I would've found myself getting a little emotional about it.

'Right,' said Danby just after ten as Steve and Kaytee returned to the table with another round of drinks. 'We've spent quite enough time enjoying Mike's birthday celebrations and now it's time for him to give us the List so that we can decide his fate.'

'I agree,' said Henshaw. 'Come on, Mike, hand it over.'

I pulled out the List from my jacket pocket. I was about to hand over something private for my mates to scrutinise and I had no choice. This was what we had agreed.

'Fine,' I said. 'But while you're going over it I'm going to sit outside in the beer garden until you're done. If you've got any queries, they should be covered by this.' I pulled out a small exercise book and handed it over along with the List.

'What's this?' asked Danby.

'Something I spent half of last night doing when I should've been sleeping: brief explanations of how I went about doing everything on the List that I think I've ticked off.' I left the room.

The beer garden was full of shivering smokers who had been banished to this concrete wasteland since the smoking ban had come in over the summer. Amongst them were friends of friends who, unaware of my To-Do-List attempt, provided me with a welcome distraction from what was going on inside.

It was nearly eleven by the time Arthur called me to come back inside so I finished my pint and made my way back to my friends.

'Okay,' said Jo. 'We're pretty much done with the counting up but we do have a few queries.'

'Fire away.'

'Well, Gary has a problem with your explanation of Item 416: "Overcome prison phobia so that you can sit down and watch Season One of *Prison Break*".'

'What possible problem could there be? You know I've always had a prison phobia and since starting the List I have watched *Papillon*, *Scum* and *McVicar* on DVD, visited a real prison in Derbyshire and met a real-life murderer. Now if that's not overcoming a phobia I don't know what is.'

'Yeah,' replied Gary grinning, 'but my point was more along the lines that it didn't say you'd actually watched *Prison Break*.'

'There's no way that you can disallow that tick.' I appealed to Jo in her role as adjudicator.

'Nice try, Gary,' said Jo, 'but I think Mike's definitely earned that one. Now moving on to 833 to 842: "Sew missing buttons back on items of clothing".'

'I did that!' I protested. 'It took ages to find matching buttons for some of them and where I couldn't I had to take off all the buttons and replace them with new ones. Have you any idea how long stuff like that takes?'

'Well, we'd love to give you the tick,' said Jo, 'but . . .'

She pointed at my midriff and I looked down to see that yes, indeed there was a button missing from my jacket.

'Now if you persuade us that it happened since you did the repair work I might be able to allow the tick.'

'I can't,' I replied, cursing both my honesty and my ineptitude. 'It was in the dry-cleaners when I was tackling the button thing and I completely forgot it.'

'I see,' said Jo with mock gravity. 'Well, that's one tick gone then.'

On and on they went questioning everything from my

green tick ('How can you say you've gone green when you flew to New York just to get a mug?') through to my second attempt at the 'learn Italian' tick (because despite being able to recall pretty much everything that I'd learned from the CD I could barely remember the Italian for 'goodbye',) and beyond until Jo announced that we had come to the end of the queries and now needed to readjust the total and work out the final percentage.

'You can take a quick walk around the block if you like,' suggested Jo.

'No,' I said. 'I'll stay here and wait it out.'

And so while my mates got out their pens and began arguing with each other in whispered tones I chatted with the lost members of the Sunday Night Pub Club (who thankfully weren't involved in the business of adjudication) until my friends were ready.

'Okay, I think we're done,' said Jo. 'Just to remind you of the rules: we agreed that a ninety-nine per cent tick rate of the 1,277-item total would be considered to be a success and anything below that mark would be considered to be a failure. Agreed?'

'Agreed. So what is it? What did I get?'

The grin on Jo's face said it all. 'You scored 1,269 ticks out of a potential 1,277 tasks which gives you a pass rate of 99.37% which I'm pleased to say means that you've made it!'

Chapter 31: 'Think about what you've learned.'

I woke up just after ten on the morning following my supremely successful To-Do-List audit. The kids were up and washed and appeared to have been fed too.

'I got your text that you'd passed your audit,' said Claire. 'Well done, babe! What time did you get in?'

'Sometime after four,' I yawned. 'Celebrations sort of carried on at Arthur's. I think there may have been some karaoke involved.'

'Not Motorhead I hope?'

'I wouldn't rule it out.'

'So, what's the first thing you're going to do with your week of freedom? Have you got any plans?'

'If it's okay with you I'm going to spend the week doing nothing. Absolutely nothing.'

My week of doing nothing turned out to be short lived. If I had only looked at my diary I'd have seen that I had a pretty busy week ahead involving a meeting with my accountant, a library event in Sheffield and an appearance on Radio Four. On the Thursday just as I was preparing to go out to meet my accountant I got a call from Simon.

'Mike!' he boomed. 'Long time no whatsit! How are you, mate? How's this list thing of yours? It must be nearly done, surely?'

'A couple of nights ago,' I replied, 'I passed. 1,269

things fully ticked off out of 1,277 which isn't bad going I reckon.'

'That's brilliant, Mike! Absolutely brilliant! Well done you! Are you ready to write a book about it?'

This was a good question. Did I really need a thing as huge as another book to add to my To-Do List so soon after I had just ticked everything off?

'Do you know what, Simon?' I began, 'I think I really am. I had a problem with it before because I thought it would end up just being about a bloke ticking things off a list. I can see now that it will actually be about lots of other stuff too like family and friendship, overcoming obstacles, growing up, taking risks and learning about the things you're really capable of.'

There was a long pause, the sound of Simon thinking.

'I can see where you're going with this, Mike, and I like it. One man attempts to overcome a set of extreme adversities and in the process learns a number of life lessons along the way? Kind of like Bridget Jones meets Andy McNab by way of J.K.Rowling?'

I hoped Simon's tongue was firmly lodged in his cheek.

'Just a bit higher.'

'Like this?'

'No, a bit lower.'

'Like this?'

'No, a bit higher than that but lower than it was before.'

It was just after six a.m. on Maisie's first birthday and Claire and I, rather than being in bed like any normal parents who had been up half the night administering Calpol to the troops, were downstairs in the living room making it suitably birthday like. We were currently standing on chairs trying to hang a banner across the bookshelf that proclaimed to anyone who cared to read it (which excluded both Lydia and Maisie): 'Happy Birthday! You are 1!'

Life had been good these past few weeks. I was reasonably confident that I was going to make my self-imposed Christmas deadline for the novel I had been working on all year, I'd managed to clear some of the backlog of my work-related To-Do List that had been neglected and the week before last I had had a call from Simon saying that my publishers had loved the new direction that I was thinking of taking the To-Do List book.

Deciding that enough was enough, I climbed off the chair and surveyed our handiwork: three banners, sixteen balloons, and some twizzly glittery things hanging from the lampshade.

'You do realise that you're insane, don't you?'

Claire nodded.

'You do realise that because I'm here helping you I'm as insane as you are?'

Claire nodded again.

'Good,' I proclaimed. 'Just so long as we both know that it's completely insane to get up at six in the morning to decorate a room for a child that hasn't the faintest clue what month it is let alone what day.'

'You're right, we are insane and though it would have been marginally less insane to have done it last night before we went to bed it wouldn't have been quite as much fun. Anyway, it's all for a good cause.' Her bottom lip started to tremble. 'It's for our little girl.' The lip was now in full quiver mode. 'She's one today, Mike. This is her first birthday and I just want her to know . . . I want her to know . . .' Claire's lips were now quivering nineteen to the dozen and joined by sniffing and then real lady tears, '. . . how special we think she is.'

'I know, babe.' I gave her a big hug as I felt a small lip-quiver of my own.

Still holding Claire I joked that as we'd done so well with the first two perhaps we ought to try to make a third. Claire didn't even crack a smile.

'I love them, you know I do, but that's one part of our own personal To-Do List that you can consider having been fully ticked off.'

Returning wearily upstairs in the hope of getting a few moments to ourselves before the day kicked in, we were met by a delighted giggle coming from the birthday girl's room. Not only was she sitting up but somehow she had managed to pull every last one of her soft toys (from Baloo the Bear to Shaun the Sheep) off the chair into her cot and was now babbling avidly as though they were long-lost friends. When she noticed us she let out an extra loud squeal, pushed Baloo out of the way and waved both hands in the air, demanding in the way that only the cutest of tiny dictators can do, to be picked up.

Collecting Lydia along the way we headed back to our bedroom, took all of Maisie's presents out from their hiding place in the wardrobe and proceeded to deliver our very best rendition of 'Happy Birthday', before handing her the first item from her present payload. Maisie, though mildly interested in the wrapping paper, reached present fatigue very quickly and it was left to the three of us who knew what was going on to help her out.

'It's like it's our birthday too, isn't it, Daddy?' observed Lydia as she tore into the wrapping on the largest of the presents.

'Yes,' I replied. 'I suppose it is.'

Later, when things were in full swing at Maisie's birthday party, I found myself thinking about the day, getting older and the To-Do List. I concluded that much of my initial impetus in undertaking the To-Do List was about trying to be something that I wasn't: some stereotypical version of an adult that I was never going to conform to. I was never going to have a house that was always tidy and, try as I might, I couldn't see the day coming when I wouldn't look like an overgrown student. Though I could hold my own in a conversation about the state of the nation, I was more confident talking about the state of the couple on last night's *Property Ladder*. As lamentable as that might sound, I was fine with it. And if one day (more likely than not on the eve of a birthday) I reached the point again where I'd got so sick of everything (the untidy house, the unsuitable clothes, the over-reliance on property programmes for entertainment) that I ended up writing yet another list, I was fine with that too because at least this time I'd be more aware of what I was letting myself in for.

Afterword

And what of the List? Well the List itself is in the top right-hand drawer of my desk in the office and from day to day it sits there unopened with its crumpled,barely-hanging-together-cover loosened at the staples. Occasionally when I'm looking for something else (stamps, paperclips, bank statements or lost bars of chocolate) I'll think about opening it but I never do because I feel as though that part of my life is over now. As for the ticks I achieved that were ongoing, some are ticking over and others have fallen by the wayside. Yes, I try to be as green as possible, and the wormery is still going a treat, but beyond being a bit more rigorous about rejecting needless plastic bags and recycling, everything else has ground to a halt. A few of the old friends I caught up with still exchange emails and leave comments on Facebook, and I'm planning to head up to Leeds to see Sam sometime over the summer. Yes, I'm still making an effort to see more of my parents; no, the drawer by the back door isn't quite as tidy as it was and, as for the attempts to lose weight . . . well let's just say it's an ongoing battle.

So as I begin typing, I feel I ought to be saying something wise and clever that will make you reflect on everything you've read and fire you up about life, no mean feat.

Having mulled over the problem, this is what I've decided to leave you with:

1. Make a list
2. Do it.

Go on, you know it makes sense.

Appendix

1. Eat more salad.
2. Frame print bought for my birthday.
3. Spend more time with number-one child.
4. Back up hard drive.
5. Make compilation CD for Jackie.
6. Find some way of commemorating 10-year wedding anniversary.
7. Change to low energy light bulbs where possible.
8. Repaint front door.
9. Read poetry.
10. Watch *Omen*.
11. Read something by Margaret Atwood.
12. Be nicer to wife.
13. Give Harry Potter a chance.
14. Watch *The O.C.* season one.
15. Watch *The O.C.* season two.
16. Finish off the first *Tomb Raider* game without recourse to cheats found on the internet.
17. Replace dodgy fence panel on old neighbour's side.
18. Reseed the lawn.
19. Restock garden.
20. Make a Will.
21. Get rid of ivy growing over front window.

22. Buy an antique.
23. Wear sunscreen.
24. Set up a birthday reminder service.
25. Sport a tie more often.
26. Spend more time with parents.
27. Wear proper shoes more.
28. Declutter office.
29. Learn to use Photoshop . . .
30. And Illustrator . . .
31. And Quark XPress.
32. Read more Paul Auster.
33. Check mortgage deal.
34. Sort out under-eaves loft space.
35. Work out system for records.
36. Fix broken guttering.
37. Breathe more deeply.
38. Go to the cinema more.
39. Do some finger painting with daughter.
40. Improve posture.
41. Join the library.
42. Catch up with rubbish summer job lost friends like Ian and Scott . . .
43. And over-worked and under-paid bar job lost friends like Monica and Paige . . .
44. And camping holiday in Anglesey lost friends like Jane, Mia and Simon . . .
45. And teen magazine lost friends like Sarah, Alex and Maria . . .
46. And lost friends inherited from other lost friends like Sam, Richard and Tall Mike . . .
47. And university lost friends like Emma, Jo, Anthony and Alison . . .

48. And sixth-form lost friends like Cath, Susie and Sarah . . .
49. And secondary school lost friends like Mick, Mark and Simon . . .
50. And finally early days in London lost friends like Lisa, Steve and Jen.
51. Learn how to use Excel (or at least open it).
52. Stop falling asleep in front of the TV.
53. Empty office drawers.
54. Empty office filing cabinet.
55. Go Salsa dancing.
56. Use my computer flat bed scanner or get rid of it.
57. Clean out drain near back door.
58. Spend more time with Mum.
59. Spend more time with Dad.
60. Same goes for elder brother.
61. Same goes again for middle brother.
62. Clean out U-bend under bathroom sink.
63. Change fuse in the shredder (to see if it's really dead or just playing possum) . . .
64. And do same with the old PlayStation . . .
65. And Claire's old-fashioned-looking radio/cassette player . . .
66. And Claire's hairdryer . . .
67. And my hair clippers . . .
68. And the bass amp for the electric guitar.
69. Use up compost bought two summers ago.
70. Lose weight.
71. Extend warranty on freezer . . .
72. And washing machine . . .
73. And cooker.
74. Put bags of wood chippings bought two years ago onto garden.

75. Talk to friends' kids more.
76. Clean under cooker.
77. Put up curtains in the loft.
78. Have a mid-nineties Indie moment.
79. Play make-believe more.
80. Take up painting.
81. Put numbers onto front door.
82. Replace missing pins in living-room light fittings.
83. Finish painting the ceiling around living-room light fittings.
84. Work out why people like Wes Anderson films.
85. Make back gate open in the winter as well as the summer.
86. Read Alan Moore's *Watchmen*.
87. Discover something new.
88. Bank cheque from short story bloke.
89. Give Radiohead another chance.
90. Clear out coat/shoe storage area at top of cellar steps.
91. Replace missing toggle from living room blinds.
92. Put hook on back of loft door . . .
93. And bedroom doors . . .
94. And cellar door.
95. Stop buying things I don't need with money I don't have.
96. Speak to checkout staff more.
97. Have a conversation with the woman who works at the Queen's Head.
98. Sit down with accountant.
99. Learn the name of the newsagent's wife . . .
100. And the postman's name . . .
101. And the name of the Parcel Force guy.
102. Put Blu-Tack in place where it can be found.

103. Put up towel rail bought six years ago.
104. Overcome fear of friends' pets especially Jim, the overly groin-orientated Labrador . . .
105. And Beth's evil-eyed terrapin . . .
106. And Flavia's budgie with the strange growth on the side of its head . . .
107. And Tim and Sharon's fat cat.
108. Attempt to overcome general animosity towards the entire animal kingdom.
109. Be a better correspondent.
110. Sort out takeaway menus shoved in drawer by back door.
111. Come up with a system for organising household washing . . .
112. And bill paying . . .
113. And children's clothes (passing down/throwing out/ keeping for sentimental reasons) . . .
114. And Lydia's artwork . . .
115. And food cupboard . . .
116. And freezer . . .
117. And recycling.
118. Work out why the freezer keeps beeping at 2.00a.m.
119. Remove crap from parents' house that you've been meaning to take since you first moved out.
120. Print out all digital photographs.
121. Do more cultural stuff.
122. Play more board games . . .
123. And parlour games.
124. Find out what a parlour game actually is.
125. Fix damp patch in bathroom.
126. Find out what to do with old electrical items.
127. Reset time for Los Angeles clock . . .

128. And Sydney clock . . .
129. And clock on cooker . . .
130. And microwave.
131. Light candles more often.
132. Buy a fire extinguisher.
133. Find a use for balsamic vinegar.
134. Empty boot of Claire's car.
135. Sort out eczema on arm.
136. Change car CDs.
137. Prune plum tree.
138. Make rooms not policed by Claire smell nice.
139. Plant bulbs bought by Claire's gran.
140. Get copy made of picture of Claire's gran and grand-dad's wedding.
141. Re-hang picture that fell down.
142. Find use for herb-infused olive oil bought as a present for us from friends who went to Italy.
143. Overcome fear of being poisoned by botulism, which may or may not be present in said herb-infused olive oil.
144. Use UV pen to mark valuables with postcode.
145. Find a reason to drink the 3 bottles of champagne gathering dust on the shelf.
146. Learn how to operate the washing machine.
147. Grow some herbs.
148. Learn how to look after cactus.
149. Unpack box marked 'loft' still unpacked from our house move 6 years ago.
150. Unpack box marked 'shed' still unpacked from our house move 6 years ago.
151. Unpack box marked 'stuff' still unpacked from our house move 6 years ago.

152. Make interesting lunches more often.
153. Stop eating McDonalds.
154. Empty drawers under our bed.
155. Play chess more.
156. Teach Claire how to play chess.
157. Become ambidextrous.
158. Read *Feel The Fear And Do It Anyway.*
159. Be more adventurous in the supermarket.
160. Write to my MP.
161. Create a scrapbook.
162. Buy a squirrel-proof bird feeder.
163. Finish Sudoku puzzle started last January.
164. Re-watch *Scrubs.*
165. Play Consequences.
166. Go green.
167. Convert CDs to MP3.
168. Buy cover for Lydia's bike.
169. Make a family Christmas card.
170. Clear Claire's student loan once and for all.
171. Increase web traffic to website . . .
172. . . . and update it.
173. Sort out garden because it's a jungle out there.
174. Wonderweb curtain hems in living room . . .
175. And suit trousers . . .
176. And Lydia's dress from Selfridges.
177. Purchase handy-sized bottle of washing gel as a preemptive measure against potential diseases.
178. Get a tetanus jab . . .
179. And if possible a chicken pox jab.
180. Replace rear left indicator bulb in Claire's car.
181. Start assembling collected works for children to inherit.

182. Get black suit dry cleaned . . .
183. And the brown one . . .
184. And the grey one . . .
185. And the blue one . . .
186. And the grey jacket with the flecks of toothpaste on it.
187. Buy something to clean shoes with and then clean them.
188. Clear in tray completely (and that includes finally replying to the woman who wanted the naked pictures of you).
189. Buy demisting spray for glasses.
190. Trace family tree.
191. Clean garden furniture.
192. Put garden furniture away in the winter.
193. Remember to get garden furniture out in the summer.
194. Find home for French editions of books.
195. Same for Italian . . .
196. Dutch . . .
197. Polish . . .
198. Japanese . . .
199. Portuguese . . .
200. And German editions.
201. Re-varnish old dining table.
202. Trim hedges.
203. Buy extendable hedge trimmer.
204. Purchase an SLR camera.
205. Buy new Christmas tree lights.
206. Clean stain from sofa.
207. Take up a new hobby.
208. Stop spraying clothes with toothpaste.
209. Put tissues in every room.
210. Take down bed in front room.

211. Reassemble bed in loft room.
212. Buy garden toys for the kids to play with.
213. Find out if huge tree at side of house is safe.
214. Scan some family photos.
215. Send Sidney a thank-you note.
216. Find out what happened at the end of *Six Feet Under*.
217. Decide what to do with the rest of my life.
218. Look into hiring a cottage for next summer.
219. Manage my time better.
220. Get some kind of receptacle for Claire's beauty products.
221. Spend longer cleaning teeth.
222. Work out what occasional pain in left shoulder might be related to.
223. Make kite with kids.
224. Perfect the art of the boiled egg.
225. Get new fence at the bottom of the garden.
226. Buy a meat thermometer.
227. Re-grout tiles in shower.
228. Find out who owns the fence on the left-hand side of the house.
229. Have a go at watching the TV cable channels you always ignore like Teacher's TV . . .
230. And the Biography Channel . . .
231. And Bloomberg.
232. Put all important dates (birthdays, holidays, appointments) on calendar rather than relying on guess work.
233. Change charcoal filter on cooker hood.
234. Get watch professionally cleaned.
235. Learn to use graph function on calculator.
236. Decide if I want to be buried or cremated.

237. Learn how to change a tyre.
238. Write letter of complaint to BQ.
239. Chase Amazon about the £1 refund.
240. Tie up loose ends.
241. See more of Jackie.
242. Wear a suit just for the heck of it.
243. Clean up spilt milk under fridge.
244. Fix wobbly garden bench.
245. Get Hannah's wedding present in time for their third wedding anniversary.
246. See more of Parker Bum.
247. Spend the three £1 BQ vouchers that you found in your desk last week.
248. Learn more about yourself.
249. Finish novel.
250. Come up with idea for next novel.
251. Take more responsibility for dishwasher (loading/ unloading etc.).
252. Take daughter swimming.
253. Get old baby clothes out of cupboard in loft.
254. Have a go at growing a beard.
255. Investigate laser eye surgery.
256. Buy emergency pyjamas . . .
257. And a dressing gown . . .
258. And possibly slippers.
259. Collect more pub facts.
260. Do something nice for Arthur . . .
261. And Gary . . .
262. And Jo . . .
263. And Danby . . .
264. And Henshaw . . .
265. And Amanda.

266. Try ordering something different from the Chinese takeaway . . .
267. And the Indian takeaway . . .
268. And Domino's Pizza.
269. Expand vocabulary.
270. Get a wall planner/diary . . .
271. And use it.
272. Book more holidays.
273. Mark down dates of next year's holiday on wall planner.
274. Do something about the enormous bush at the side of the house . . .
275. And the enormous tree.
276. Buy some new bowls that are less like vats.
277. Add Google maps to my browser favourites.
278. Meet people for lunch.
279. Be the one who volunteers.
280. Get rid of all the bits of left-over MDF from when we had the shelves fitted in the basement.
281. Write to the school at the end of our garden about the demon tree.
282. Bluetooth all photos taken on your phone on to your computer.
283. Find out how to bluetooth all your photos taken on your phone on to your computer.
284. Arrange all your journalism cuttings into something resembling an order.
285. Assemble and paint silver surfer.
286. Buy spare mini-DV tapes.
287. Clean office rug as there's still a slight stain left over from winter vomiting bug of 2002.
288. Buy a Moleskine notebook because Hemingway had one.

289. Use fountain pen.
290. Keep sharp pencils and notepad by bed.
291. Buy a first aid kit.
292. Get rid of all half-empty cans of Lynx body spray . . .
293. And decades' old Kouros aftershave . . .
294. And all the videotapes containing episodes of *Seinfeld* taped off the TV made redundant by the advent of DVDs.
295. Stock up with clean drinking water in case of emergency.
296. Find out what else you might need in case of emergency.
297. Read scary government leaflet about what to do in an emergency that you shoved in the drawer by the back door.
298. Wash car more . . .
299. And check tyre pressure . . .
300. And tread depth.
301. Have driveway widened.
302. Find plum-related recipes in hope of using up the twelve containers of plums in the freezer left over from last year's harvest.
303. See Nadine.
304. Have John and Sue over for dinner . . .
305. And Dave and Maz . . .
306. And Chris and Alison . . .
307. And James and Angie.
308. Read something by Freud.
309. Buy some vests/thermal underwear.
310. Be kinder to old people.
311. Use less paper.
312. Stop hoarding.

313. Get rid of accounts and receipts relating to the year 99/98 . . .
314. And the year 98/97 . . .
315. And the year 97/96 . . .
316. And the year 96/95.
317. Put childproof locks on kitchen cupboards.
318. Make Claire a compilation CD like I used to in the old days.
319. Buy a packet of Super White plus for spillage emergencies.
320. Close the First Direct account that you only opened because of the £20 offer.
321. Visit Nikki in Brighton . . .
322. And Richard in Cardiff . . .
323. And Dom and Sue in Reading . . .
324. And Cath in Tenby . . .
325. And Marjorie in Southampton . . .
326. And Sarah and Ben in Cardiff.
327. Find Dad's Black and Decker workmate that you lost in the move.
328. Speak to a financial advisor.
329. Find a way to move the acer from the olde-worlde-style barrel to the garden before it fully disintegrates.
330. Try to recall more stuff that you used to know like who invented the spinning Jenny.
331. And what ATP stands for . . .
332. And what the rough gist of *Das Kapital* was . . .
333. And what the Krebs cycle is . . .
334. And what the formula for velocity is . . .
335. And how to ask for a hotel room with a shower in German . . .

336. And how to work out probability . . .
337. And how the Second World War started . . .
338. And how the First World War started . . .
339. And how long the Seven Years War lasted . . .
340. And what Historical Materialism is . . .
341. And how to do a head spring . . .
342. And how to construct a thirty-three-degree angle using only a compass and a ruler . . .
343. And the plot to *Richard III*.
344. Develop a firmer handshake.
345. Try to learn Italian using the Italian-in-a-day CD.
346. Buy new head for electric toothbrush . . .
347. And new batteries.
348. Don't overfill the kettle.
349. Use the tumble dryer less.
350. Order a weekly organic vegetable box delivery.
351. Unscrew lock off bathroom door in case Lydia decides to trap herself in there one day.
352. Audition potential babysitters starting with Joe and Amy's kid . . .
353. And Kate and Dan's kid . . .
354. And John and Ruth's kid . . .
355. And Paul and Steff's kid.
356. Shred all old bank statements.
357. Complete all half-finished DIY projects like the shelves in the loft . . .
358. And painting the walls in the cellar . . .
359. And cementing the hole by the back door . . .
360. And repairing the flashing under the bedroom window . . .
361. And putting the phone extension in at your mum and dad's . . .

362. And repairing the hole you made in the plaster putting up Heather's painting . . .
363. And the hole you made putting up the framed *Tin Tin* poster.
364. Make friends with new and interesting people.
365. Find a minicab firm that will actually turn up on time.
366. Buy an Allen key.
367. Attempt to rescue the stuff that Lydia has shoved between the gaps in the floorboards in her bedroom.
368. Arrange a boys' weekend.
369. Encourage Lydia to be musical.
370. Call Del in lieu of condolence card that should have been sent five months ago.
371. Get round to countersigning Gary's passport photos.
372. Buy Gaffer tape . . .
373. And Duck tape.
374. Phone parents just for a chat.
375. Catch up with Scottish Helen.
376. Post Jackie and Mark's unposted Christmas card . . .
377. And Steve and Jenny's . . .
378. And Lisa and Trey's . . .
379. And Rachel and Dom's . . .
380. And Fran and Andy's . . .
381. And Emma and Justin's . . .
382. And Tessa and James' . . .
383. And Tamara and Mike's . . .
384. And Shewli and Neil's . . .
385. Find out if mole on hand is of the okay variety.
386. Be a better uncle to my nieces and nephews.
387. Get cholesterol level checked.
388. Talk to bank about extending overdraft facility . . .
389. And claiming back overzealous charges.

390. Take Lydia to see her first film.
391. Return Lydia's faulty Christmas slippers to Woolworth's.
392. Listen to more mid-period Rod Stewart.
393. Get some proper suitcases.
394. Find a new home for the eight boxes of Scalectrix that you bought from eBay during your 're-create your childhood' phase.
395. Replace broken glass on frame of picture taken on day before wedding.
396. Watch Martin Luther King's I have a dream speech all the way through.
397. Start a pension.
398. Buy new pants.
399. Tell Mum that I love her.
400. Read one of the baby books Claire told me to read last time around.
401. Attend Neighbourhood Watch meeting.
402. Buy a family calendar now that Lydia has her own social life.
403. Buy miniature screwdriver to tighten glasses that keep falling off nose.
404. Write letter to Uncle Churchill . . .
405. And Aunt Esther . . .
406. And Aunt Lorna.
407. Fix back door.
408. Finally see Dr about dodgy knee.
409. Take all unwanted books to Oxfam.
410. Get subscription to *Vanity Fair*.
411. Start reading *Private Eye*.
412. Give blood.
413. Try wearing hats more.

414. Put pens in every room.
415. Tidy Lydia's crayon sets.
416. Overcome prison phobia.
417. Have a facial.
418. Sample all the milks.
419. Be someone's mentor.
420. Be more efficient.
421. Find replacement TV remote control.
422. Find a home for the five billion CD-Rs that you've burned but no longer listen to.
423. Find out what the big fuss is about Pink Floyd.
424. Get rid of typewriter.
425. Get rid of AOL.
426. Spend whole day with new kid trying to make her smile.
427. Fix broken kitchen door.
428. Redeem all Tesco Club card points . . .
429. And Nectar points . . .
430. And Boots points . . .
431. And Premier points . . .
432. And Café Coffee loyalty card.
433. Buy extra printer toner.
434. Upload photos to Flickr.
435. Repair Dave and Maz's Super 8 camera.
436. Go to one of artist friend Heather's shows.
437. Clear under sink cupboard.
438. Buy can of 3 in 1 and then use it to stop squeak on living room door.
439. Find right photo to go in silver frame Lauren bought us.
440. Buy a frame that actually fits the 'scary Polish' print.
441. Have Christmas dinner at home.

442. Superglue the Six Million Dollar man's arm back on.
443. Get Danny and Mrs Danny to come up to Brum.
444. Change default web browser on computer.
445. And media player.
446. Get round to using unopened wedding presents like the cookbook stand . . .
447. And the 'dips and chips' tray . . .
448. And the food mixer . . .
449. And the purple heart-shaped vase . . .
450. And the electric salt and pepper mill . . .
451. And the burnt orange toilet seat cover and pedestal mat.
452. Take more photos of Lydia.
453. And more video.
454. Watch *Battlestar Galactica Season One*.
455. Watch *Battlestar Galactica Season Two*.
456. Watch *Battlestar Galactica Season Three*.
457. Freecycle.
458. Buy a huge book of stamps and keep somewhere safe.
459. Take all pre-recorded videos to the charity shop.
460. Look better naked.
461. Clean hallway carpet . . .
462. And carpet in loft.
463. Make appointment with dentist about that overly sensitive rear molar.
464. Write thank-you notes.
465. Stop leaving pants on floor in bathroom.
466. Get to know myself better.
467. Finally win at local pub quiz.
468. Try to improve memory.
469. Clean self-cleaning oven.

470. Defrost frost-free freezer.
471. Learn wife's mobile phone number . . .
472. My mobile phone number . . .
473. And my home number . . .
474. And my parents' new phone number.
475. Work out how long it actually takes to write a novel.
476. See if you can buy Novi on the internet.
477. Clean hallway skylight.
478. Buy and use air-freshener.
479. Clean out back of radiator in living room.
480. Try to retrieve the hi-fi remote that Lydia dropped down the back of the radiator.
481. Spend less money.
482. Conduct a full family expenditure overhaul.
483. Drink more water.
484. Put a notice board up in the kitchen.
485. Get round to putting money into Lydia's Child Trust Fund account.
486. Dust top of bookshelf.
487. Eat out of Dalek eggcup bought for Easter.
488. Drink out of mug Lydia made me at pre-school.
489. Work out what the other 16 programmes on the washing machine dial actually do.
490. Confess to wife about how her favourite episode of *Oprah* really came to get taped over by a repeat of *Xena – Warrior Princess* all that time ago.
491. Watch unopened *Die Hard* trilogy box set.
492. Put a plant next to computer to reduce exposure to radioactive stuff.
493. Cook using a recipe from one of the ten-gazillion cookbooks Claire's bought you.
494. Disassemble Claire's desk.

495. Find place to store Claire's work/university stuff (not loft!!!).
496. Buy smaller dinner plates.
497. Get into habit of checking appearance in hallway mirror before leaving the house.
498. Empty drawer by back door.
499. Identify what is a plant and what is a weed in our garden.
500. Return Lydia's ludicrously late library books . . .
501. And work out how to explain to them what happened to page five of *The Cat in The Hat*.
502. Buy a wheelbarrow.
503. Give old next-door neighbours back their old front door keys.
504. Put labels on all the mini D.V. cassettes . . .
505. And CD-Rs . . .
506. And keys for all the various doors . . .
507. And all the bags of Lydia's old clothes . . .
508. And all the box files.
509. Organise all photo albums.
510. Replace all the missing bits from Lydia's board games.
511. Create a childhood memory box for Lydia and kid number two like you told Claire you would rather than just dumping all the stuff in a black bin liner under the bed.
512. Get a proper winter coat.
513. Find a secret hiding place for all spare car keys.
514. Burglar-proof shed.
515. Learn how to make hot drinks for others.
516. Put down wife as next of kin in passport rather than mother.

517. Do something with small but burgeoning business card collection.
518. Cease shedding socks everywhere.
519. Buy more new music.
520. Get a new passport photo.
521. Wear proper trousers more.
522. Work out if there's actually a way of pulling off the 'double denim' look without coming off looking like Shakin' Stevens.
523. Buy de-ioniser.
524. Find out what an ion is and why they are bad.
525. Find out where local tip is.
526. Visit local tip.
527. Find someone to have the kind of water cooler chats with that normal people have at work.
528. Collect together all important car documents and put somewhere safe.
529. Reclaim that Season One of the *Sopranos* that you loaned out to Elt back in December . . .
530. And Kathryn William's first album from Jayne . . .
531. And *The Art of Guerrilla Film Making* from Rod . . .
532. And my hammer drill from Andy . . .
533. And my animal skin bongos from Phil . . .
534. And the director's cut of *Leon* from Steve . . .
535. And *SingStar Party* and *SingStar Pop* from Julian and Emma . . .
536. And my walking boots from Dan the Man . . .
537. And my six-button computer mouse from Fitzy . . .
538. And the hedge trimmers from my dad . . .
539. And the travel cot from Lynne and Foz . . .
540. And Trivial Pursuit and Pictionary from mother-in-law . . .

541. And my electronic Hulk hands from next-door-but-one's son Kieran.
542. Start an ideas folder.
543. Try writing in new places.
544. Try writing in long hand.
545. Try writing a plan before writing a book.
546. See Doctor about RSI.
547. Reread favourite childhood books to Lydia.
548. Keep a stock of envelopes.
549. Get printer for downstairs computer.
550. Open bedroom window that has been stuck shut since it got painted over two summers ago.
551. Archive the several hundred hours' worth of last year's holiday video onto DVD . . .
552. And the holiday before that . . .
553. And the holiday before that one too . . .
554. And last Christmas . . .
555. And Lydia's last three birthdays . . .
556. And the stuff I took of her riding on her bike before it got its puncture . . .
557. And the stuff I took of her pre-school nativity play . . .
558. And the stuff in the garden when we had the paddling pool out . . .
559. And the stuff I took when she stayed at Claire's mum's . . .
560. And the really cute stuff when she's just babbling all kinds of madness.
561. Try and find a pair of cords that will fit you.
562. Eat more whole grain.
563. Buy a variety of cotton reels in different colours.
564. Floss.
565. Update your CV.

566. Get gas bloke to check flue.
567. Buy a carbon-monoxide detector.
568. Check all the smoke alarms.
569. Do something about the spider infestation.
570. Change knackered front-door light fitting.
571. Buy some Baby Bio . . .
572. And use it to feed all houseplants.
573. Update virus barrier.
574. Get a place for everything and put everything in its place.
575. Wear aftershave more often.
576. Hire a skip.
577. Catch up with Hassan.
578. Find new home for sofa bed.
579. Get yourself a skin care regime.
580. Take Gary for posh meal to show him that there is life outside of KFC.
581. Get TV aerial repositioned.
582. Learn what can be tumble dried . . .
583. And then teach Claire.
584. Fix Lydia's bed base.
585. Wash curtains in bathroom . . .
586. And our bedroom . . .
587. And living room . . .
588. Tell Dad I love him.
589. Try to erase Lydia's doodling on wall next to bathroom.
590. Watch *A Clockwork Orange* . . .
591. And the first *Godfather* film . . .
592. Put all bank statements in folders.
593. Work out how to set child-lock in back of car.
594. Return Dave's copy of *Catcher in the Rye* . . .
595. And Arthur's *Blake's Seven* DVDs . . .
596. And Henshaw's copy of *Best of The Clash* . . .

597. And Amanda's bicycle pump . . .

598. And Amanda's *How To Play Bass Guitar* book . . .

599. And Steve's old Technics . . .

600. And Danby's army issue sleeping bag . . .

601. And Elt's copies of *The Host* and *Labyrinth* . . .

602. And Emma's Sylvia Plath stuff . . .

603. And Moonie's copy of *Hatful of Hollow* and his *Go Betweens* compilation . . .

604. And Jackie's *Roots* CD and her copy of *Blue in the Face* . . .

605. And Andy's Marx's brother's book . . .

606. And Manby's *Geraldine's Fortune* DVD and the book that she lent you at the same time that you can't even remember the title of . . .

607. And Fitzy's bass amp lead . . .

608. And Gary's walking boots . . .

609. And Jo's photos that you were supposed to have scanned and returned ten months ago . . .

610. And finally Charlotte's video with the last three episodes of *Thirtysomething* on it.

611. Renew passport.

612. Make an important document file/drawer.

613. Find marriage certificate.

614. Open bank account for Lydia.

615. And one for the new sprog when it arrives.

616. Develop skills in the ancient art of re-gifting.

617. Read broadsheet newspaper from cover to cover including the sport and the news stuff about countries you've never heard of.

618. Find all the missing music CDs that appear to have miraculously vanished from their cases like Bruce Springsteen's *The River* . . .

619. And Bowie's *Heroes* . . .
620. And Kings of Convenience's *Versus* . . .
621. And The Sunday's *Static and Silence* . . .
622. And Gomez's *Bring It On* . . .
623. And The Black Crow's *Amorica* . . .
624. And Gene's *Drawn To The Deep End* . . .
625. And Dinah Washington's *The Roulette Years* . . .
626. And Terry Hall's *The Collection* . . .
627. And Soul Jazz Record's *300 Dynamite* compilation . . .
628. And Erlend Oye's *DJ Kicks* compilation . . .
629. And *The Best of The Wiggles*.
630. Hand in the receipts to publishers that you forgot to hand in last summer but have been too scared to hand in ever since.
631. Give new address to all people and institutions who are still sending mail to your parents' address.
632. Get mobile phone for Mum.
633. Get mobile phone for Dad.
634. Wrestle middle brother.
635. Do something with the million and one mini-discs in the box under the bed.
636. Stop early adopting when it comes to new technology.
637. Finish off any books that you started but couldn't finish such as *Extremely Loud and Incredibly Close* . . .
638. And *My Friend Leonard* . . .
639. And *The Old Man and The Sea* . . .
640. And *The Writer's Journey* . . .
641. And *Little Dorrit* . . .
642. And *The Collected Dorothy Parker* . . .

317

643. And *Alan Titchmarsh's Complete book of Gardening* . . .
644. And *Screenwriting for Dummies* . . .
645. And *The Iliad* . . .
646. And *Middlemarch* . . .
647. And Gary Wilmot's *Guide to Doing impressions.*
648. Start reading food labels.
649. Eat less sugar.
650. Eat less salt.
651. Eat less fat.
652. Switch off electrical appliances at night.
653. Stop leaving TV on standby.
654. Install a doorbell.
655. Digitise best of old mix tapes.
656. Get a business card.
657. Get round to doing something with the speak and type software that you convinced yourself would revolutionise your writing life but you failed to even open . . .
658. And the jigsaw saw you bought after watching one episode too many of *Changing Rooms* . . .
659. And the microwave egg poacher . . .
660. And the IKEA cappuccino maker . . .
661. And the sunflower seeds . . .
662. And the cress seeds . . .
663. And the lettuce seeds . . .
664. And the pedometer . . .
665. And the ludicrously expensive cable that can attach the computer to the TV . . .
666. And the revolutionary steam cleaner you bought from the back of the *Telegraph* magazine.
667. Try to engage more people in friendly conversation.

668. Score at Monday night football.
669. Do something with the fifty billion empty jam jars and the quarter of a million empty biscuit tins Claire keeps squirrelling away around the house claiming that they'll 'come in useful' some day.
670. Get rid of weeds from front path.
671. De-stink trainers.
672. Use up all the mini bottle of toiletries that you insist on liberating from hotel bathrooms.
673. Come up with a plan B.
674. Balance chequebook.
675. Find out what balancing a chequebook actually entails.
676. Clean out microwave.
677. Take the Glucosamine sulphate tablets Claire bought for your knees.
678. Know who's who in government.
679. Buy something from a door to door salesman.
680. Replace light in microwave as I know how much you miss watching the food go around.
681. Eat more fibre.
682. Try to organise an NCT group reunion.
683. Fix kickboard in kitchen that falls down when you open dishwasher.
684. Stop to complete surveys.
685. Reduce outlay on depreciating assets.
686. Get some life insurance.
687. Be more civic minded.
688. Check my credit rating.
689. Get blinds for Velux windows in loft.
690. Get blind for window next to loo.
691. Multitask.
692. Listen to entire albums without skipping tracks.

693. Stop spending money in a bid to cheer myself up.
694. Decide what my stance is on the new iPod range.
695. Try shopping at proper market stalls.
696. Get tips from Mother about how to select good quality fruit and vegetables.
697. Get fan for loft.
698. Get new curtain rail for our bedroom.
699. Buy large whiteboard . . .
700. And set of dry wipe marker pens.
701. Decorate a room in something other than white or antique cream paint.
702. Split clothes into seasons and store accordingly.
703. Get box for shoe cleaning equipment.
704. Buy summer-weight duvet instead of sweating underneath winter one.
705. Buy a shoe horn.
706. Try to get to grips with Lydia's fascination with The Wiggles.
707. Make space in busy schedule to use voucher for luxury health spa day kindly bought for us as a wedding anniversary present last year by Claire's mum.
708. When Claire asks you what you're thinking try to have a better answer than 'nothing' at the ready.
709. Vacuum all cobwebs from the ceiling.
710. Try to say 'no' more often.
711. And 'yes' too.
712. Clean out the extractor fan in the kitchen . . .
713. And change its charcoal filter too.
714. Drink more hot drinks.
715. Take Lydia camping given that she's been begging to do it on a daily basis ever since she saw people doing it on CBBC a year ago.

716. Brush up on your degree knowledge.
717. Consider getting a pet.
718. Write a poem.
719. Try to appreciate jazz.
720. Apologise to 'M' for the time that I called him 'U'.
721. And apologise to 'D' for what I did on 12.12.92
722. And apologise to 'K' and to 'J' for that thing I did that we don't talk about.
723. And while I'm at it issue an apology to 'B' for the misunderstanding that happened a while back that means we don't talk any more.
724. Find a mentor.
725. Know about the solar system.
726. Investigate car leasing.
727. Decide if you are really ever going to watch *Matrix Reloaded* again . . .
728. Or *Leaving Las Vegas* . . .
729. Or *Shakespeare In Love*.
730. Go on professional development courses.
731. Be prepared.
732. Eat more fish.
733. Re-create first date with wife.
734. Find out parents' life stories.
735. Back up phone SIM.
736. Buy new set of everyday cutlery.
737. Empty all food cupboards and check dates.
738. Remember people's wedding anniversaries.
739. Change living room around . . .
740. And bedroom.
741. Spend less time on the internet.
742. Keep record of important numbers in case I lose bank cards.

743. Fix wonky shelf in loft.
744. Work out how to write next book whilst helping out more at home.
745. MAKE SURE YOU DON'T FORGET MOTHER'S DAY AGAIN AS CLAIRE WILL NOT BE SO FORGIVING A SECOND TIME.
746. Befriend a doctor.
747. Stop buying new pens.
748. And pencils.
749. And notepads.
750. Keep in touch with cousins.
751. Donate old spectacles to charity.
752. Try to redress work/life balance.
753. Chase year-old parking ticket that was incorrectly issued to you.
754. Get a proper wallet.
755. Set up a direct debit to pay the water rates . . .
756. And the council tax . . .
757. And the TV licence . . .
758. And telephone bill.
759. Be more romantic.
760. Try on wedding suit and see if it fits.
761. Replace gas canister for BBQ so that you'll use it this summer.
762. Make a decision about where to go on holiday next summer . . .
763. And when (or if) Claire should go back to work . . .
764. And whether we should switch to Freeserve . . .
765. And whether we should move house . . .
766. And whether we should move to the country . . .
767. And whether we should change to generic bran flakes . . .

768. And what exactly to tell Lydia about Santa . . .
769. And about the tooth fairy . . .
770. And about where babies come from . . .
771. And why we don't see the newsagent's dog taking himself for a walk any more . . .
772. And how we feel about private health care . . .
773. And organic food . . .
774. And ballet lessons for three year olds . . .
775. And what to call the new baby if it's a boy . . .
776. And what to call the new baby if it's a girl . . .
777. And if it's okay to buy barn eggs.
778. Get rid of anthill in garden.
779. Recycle old mobile phones.
780. Make more stuff (popcorn, mayonnaise, etc) from scratch.
781. Get duvets cleaned.
782. Get that really nice family photo of us all sitting on the sofa in 1970 digitally repaired.
783. And the one of my mum when she first started nursing in Wolverhampton.
784. Go to bed earlier.
785. Correct the internet rumours about my untimely demise on the Sheryl Crow message board.
786. Check fertility.
787. Decide whether or not we're having more children.
788. Back up computer hard drive.
789. Turn over mattress.
790. Use less salt.
791. Clean bathroom . . .
792. And the kitchen . . .
793. And the living room . . .
794. And the cellar . . .

795. And the conservatory . . .
796. And the bedrooms too.
797. Clean detritus from rucksack.
798. Sort out modem.
799. Clean out car.
800. Carpe diem!
801. Get boiler checked.
802. Fixed stained glass in hallway door.
803. Buy new pillows as I have no idea how old the ones we have are but I do know they feel sort of crunchy.
804. Move Lydia's bedroom.
805. Read all unread back issues of *Word* Magazine . . .
806. And *Esquire* . . .
807. And *MacUser* . . .
808. And *DVD monthly*.
809. Clean rug in living room.
810. Buy cover that you forgot to buy for Lydia's IKEA chair.
811. Catch up with John O.
812. Get mobile number for all friends whose only contact detail I have is their email address.
813. Finish watching Season One of *The Wire*.
814. Get email address for all friends whose only contact detail I have is their mobile number.
815. Make Lydia's bedroom look more like a little girl's room.
816. Get doctor to undertake review of all non-temporary medication.
817. Get a new address book and add friends' current addresses rather than walking round with a vague recollection of places my friends lived nine years ago.

818. Organise bookshelves so that you can find a specific book without turning the house upside down.
819. Get rid of all out-of-date direct debits.
820. Find a replacement solicitor for the one who retired.
821. Finish painting the cellar.
822. Institute TV-free nights.
823. Find out what all the extraneous switches in the kitchen are for.
824. Teach wife the art of self-defence.
825. Read all articles torn out of newspapers for later consumption . . .
826. Do same for those torn out of magazines.
827. Get in touch with people we met on holiday and really liked and exchanged email addresses with but never did anything about like Stan and Beth from New York . . .
828. And Andreas and Arva from Cyprus . . .
829. And Olga and Alyosha from Russia.
830. Re-hang bathroom door.
831. Work out how to download a podcast.
832. Have a go at learning basic HTML.
833. Replace missing buttons from pinstripe jacket . . .
834. And grey shirt . . .
835. And those cheap jeans you bought . . .
836. And from your grey jacket . . .
837. And from your grey overcoat . . .
838. And from your black cardigan . . .
839. And from your black jacket.
840. And from your white button-down shirt . . .
841. And from your black winter coat . . .
842. And from your grey cardigan . . .
843. Find out what the big fuss is about Bob Dylan.

844. Learn to identify names of plants and shrubs.
845. Go to more gigs.
846. Buy new glassware.
847. Fix missing roof tile.
848. Investigate school for Lydia.
849. Take more baths.
850. Sample more world cuisine like Iranian food . . .
851. And Nigerian . . .
852. And Polish . . .
853. And Lithuanian.
854. Visit Loch Ness.
855. Keep travel sweets in the car.
856. Come up with a title for new book.
857. Collect together all loose change in house . . .
858. And then do something with it.
859. Double-check the rules of box junctions.
860. Paint over former damp patch in hallway.
861. Clean all downstairs windows.
862. Try and break a world record (yes I know!).
863. Eat less meat.
864. Throw a *Seinfeld* appreciation night.
865. Work on alternative routes to routine destinations.
866. Fully utilise all of the different attachments that came with the vacuum cleaner that you never give a second glance.
867. Find the plug bit for the baby monitor . . .
868. And the missing speaker for the surround sound . . .
869. And disc one from DVD box set of season four of *Buffy the Vampire Slayer* . . .
870. And the re-install discs for the computer . . .
871. And the piece of paper that you wrote Dave's mobile number on . . .

872. And the instruction manual for the breadmaker . . .
873. And the £52 charity sponsorship money that you put in a safe place and then promptly forgot about . . .
874. And the battery for the old digital camera . . .
875. And the charger for the old digital camera . . .
876. And the 2GB memory stick you bought back in March . . .
877. And the special nut thing without which it's impossible to take the wheels off the car . . .
878. And your car's V5 document . . .
879. And the receipt for the washing machine to prove that it really is less than six months old and therefore should not be giving up the ghost just like that.
880. Find out how to responsibly get rid of low-energy light bulbs.
881. Try to like cricket.
882. Go jogging.
883. Have family portraits taken.
884. Plan more day trips.
885. Buy a coffee table book.
886. Buy a coffee table.
887. Come up with a five-year plan.
888. Get more discounts.
889. Learn how to fold clothes properly like they do in posh clothes shops.
890. Be a better son . . .
891. And a better brother.
892. Ask more questions.
893. Try to make miserable check-out lady smile.
894. Meet bank manager.
895. Remember Phillip's birthday.
896. Look after the pennies.

897. Get round to watching Danby's art videos.
898. Buy in bulk.
899. Replace wife's Dean and Deluca mug
900. Get the city council's building regulations people in to finally check all of the changes to the house like you should have done a few years ago.
901. Investigate getting cheaper offers on mobile phone insurance.
902. Take Lydia on to upper deck of double-decker bus to prove to her that there is no shop up there.
903. Get planning permission for loft.
904. Bleed radiator.
905. Ask to see my medical records.
906. Finish *Guardian* quick crossword begun back in April.
907. Overcome embarrassment about middle name.
908. Use handkerchiefs.
909. Carry an umbrella.
910. Buy a tablecloth . . .
911. And serving dishes . . .
912. And proper serving spoons . . .
913. And a proper dinner service . . .
914. And napkins . . .
915. And a proper tea set . . .
916. And a proper coffee maker . . .
917. And a canteen of cutlery with no missing teaspoons.
918. Replace all horrible 80s style Chinese lantern lampshades.
919. Watch first series of *Spooks*.
920. Be a calmer driver.
921. Read *The Lovely Bones* even though it's at least four years too late for it to be current fodder for dinner party conversation . . .

922. And *We Need To Talk About Kevin* . . .
923. And *Small Island* . . .
924. And *Stuart: A Life Backwards* . . .
925. And *Notes on a Scandal* . . .
926. And *The Shadow of The Wind* . . .
927. And *The Da Vinci Code* . . .
928. And *The Kite Runner*.
929. Start a blog.
930. Become the kind of man who isn't fazed by the idea of buying his wife underwear from Agent Provocateur.
931. Learn wife's bra size . . .
932. And her dress size . . .
933. And her shoe size . . .
934. And her ring size . . .
935. Change mobile phone provider.
936. Review cable package.
937. Consider Sky+.
938. Be open to suggestion.
939. Cease and desist from buying dry-clean-only clothes.
940. Speak to overseas friends via Skype.
941. Eat more nuts.
942. Find left hand of ski gloves.
943. Find the instruction manuals for the video recorder . . .
944. And DVD player . . .
945. And then correct the time on both as they have been displaying the wrong time for the past five years.
946. Remember to take address book on holiday . . .
947. So that we can send postcards home.
948. Let the Chadwicks finally know that the Smiths have moved house.
949. Find out actual neck size so that I don't carry on buying shirts that are too small.

950. Put door closers on loft bedroom door as requested by building regulations . . .
951. And Lydia's bedroom . . .
952. And Claire's old office . . .
953. And our bedroom . . .
954. And the living room . . .
955. And the kitchen.
956. Find plug for electric breast pump.
957. Take better care of feet.
958. Buy a pair of proper ladders . . .
959. And a pair of smaller ones too.
960. Visit mother-in-law more.
961. Find out who insures house . . .
962. And who insures contents . . .
963. And make sure that we're fully covered.
964. Write love letters to wife like I did in the old days.
965. Descale kettle . . .
966. And the iron.
967. Use Debenhams vouchers bought by Claire's auntie for our wedding ten years ago.
968. Descale shower head.
969. Make receptacle for work-related receipts.
970. Clear leaves from gutter.
971. Find removal van number that Jo asked for months ago.
972. Put preservative on shed.
973. Make an effort to go to London more.
974. Join online DVD club.
975. Use *Final Draft*.
976. See if there's a device for taking out screws that no longer have a head so that you can unscrew the one that broke while fixing the bed.

977. Alphabetise CDs.
978. Either get rid of or consume all impulse duty-free purchases of the alcoholic variety like the bottle of Peach Schnapps from Innsbruck Airport . . .
979. Or the 2 bottles of Dream Island Cocktail mix from Seychelles International Airport . . .
980. Or the bottle of Mount Gay Rum from Grantley Adams International Airport . . .
981. Or the bottle of Ouzo from Larnaca Airport . . .
982. Or the bottle of Tequila from Mexico City International Airport . . .
983. Or the bottle of Banana Liqueur from Birmingham International Airport.
984. Fix wardrobe sliding door.
985. Find 'A' level certificates . . .
986. And 'O' level . . .
987. And Post Graduate Diploma . . .
988. And Sociology degree . . .
989. And 5m swim badge.
990. Indulge wife's increasing fondness for throws without complaint.
991. Understand the point of kitchen roll.
992. Buy an Oxford English Dictionary . . .
993. And refer to it rather than relying on Google.
994. Buy a bradawl.
995. Shop locally.
996. Come up with idea for play . . .
997. And a screenplay . . .
998. And a non-fiction book.
999. Get low-maintenance pet for Lydia that neither of us are frightened of or allergic to and that is minimally annoying.

1000. Locate and read Mark Forster's book *Get Everything Done And Still Have Time To Play*.
1001. Visit chiropodist.
1002. Buy collection of birthday cards so that all I have to do is search out the address and slap it in the post . . .
1003. And collection of 'sorry you're leaving' /'It's a boy!' 'Hope you're happy in your new house' type cards.
1004. Buy a water feature.
1005. Learn to catch fish.
1006. Build something out of wood for Lydia.
1007. Get citronella candle or similar for garden.
1008. Be more open.
1009. Buy flowers for wife for no reason.
1010. Work out what the mysterious splatter that goes up to the ceiling is on the wall in the hallway.
1011. Get a second opinion.
1012. Stop missing appointments.
1013. Purchase an extra dustbin.
1014. Watch *24* season four.
1015. Investigate Bolivian food shop that always piques your curiosity given the low density of Bolivian families in your local community.
1016. Practise Heimlich manoeuvre.
1017. Replace all missing light bulbs.
1018. Finally take up Mum's offer to teach me how to make rice and peas . . .
1019. And her infamous 'boozy cake' . . .
1020. And that thing she does with okra, tinned tomatoes and bacon.
1021. Read *War and Peace* because it will make you look smart . . .

1022. As will *Of Mice and Men* . . .
1023. And *Lucky Jim* . . .
1024. And *Catch 22* . . .
1025. And *Moby Dick* . . .
1026. And *Frankenstein* . . .
1027. And *Brave New World* . . .
1028. And *David Copperfield* . . .
1029. And *Madame Bovary*.
1030. Rediscover and consume all lost freezer food.
1031. Get up to date with current music.
1032. Stop wife buying any more hand cream seeing that we have enough to soften her hands well into her eighties.
1033. Stop wife buying any more lip balm. (See above but in relation to lips.)
1034. Stop wife buying any more lady razors. She's not *that* hairy.
1035. Turn down thermostat.
1036. Learn the rules of backgammon.
1037. Plan more.
1038. Increase punctuality.
1039. Drink less alcohol.
1040. Find out from GP what I am genuinely allergic to.
1041. Find out what happened in the last episode of the *X-Files* . . .
1042. And *Twin Peaks* . . .
1043. And *Friends* . . .
1044. And *Happy Days* . . .
1045. And *Alias* . . .
1046. And *Xena: Warrior Princess* . . .
1047. And *The West Wing* . . .
1048. And *The Fresh Prince of Bel-Air* . . .

1049. And *Dallas* . . .
1050. And *Cheers* . . .
1051. And *The Golden Girls*.
1052. Remove my name from all of the email newsletters subscription services that I unwisely signed up for.
1053. Keep up with current affairs.
1054. Get rid of left-over currency from previous holidays and foreign trips . . . including US dollars . . .
1055. And French francs . . .
1056. And Spanish pesetas . . .
1057. And Swedish kroners . . .
1058. And Singaporean dollars . . .
1059. And Cypriot pounds . . .
1060. And Australian dollars . . .
1061. And Russian roubles.
1062. Do something with all the stamps that you've been tearing off envelopes for charity but then fail to take to a charitable concern.
1063. Open a savings account.
1064. And a joint account for bills and stuff.
1065. Take out all the spooky red eye from all digital photos.
1066. Learn to appreciate Raymond Carver.
1067. Grow rhubarb.
1068. Read more non-fiction.
1069. Whilst I'm happy with Dr M's work start trying out other GPs, just in case.
1070. Get batteries for the spare car keys that haven't worked since the summer before last.
1071. Ask around for recommendations for a decent electrician . . .
1072. And a plumber . . .

1073. And a children's party entertainer . . .
1074. And a cleaner . . .
1075. And a tree surgeon.
1076. Write to that address that stops junk mail being sent to you.
1077. Learn how to properly use your current mobile phone.
1078. Do more boring stuff online like filing tax return . . .
1079. And paying bills . . .
1080. And paying car tax . . .
1081. And food shopping . . .
1082. And banking.
1083. Get the wiring in the house checked to find out why the toaster keeps triggering the trip switch.
1084. Fix broken slat on our bed.
1085. Add dishwasher salt to dishwasher.
1086. Return all stray tools to the toolbox.
1087. Thin out CD collection – is there really any need to keep that Light House Family CD any longer?
1088. . . . and do the same for your vinyl. No one needs two copies of *I Should Be So Lucky*.
1089. Choose date for gathering of the Gayle clan.
1090. Give in to publisher's demand for new author photo.
1091. Get to know cheese.
1092. Watch all remaining Woody Allen films in hope that at least one of them will prove to be a return to form.
1093. Buy more shelving.
1094. Find out which one of your neighbours has a wi-fi network called 'electricvagina2' and why.
1095. Find lids for all plastic storage containers. Bin ones without.

1096. Wash out and fill the bird feeder.

1097. Get a knife sharpener.

1098. Sharpen all knives.

1099. Try to choose wine without relying on the attractiveness of the label or the fact that it costs less than a fiver.

1100. Buy new non-stick frying pans to replace old extra-sticky frying pans.

1101. Buy a new set of saucepans and dump all the battered mangled old things we have been coping with for the last ten years.

1102. Get rid of all out-of-date spices.

1103. Buy jar of Ras el Hanout . . .

1104. And cumin seeds . . .

1105. And smoked paprika.

1106. Try to address wife's complaint that I don't talk enough.

1107. Have longer phone conversations with male friends.

1108. Read Claire's lady magazines without recourse to mocking.

1109. Occasionally listen to music in the evenings rather than just switching on the TV.

1110. Try to like new neighbours more.

1111. Find out what the strange smell is coming from the basement.

1112. Find the memory card for the old camera that's got the photos of Gina and Paul's wedding on it.

1113. Seek and destroy the slug that's been leaving its trail over the welcome mat.

1114. Use public transport more.

1115. Borrow Dad's garden hose . . .

1116. And his lawn-edging tool.

1117. Make peace with enemies.
1118. Try to look slightly less 1997 when getting ready for a big night out.
1119. Get eye test.
1120. Have shorter meetings.
1121. Eat outdoors more.
1122. Deal with mail as soon as it comes through the door. Failing that, find a receptacle for mail rather than leaving it on the stairs to be tripped on, scribbled on or lost.
1123. Find bank statements 145 and 146 that the accountant has been asking about since January.
1124. Try to understand the plot to *Donnie Darko* without recourse to the internet.
1125. Speak to a life coach.
1126. Help Claire to cancel her Next Directory as there are at least 12 editions of it a year and I am sick and tired of trying to find somewhere to store them seeing as she never orders anything from any of them.
1127. Remember that your home is not a museum . . .
1128. Or a library.
1129. Get a hands-free set for mobile phone.
1130. Change burglar-alarm code to something slightly less obvious . . .
1131. And my email password.
1132. Replace watch battery.
1133. Get a proper bag not a rucksack seeing as you are neither a hiker nor a skateboarding student.
1134. Give the man-bag a chance.
1135. Do something with the leftover gravel that's at the bottom of the garden.

1136. Get outdoor plug socket fitted so that I don't have to do scary things with extension leads when I want to cut the grass.
1137. Wash out the outside bin . . .
1138. And the recycling boxes too.
1139. Make DVD of kids for mother-in-law as promised last Christmas.
1140. Try to like something by Leonard Cohen other than 'Famous Blue Raincoat'.
1141. Fix parents' front door bell.
1142. Watch *Citizen Kane* . . .
1143. And *The Shawshank Redemption* . . .
1144. And *Hotel Rwanda* . . .
1145. And *Raging Bull* . . .
1146. And *The French Connection* . . .
1147. And *The Deer Hunter* . . .
1148. And *Jean de Florette* . . .
1149. And *The Exorcist* . . .
1150. And *Don't Look Now* . . .
1151. And *Breathless* . . .
1152. And *Easy Rider* . . .
1153. Find out what the dozen or so random keys in the key drawer actually open.
1154. Get new back-door key in case we lose the original.
1155. Drop a set of spare keys at my parents.
1156. And another set at Andy's.
1157. Give Damian Rice's second album a chance . . .
1158. And Stone Rose's one . . .
1159. And the Strokes' one too . . .
1160. And while we're at it, Goldfrapp's entire output since that first one.

1161. Work out how to stop texting like an old man whilst still avoiding irksome phrases like 'c u l8tr' and 'lol'.

1162. Find out why wedding ring is turning skin funny.

1163. Get into reading and checking bank statements.

1164. Arrange for builder to quote for new roof that has been looking decidedly dodgy since we first bought the house.

1165. Fly kite with child.

1166. Now that you have perfected the three-pint triangle manoeuvre, try the four-pint square.

1167. Stop bingeing.

1168. Fix puncture on Lydia's bike rather than pumping it up all the time as you have been doing since May.

1169. Eat less bread.

1170. Use electric toothbrush.

1171. Eat more soup.

1172. Put preservative on lawn edging.

1173. Listen to more classical music . . .

1174. And opera.

1175. Indulge wife's increasing fondness for scatter cushions without complaint.

1176. Re-pot the spider plant . . .

1177. And the Aloe Vera plant . . .

1178. And the potted palm in the bathroom . . .

1179. And the other potted palm in the bathroom . . .

1180. And the plant with the big leaves that keep dropping off . . .

1181. And the umbrella plant . . .

1182. And the cheese plant . . .

1183. And the fern . . .

1184. And the potted palm in the living room . . .

1185. And the yucca.

1186. Ebay golf set . . .
1187. And broken digital camera . . .
1188. And old iPod . . .
1189. And bass guitar . . .
1190. And season one of *House* . . .
1191. And my old SLR camera . . .
1192. And old miniDV camera . . .
1193. And those ridiculously expensive Maharishi trousers you bought and wore only once . . .
1194. And the grey John Smedley jumper that Claire shrunk in the wash . . .
1195. And the black John Smedley jumper that Claire shrunk in the wash . . .
1196. And the grey and yellow striped John Smedley jumper that Claire shrunk in the wash . . .
1197. Buy a shirt requiring cuff links.
1198. Get an Oyster card for when I'm in London.
1199. Find extended warranty for iPod . . .
1200. And for new digital camera . . .
1201. And for the old TV.
1202. Try and work out who's who on *EastEnders*.
1203. Buy new festive outdoor lights.
1204. Do the lottery if only because it'll give me and Dad something extra to talk about.
1205. Stop thinking a meal isn't complete without pudding.
1206. Eat more raw food.
1207. Try Goji berries.
1208. Eat more fruit.
1209. Listen to the *Today* programme.
1210. And the *Archers*.
1211. And in fact more radio in general.

1212. Get Leeds-based car showroom to change their burglar alarm dialler number which has been phoning my mobile phone on and off since February.
1213. Learn to enjoy surprises.
1214. Buy subscription to *Men's Health*.
1215. Edit wardrobe.
1216. Buy tie hanger.
1217. Buy digital thermometer.
1218. Listen to Claire's medieval music without grimacing.
1219. And again on behalf of wife try to listen to Crash Test Dummies without yelling, 'Will someone stop this racket now!'
1220. Work out my carbon footprint.
1221. Try to eat daily 5 portions of fruit and veg.
1222. Be more encouraging.
1223. End fatwa against Royal Sun Alliance . . .
1224. Set clock in conservatory to the right time.
1225. And the one with Indesit . . .
1226. And the one with BQ's kitchen installation service.
1227. And the one in our bedroom . . .
1228. And the one on the CD player.
1229. Tune in Channel Five properly on the TV.
1230. Transfer ISA to one with a better rate.
1231. Institute a casual Friday policy at work.
1232. Stop worrying about death . . .
1233. And the likelihood of people trying to steal your identity . . .
1234. And potentially fatal diseases . . .
1235. And whether or not you're a good dad.
1236. Worry more about eating properly . . .
1237. And the meaning of life . . .

1238. And how you're going to get this next novel finished on time.

1239. Look after your lips.

1240. Stop being tied to your mobile.

1241. Try to buy more seasonable products.

1242. Find out exactly what Hedge Fund managers do to make all that cash.

1243. Chillax more.

1244. Collect together all the random photos lying about the house without a frame and frame them.

1245. Do something with the old Christmas wrapping.

1246. Buy tube of Superglue.

1247. Clear out shed.

1248. Pick up Lydia more often from pre-school.

1249. Do something with huge rubber band ball on desk.

1250. Work out how to transfer calls from one telephone handset to the other so that when Claire's mates call I don't have to get up and find her.

1251. Label one of our two cordless phone 'his' and the other 'hers' so that if I ever do need to answer a call I'll know where my phone actually is rather than chasing around the house with my ear to the ground like some kind of idiot.

1252. Increase iron levels.

1253. Finish off the huge tub of multivitamins that you bought when the news about 'bird flu' first broke.

1254. Take a bag with me whenever I go shopping.

1255. Spend more time doing nothing.

1256. Buy a humane spider catcher.

1257. Clean under microwave.

1258. Create a weekly spending budget and stick to it.

1259. File Claire's old tax statements because if you leave it to her it will never happen.

1260. Get rid of all joke presents of the fluffy washing-up gloves/executive miniature snooker table variety.

1261. Be more generous.

1262. Talk less. Listen more.

1263. See if conditioning hair makes ANY difference whatsoever.

1264. Try to reduce your water consumption.

1265. Do something with last year's Christmas cards instead of just leaving them stuffed in the cupboard where you keep the board games.

1266. Visit the RSC.

1267. Sort out dodgy toenail.

1268. Compost.

1269. Go ice-skating.

1270. Record new out-going message on home phone.

1271. Record new out-going message on office line that doesn't state your mobile phone number incorrectly.

1272. Get rid of all audiotapes since you no longer have a tape deck.

1273. Discover something new about your locality.

1274. Delete all old files from laptop hard drive.

1275. Delete all old files from desktop hard drive.

1276. Watch *Ghost World* DVD.

1277. Clean windows.